IMAGES
of America

DAVIE COUNTY

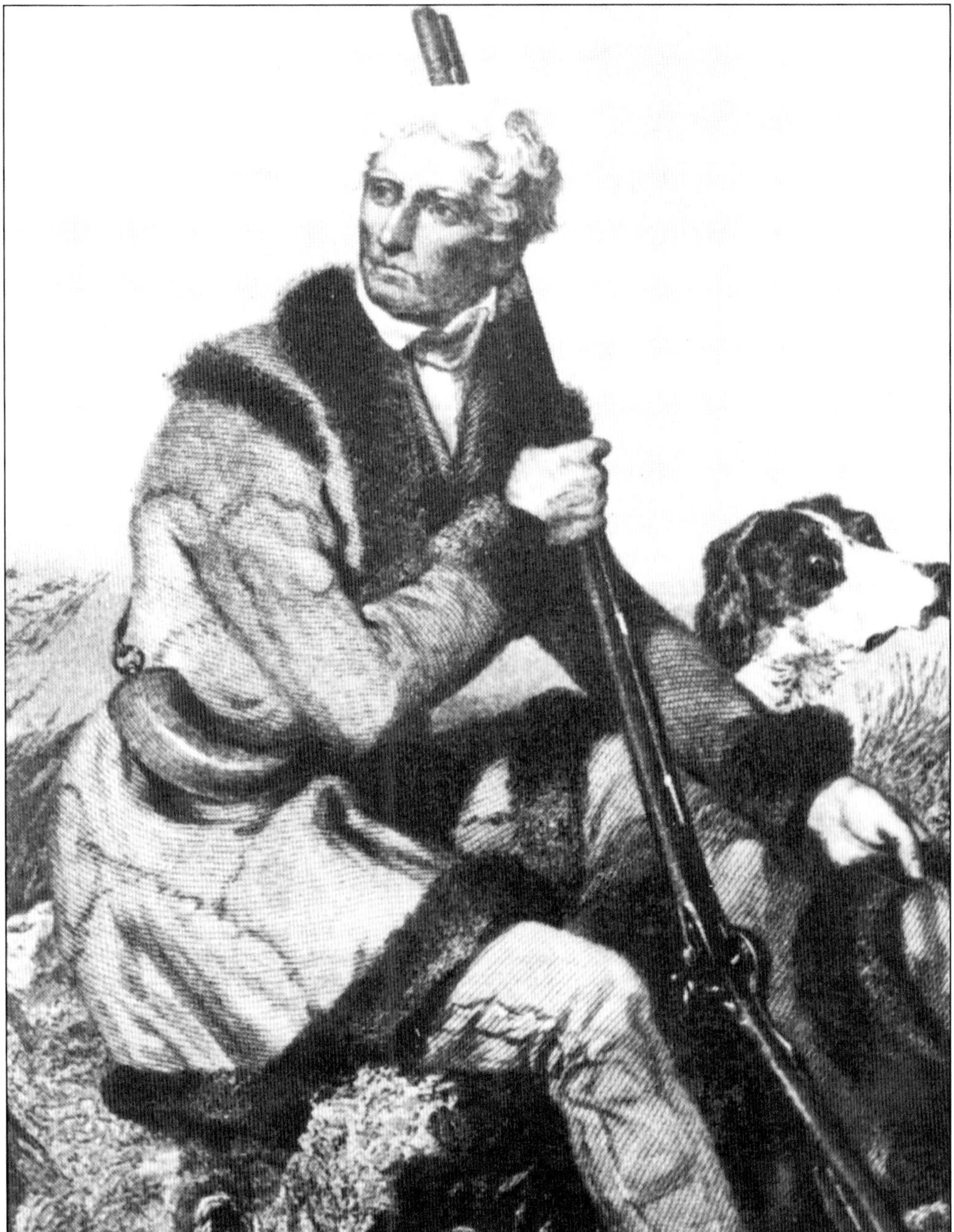

Daniel Boone Portrait. This undated engraving from around 1861 derives from a painting by Alonzo Chappel (1828–1887). (Courtesy of Archiving Early America.)

On the Cover: Schoolchildren pose in front of the old Sunnyside Seminary building around 1908, when it was used during the construction of the Mocksville Graded School on Cherry Street (1907–1911). Teacher Mattie Eaton stands in the left background and teacher Pattie Battle, with her arm extended, to the right of the tree. Bailey Clement holds on to his dog. (Courtesy of the Davie County Public Library.)

IMAGES
of America

DAVIE COUNTY

Jane Satchell McAllister
Debra Leigh Dotson

ARCADIA
PUBLISHING

ISBN 978-0-7385-6797-6

Published by Arcadia Publishing
Charleston, South Carolina

Printed in the United States of America

Library of Congress Control Number: 2009923610

For all general information contact Arcadia Publishing at:
Telephone 843-853-2070
Fax 843-853-0044
E-mail sales@arcadiapublishing.com
For customer service and orders:
Toll-Free 1-888-313-2665

Visit us on the Internet at www.arcadiapublishing.com

We dedicate this book to historians James W. Wall and the late Flossie Martin, whose dedication and hard work recorded and preserved Davie County history.

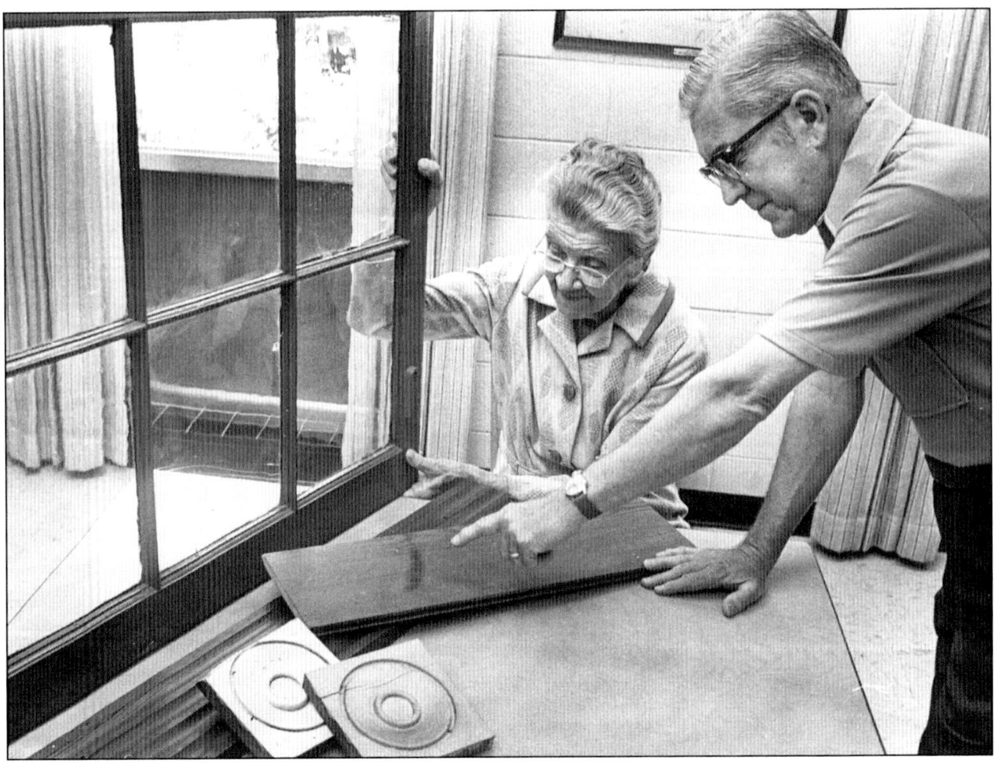

CONTENTS

ACKNOWLEDGMENTS

The authors acknowledge the contributions of several people who made this book possible: librarian Doris Frye and History Room volunteer Flossie Martin for ensuring that a cache of historical Davie County photographs remains available for this project and others; Lynn Rumley of the Textile Heritage Center at Cooleemee for generously contributing materials and text on the town of Cooleemee; James Wall, distinguished county historian, for his continuing interest in and enthusiasm for Davie County projects; Peter Hairston Jr., who graciously opened his home and provided hundreds of family photographs; Dr. Charles McAllister for being our editor of first resort; and others who graciously shared their photographs and extensive historical knowledge: Neil Anderson, Archiving Early America, Lucy Barney, James Barringer, Larry Cope, William Ferebee, Forsyth County Public Library Photo Collection, Gwynn Meroney, Jack Pennington, Charles "Muggs" Smith, Robin Snow, John and Susan Stowers of Plantation Antiques, and Charles Odell Williams. Unless otherwise noted, all images appear courtesy of the Davie County Public Library. The authors regret being unable to use all the photographs submitted as a result of limited space.

INTRODUCTION

This illustrated history celebrates the rich traditions of a proud people in a small North Carolina county. Though the precious old photographs cannot tell the full story of Davie County, they draw us into the past by evoking a wide variety of responses: curiosity about the historical and cultural contexts, amusement at moments still funny even several generations later, appreciation for the quality of the images, and reflections on our own lives compared to those of the folks who shaped our community over the past 200 years.

Situated in the central piedmont area of North Carolina, Davie County rests in the forks of the Yadkin and South Yadkin Rivers. The earliest known history of the area dates back 10,000 years, with Native American arrowheads, tools, and broken pottery providing evidence of camps and trading posts, particularly along the riverbeds.

European settlers began settling the area in the mid-1700s, following the Great Wagon Road south from Pennsylvania. Plentiful hunting, abundant forests, and fertile land for farming supported a growing population. The Morgan Bryan family arrived in 1748 and became one of the largest local landowners, with 2,200 acres known as Bryan Settlement, now Farmington. Squire and Sarah Boone, acquaintances of the Bryans, migrated into the area around 1752, acquiring land in 1753. Their son Daniel reveled in the good hunting. Daniel and Rebecca Bryan married in 1756 and lived in a log cabin on Sugartree Creek in Bryan Settlement. Daniel Boone resided in the area for over a decade before moving west into Kentucky. Squire and Sarah Morgan Boone lie buried in Joppa Cemetery in Mocksville.

In December 1836, the North Carolina Legislature named a new county carved from Rowan after William R. Davie, a Revolutionary War hero and North Carolina governor. Three years later, Mocksville became the seat of Davie County, building the original courthouse in the center of the town square. In 1909, a new courthouse building replaced the old one, which survived until the paving of Main Street in 1922. The National Park Service added the current courthouse to the National Register of Historic Places in 1979.

Peter Hairston purchased the 2,500-acre tract of Cooleemee Plantation in 1817. His great-grandson Peter Wilson Hairston expanded the tract to 4,200 acres and constructed the imposing Greek Revival–style plantation house from 1853 to 1855. The house stands 50 feet tall with 12 rooms, a large central hall, and a self-supporting wooden staircase. Additional features include woodwork by Philadelphia craftsmen and plasterwork by Italian workmen. The house, listed on the National Register of Historic Places in 1973, remains private property of the Hairston family.

The year 1878 marked the beginning of the Masonic Picnic in the county. First held at the Shoals in Cooleemee, the picnic was sponsored by the Mocksville Masonic Lodge to benefit the Oxford Orphanage. The picnic moved to Clement Grove in Mocksville in 1883, where it continues today. Speakers at the picnic have included governors, senators, and other dignitaries. The Local Legacies project of the Library of Congress includes the Mocksville Masonic Picnic in its listings.

The Erwin Mills Company established the town of Cooleemee, building the cotton mill on the South Yadkin River in 1899. In peak operation, the mill employed 1,800 workers. Until closing in 1969, the mill sponsored a broad range of recreational, social, religious, civic, and educational opportunities. The Textile Heritage Center at Cooleemee documents and preserves the history of the mill's relationship to the community.

Education played an important role from the beginning of the county. More than 60 public and private schools, seminaries, and academies taught local youth in the early 1900s. Today the county boasts six elementary schools (Cooleemee, Cornatzer, Mocksville, Pinebrook, Shady Grove, and William R. Davie), three middle schools (North Davie, South Davie, and William Ellis), Central Davie Academy, Davie High School, Davie County Early College High School, and an extension of Davidson County Community College.

Pioneers, public servants, lawyers, doctors, and businessmen shaped the history of our county and nation. The 18th-century pioneer Daniel Boone spent his teenage years here before helping open the West. Davie County sent several native sons to North Carolina state government, including state Supreme Court justices Richmond M. Pearson and David Moffatt Furches, and state representative and senator William Booe March. Peter Stuart Ney, reputedly a former general in the army of Napoleon, mystified area residents. Hinton Rowan Helper's *The Impending Crisis* inflamed political sentiment leading to the Civil War. And Thomas Ferebee, the *Enola Gay* bombardier, dropped the first atomic bomb on Hiroshima, Japan, in 1945.

Davie County today remains true to its agricultural heritage while balancing commercial and industrial development. Community traditions featured in this book, including fairs, parades, holiday observances, and the Masonic Picnic, still frame county life. We hope you enjoy these glimpses into the story of our county.

One

Mocksville

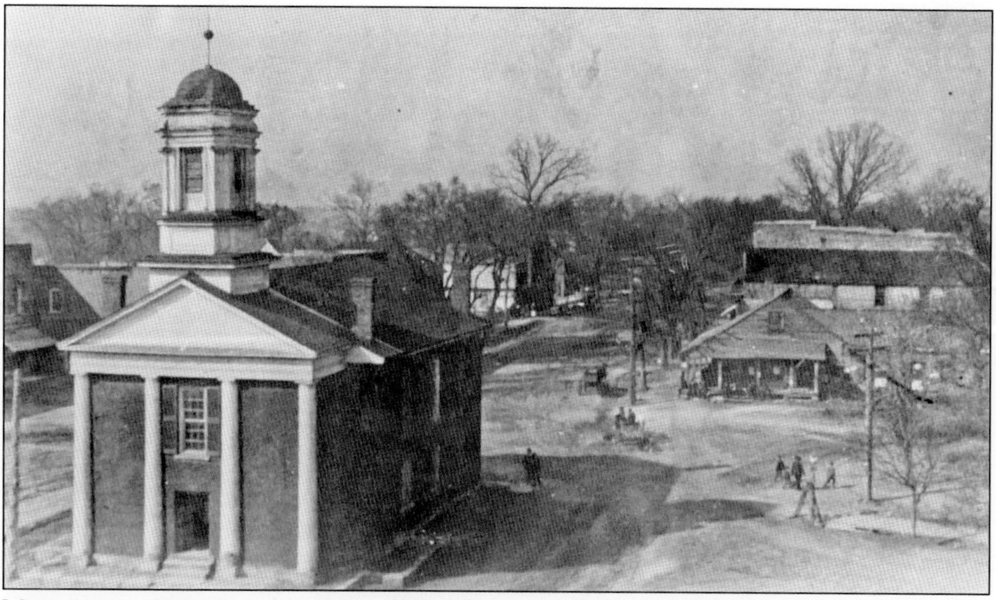

Mocksville, 1914. Named for the settlement known as Mocks Old Field, Mocksville incorporated in 1839. Civic leaders erected the courthouse in the center of the 1.5 acres set aside as a public square and business district. The business center of town shifted to the downtown square from present-day Salisbury Street. Town limits radiated one half mile in every direction from the new courthouse.

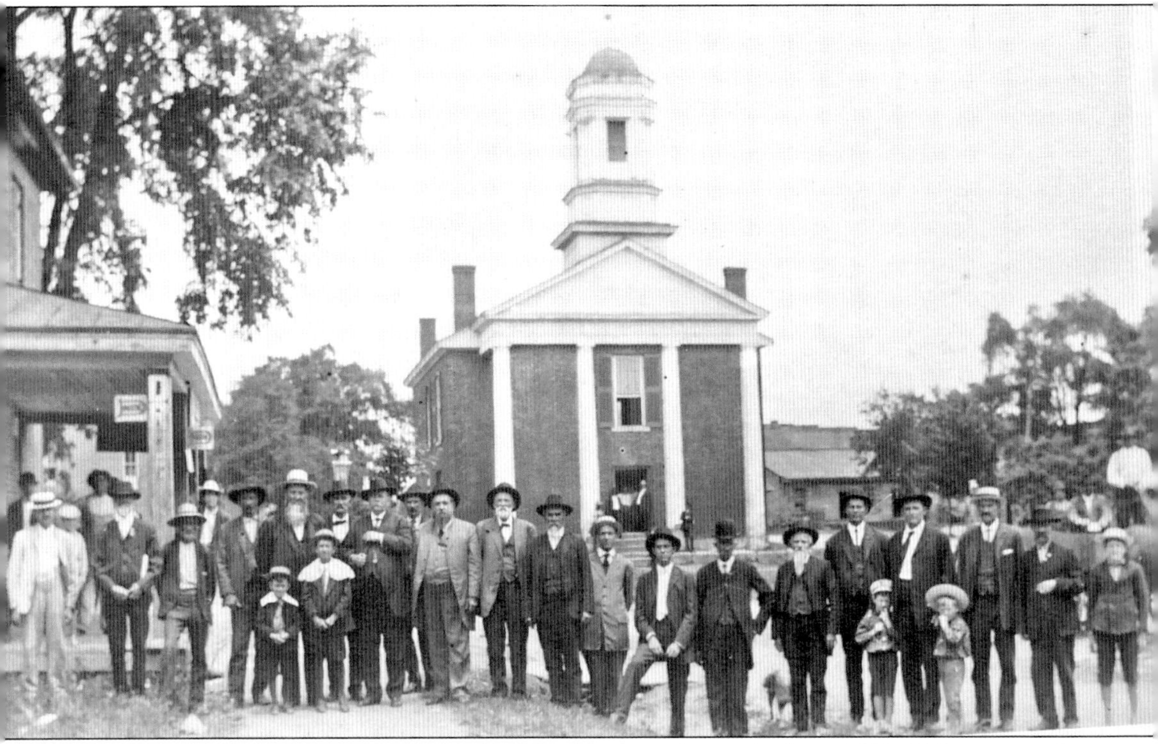

Davie County's First Courthouse. The first courthouse, built in 1837–1839, remained in use until 1909. This picture, likely from the early 1900s, shows the old Masonic Hall to the left. Capt. Wiley Clement's store lies beyond the courthouse to the right. From left to right are Henry Howard (white suit, operated a jewelry store), Chief W. C. P. Etchison (white beard, the town policeman), Chal Brown (short, father of Frank and Hugh Brown), Poss Harbin (black hat), Enoch Smith (white hat and beard), John Sprinkle (black bow tie, the sheriff), Moffit Sprinkle (boy), Blackburn Sprinkle (boy), Alec Bailey (crossed arms), George Freezor, Capt. ? Bailey, A. T. Grant Sr. (white beard, clerk of court), Ben Stonestreet, Charlie Cherry, A. T. Grant Jr., Marshall Bailey, Dr. John M. Cain (beard), John Current, Jim Moore (Register of Deeds), Jimmy Moore (boy), Paul Moore (boy), John W. Etchison (straw hat), Jim Harbin (jailer), and Carl Harbin.

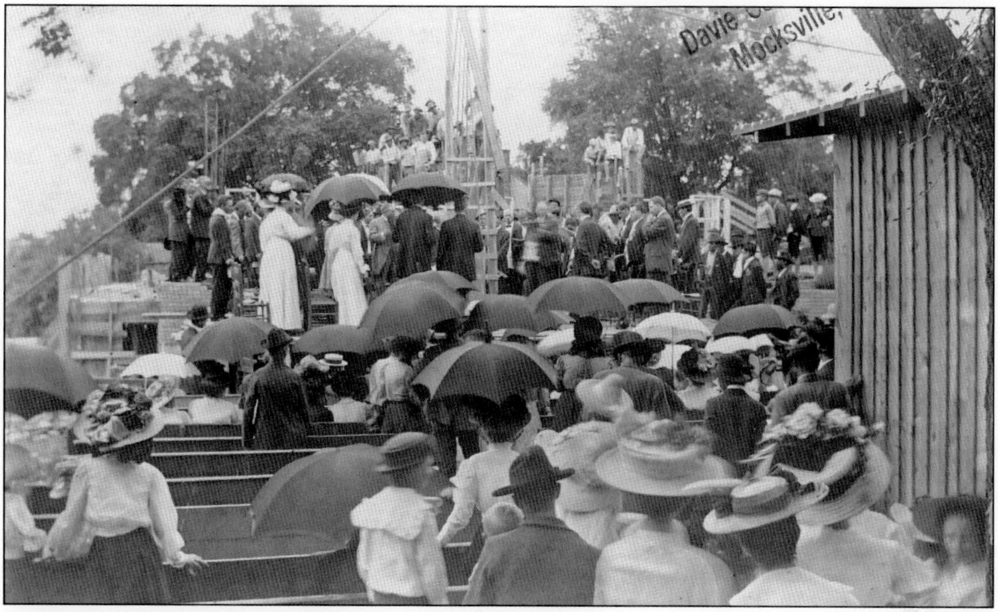

CORNERSTONE CEREMONY, 1909. This image may depict the ceremony to lay the cornerstone of the new courthouse. The local Masonic Lodge laid the cornerstone, assisted by Masons from other areas of the state.

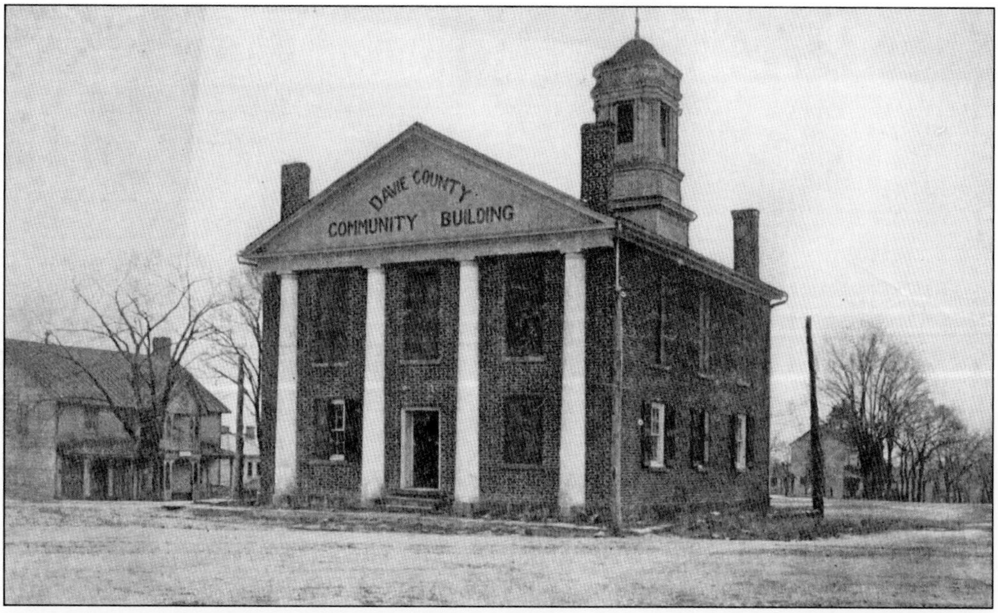

DAVIE COUNTY COMMUNITY BUILDING, EARLY 1900S. The old courthouse became the Davie County Community Building in 1915. The March House, to the left in the photograph, served as a residence on the top floor and a tin shop on the ground floor, owned by Hilary Meroney. A fire in 1939 destroyed the March House along with the weather vane from the top of the old courthouse, which was in the tin shop for refurbishment. The building to the right housed Dr. James McGuire's office and residence in his later years. (Courtesy of Gwynn Meroney.)

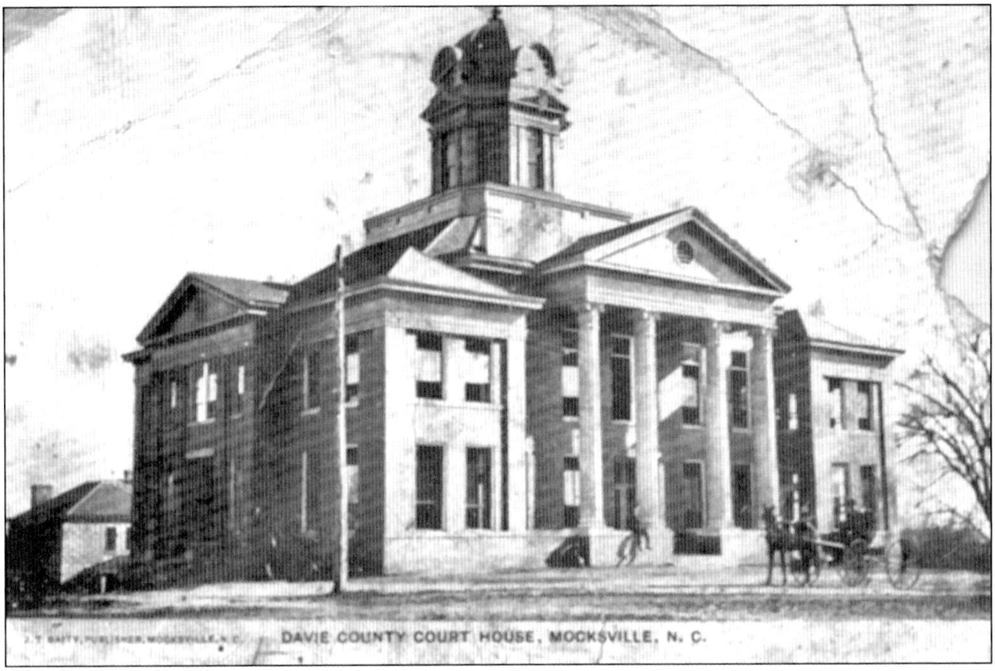

COURTHOUSE PRIOR TO THE 1916 FIRE. The county constructed a new courthouse and jail in 1909 on the southeast side of the square, partially on the site of the Davie Hotel, purchased from Gaston Horn for $4,000. Many community events transpired on the upper floor of the new courthouse, like the Chautauqua, three nights of entertainment by actors who traveled to Mocksville. Louise Stroud wrote of another time when sheets and quilts covered the upstairs floors and a large number of children had their tonsils removed on the same day. (Courtesy of Jack Pennington.)

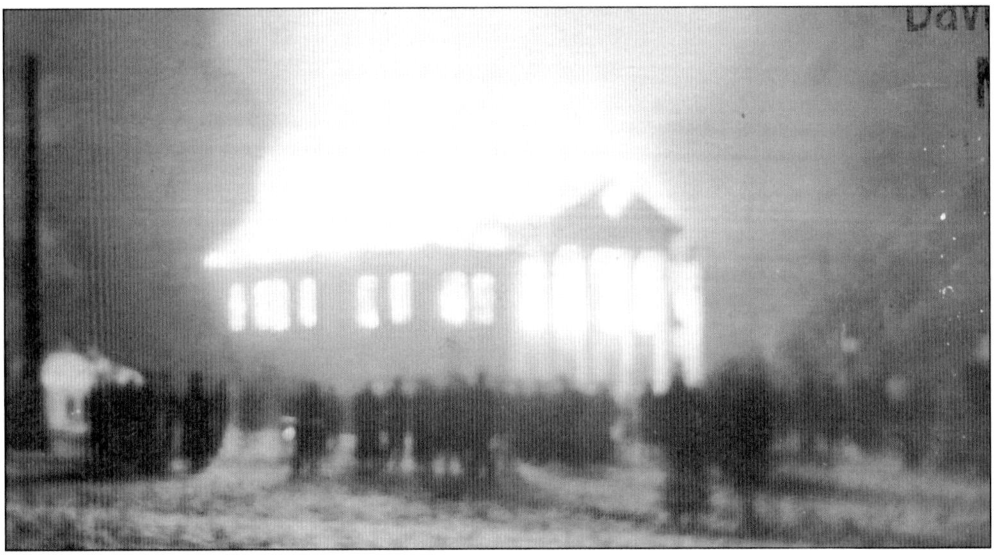

COURTHOUSE FIRE, FEBRUARY 28, 1916. The top floor of the courthouse, badly damaged by the fire, required extensive rebuilding. J. L. Crouse of Greensboro, submitting the lowest bid of $24,594, repaired the damage. The complete cost to repair the building, including heating, plumbing, electrical, furnishings, and a new clock, totaled about $30,000, paid for by bonds sold to Wachovia Bank and Trust Company of Winston-Salem.

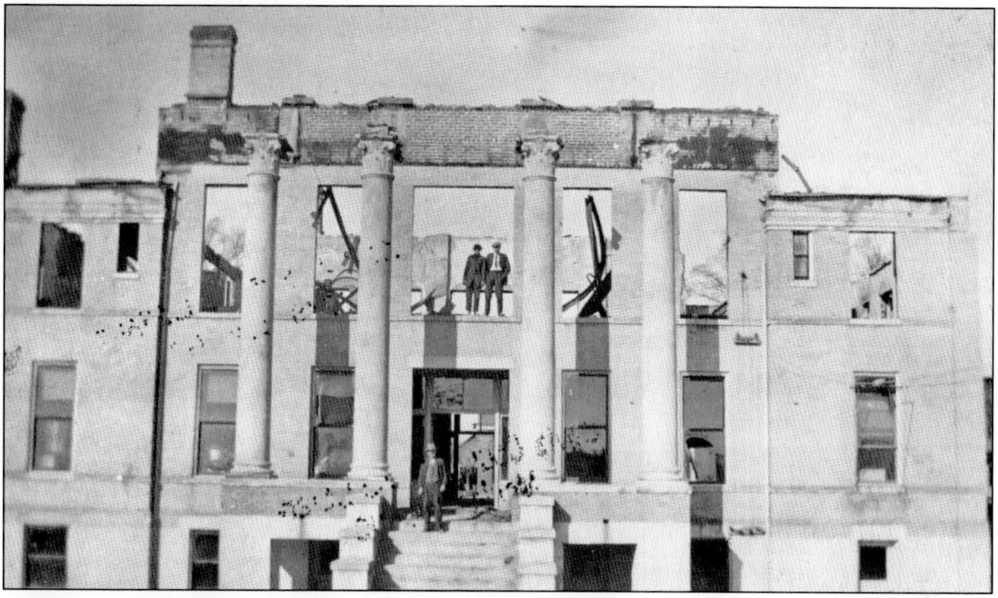

Mocksville Courthouse. These images show the damaged courthouse after the February fire. By June 1916, the courthouse remained in disrepair because county commissioners delayed, judging the bids too high. However, impatient county residents wanted the courthouse rebuilt before the end of the summer because rain ruined furniture and other contents.

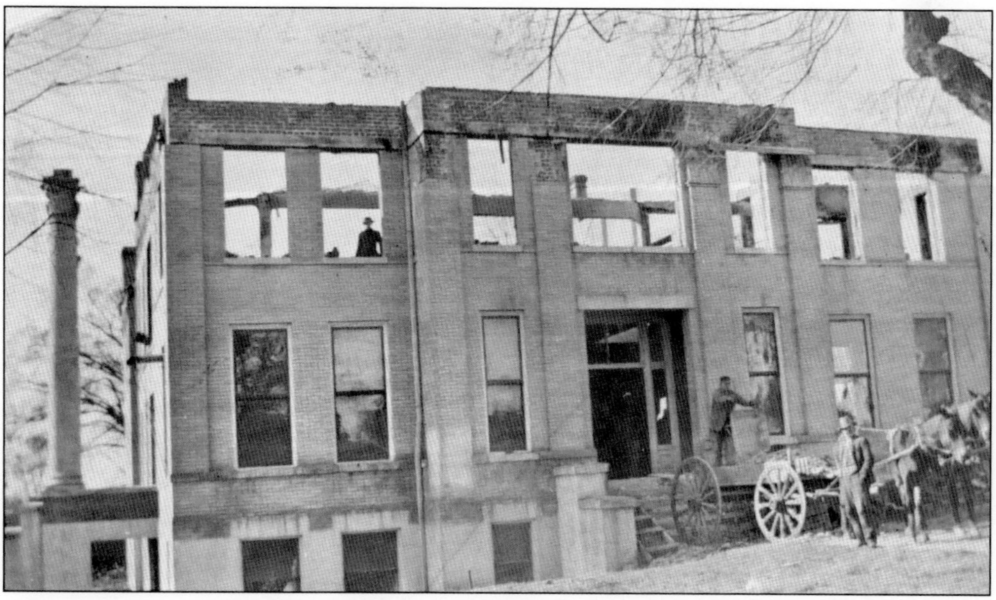

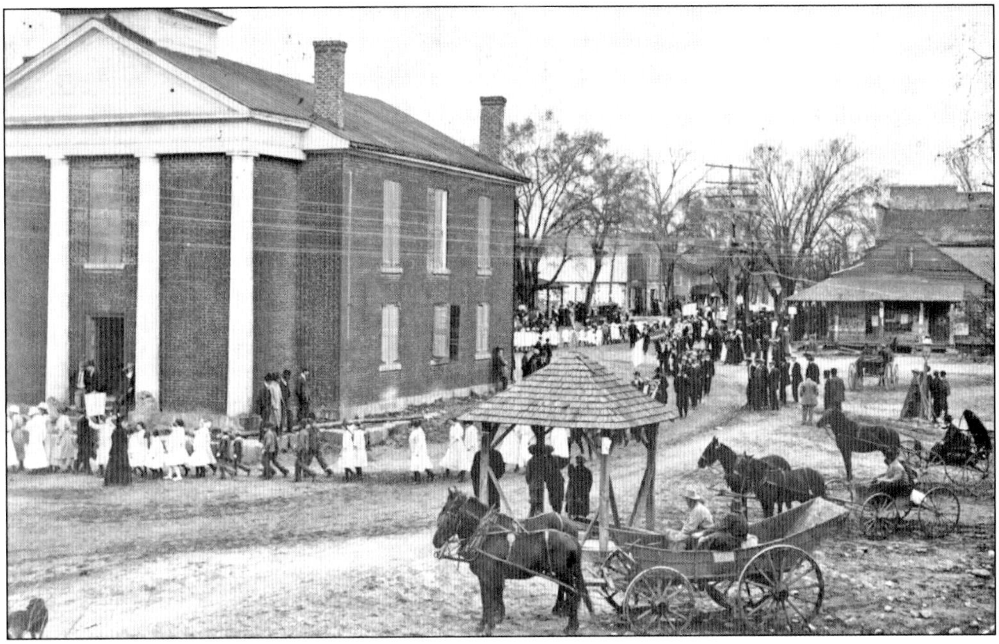

Commencement Parades. The one- and two-teacher schools in the county observed combined commencement day festivities in Mocksville, complete with a parade, floats, and a program. The parade began at the school building on Cherry Street, proceeded south on Main Street, circled the community building, and returned up Main Street to the arbor at the Masonic Picnic Grounds for the program. The boys wore denim overalls and white caps; the girls, chambray dresses and white shoes. Note the well and well house in the foreground of the above photograph. The photograph below dates to Easter Monday 1917.

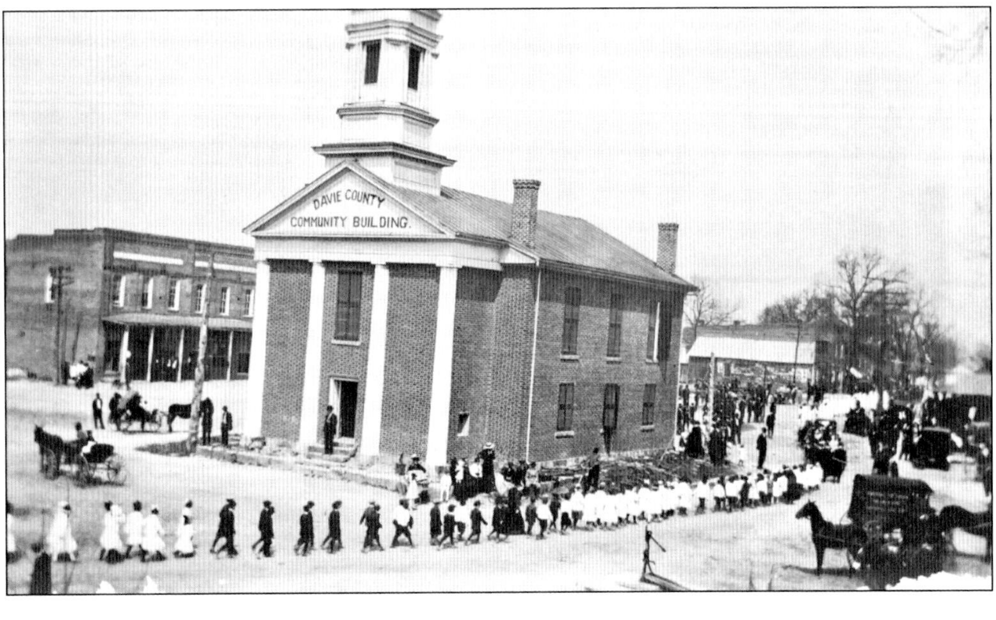

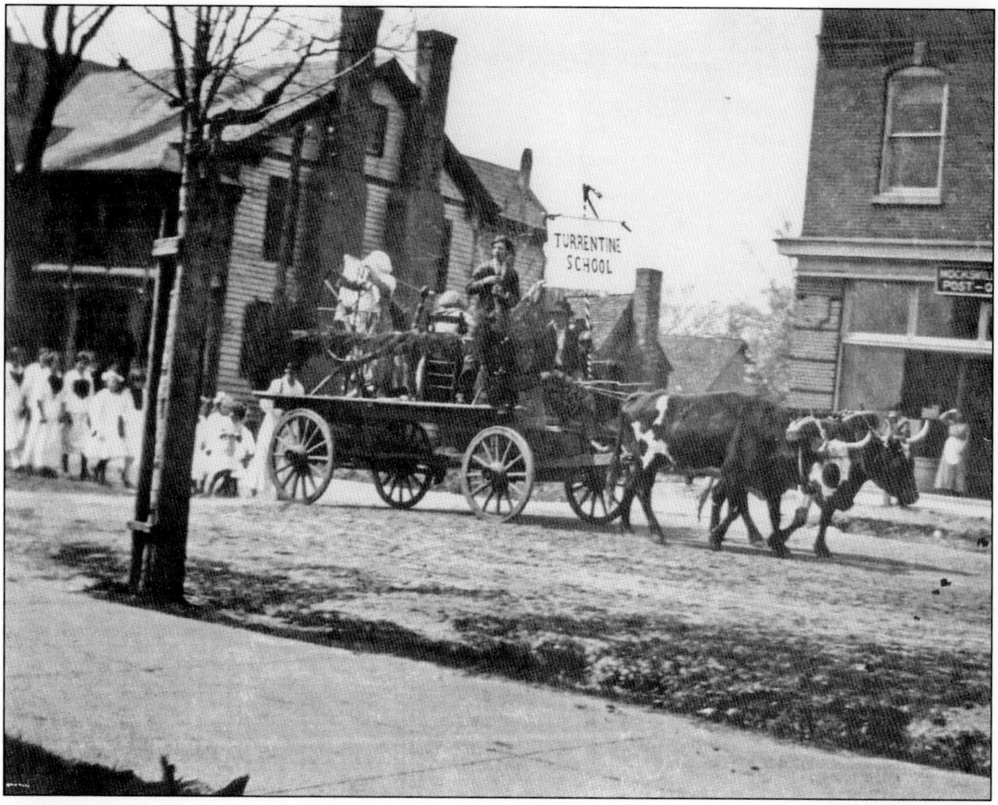

School Parades. In the photograph above, oxen pull the Turrentine School float in a Mocksville parade in the early 1900s, with the Swicegood Hotel and Mocksville Post Office in the background. The photograph below shows the parade passing in front of the Mocksville Hotel around 1915.

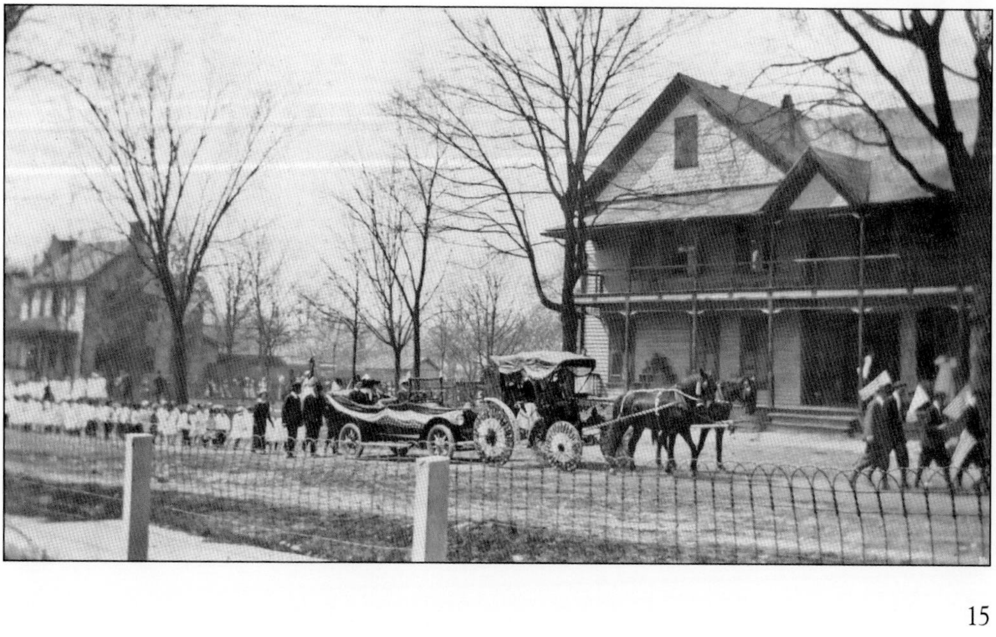

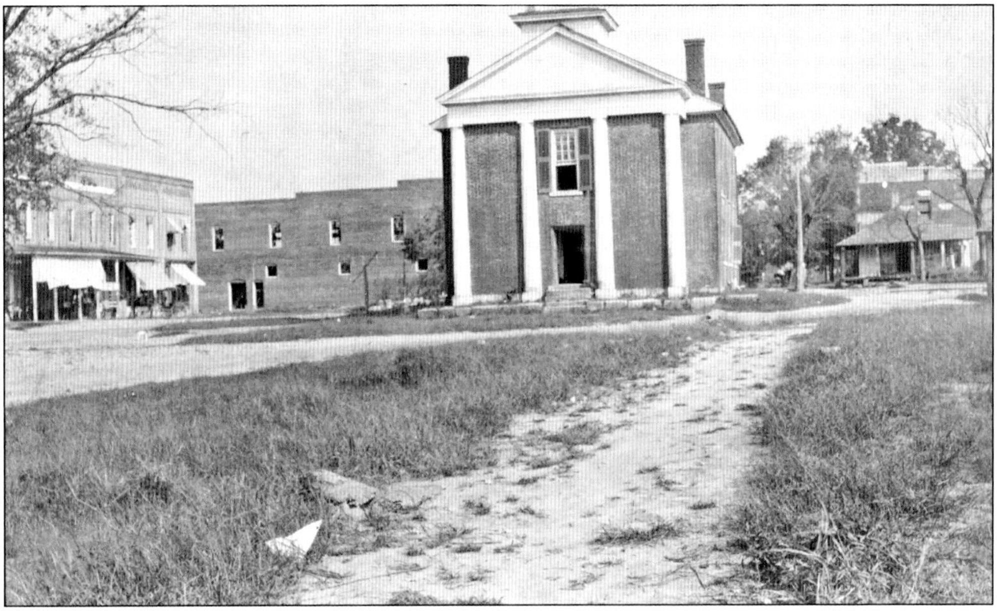

Dirt Roads. The image below looks up Main Street from the square at the dawn of the 20th century. Residents complained that dust from the dirt roads blew so thick that it coated furniture inside homes even with doors and windows tightly closed. Mocksville paved the downtown roads during the 1920s.

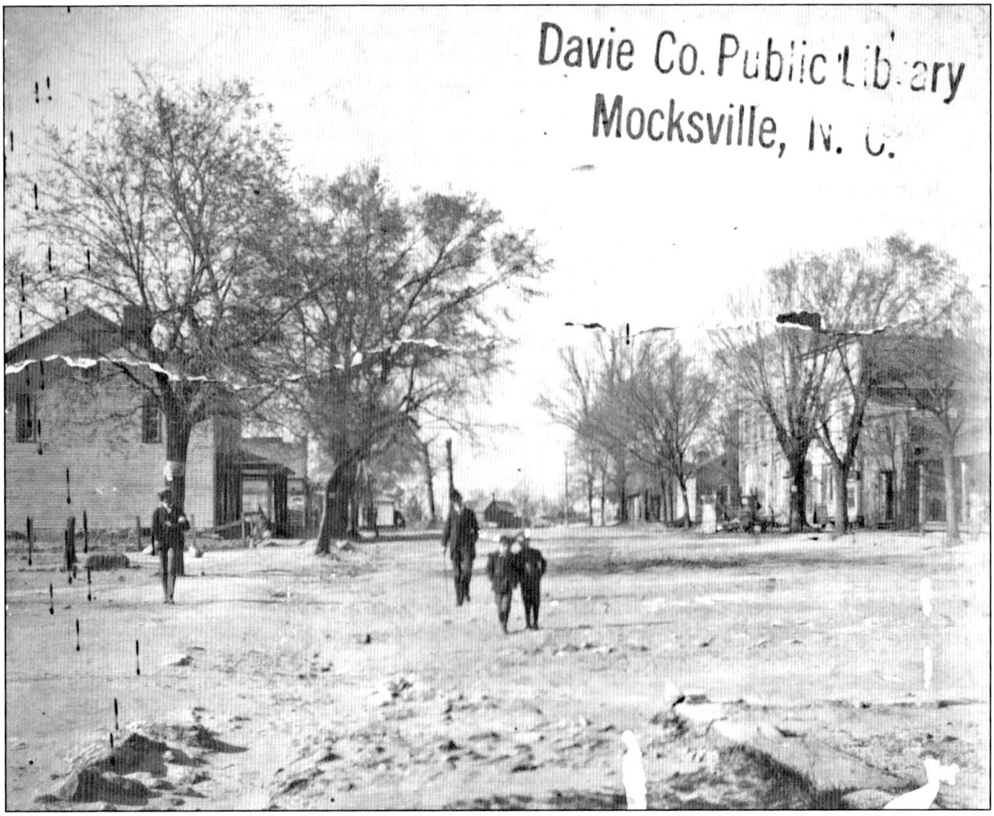

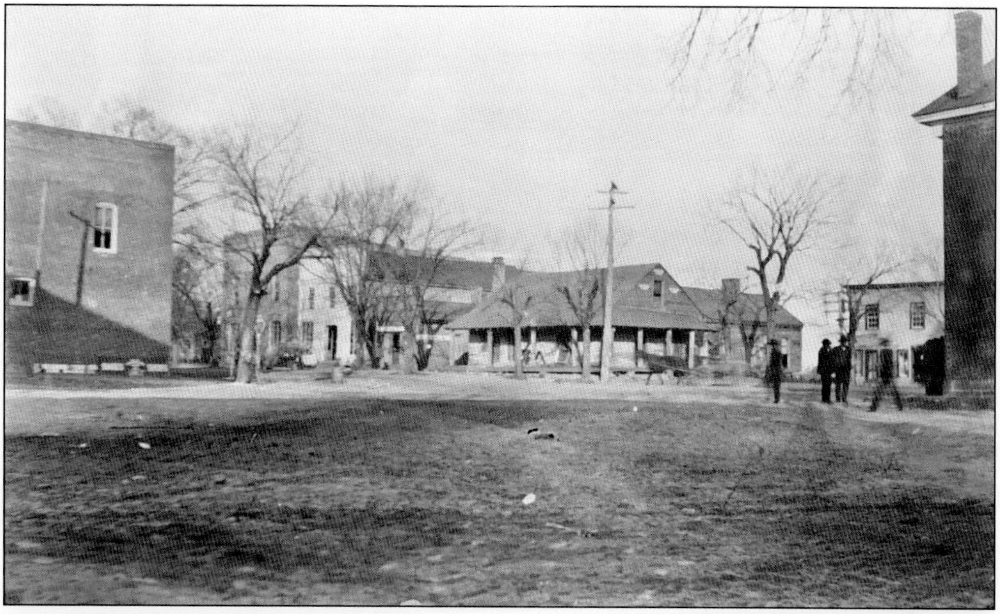

North Main Street, Mocksville. The extensive porches of Capt. Wiley Clement's store (center) provided a meeting place for politicians, traders, and townsfolk. After Clement died, the store housed successively a meat market, a soda bottling business, and finally the Farmer's Alliance Store. The small brick building adjacent to Clement's store on the left contained a barroom and later a barbershop. The next two buildings to the left held the E. E. Hunt Store and the Gaither Tobacco Factory.

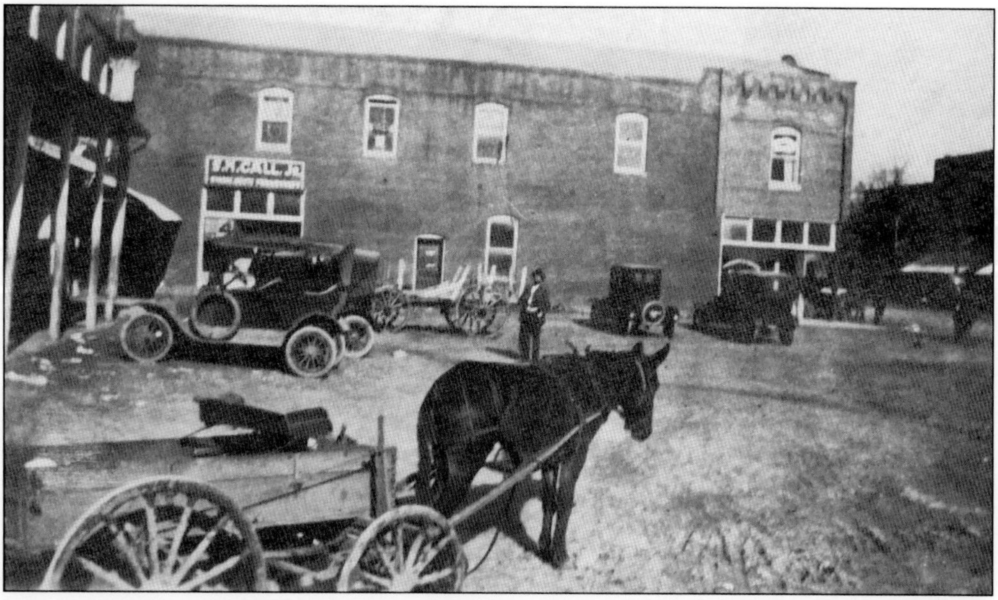

Mocksville Square. Pictured around 1914, the northwest corner of the square included S. M. Call's store in the Anderson building and the C. C. Sanford and Sons Company on the immediate left.

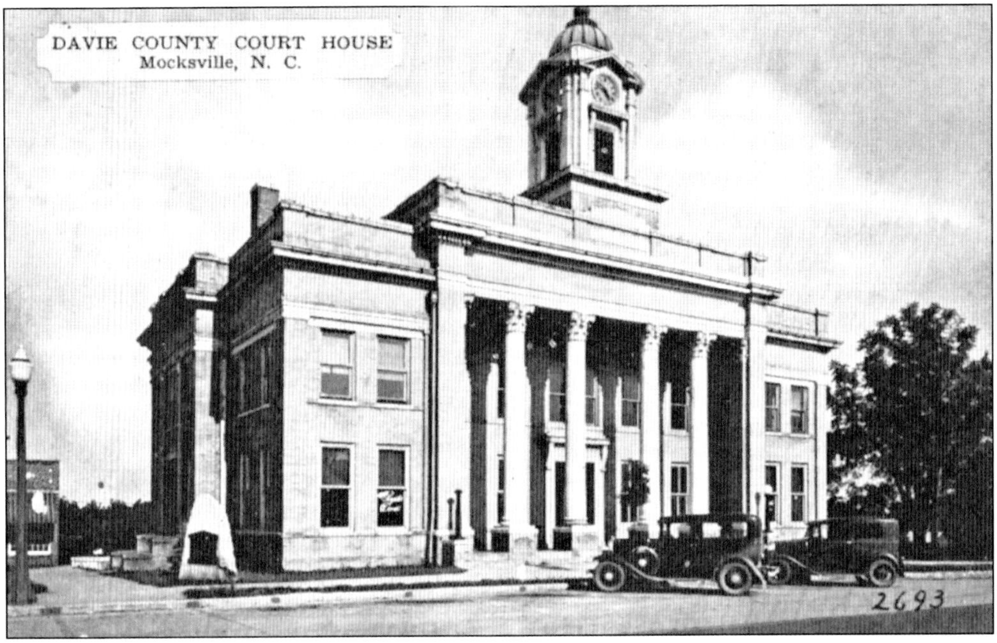

MOCKSVILLE COURTHOUSE AND SQUARE, C. 1920. The downtown square saw much traffic as county residents visited for court, business, and community events.

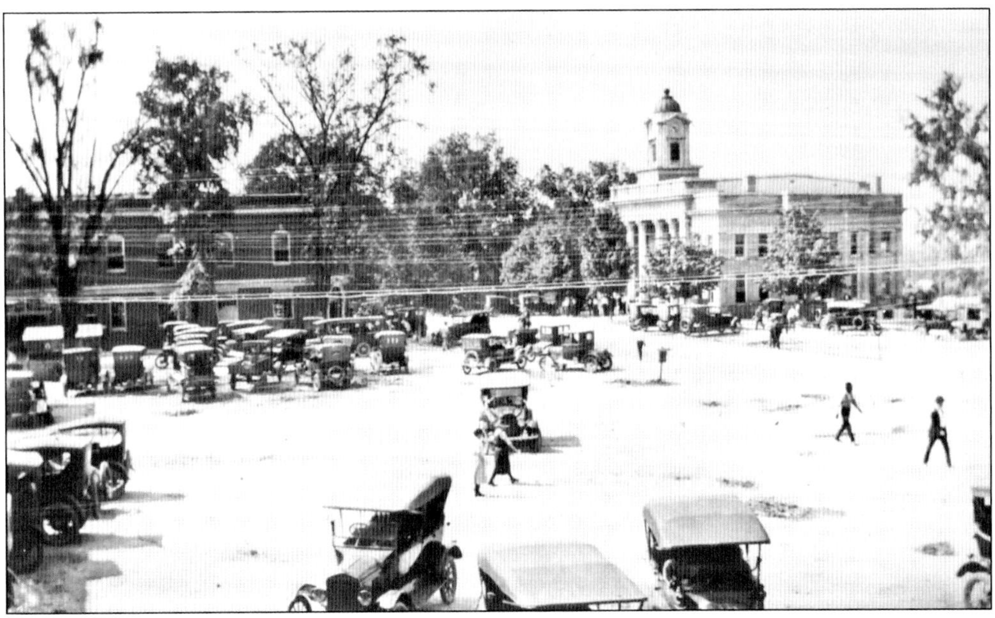

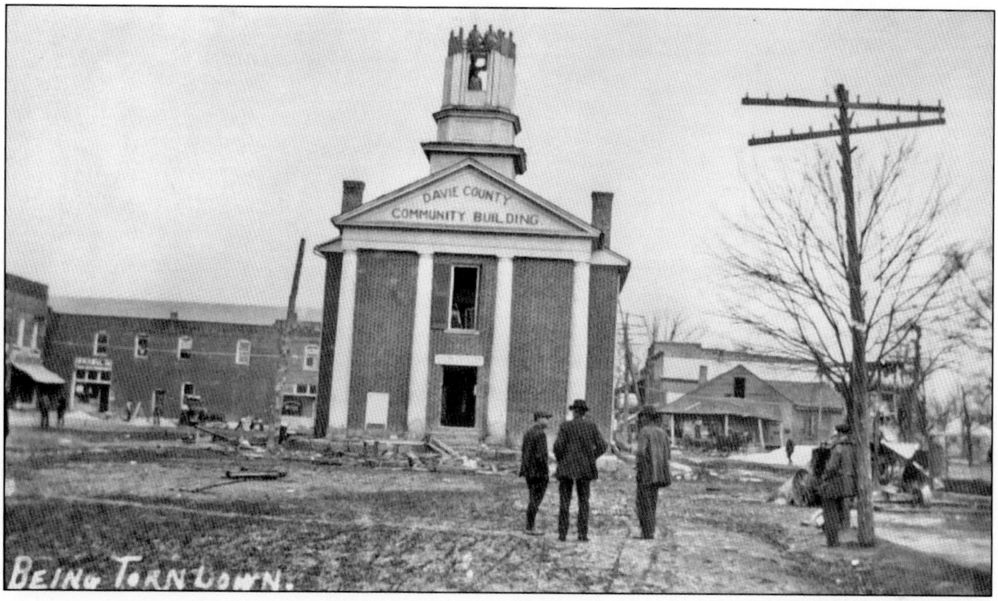

Razing of the Community Building, 1922. A. T. Grant Sr. and two unidentified men watch the razing of the Davie County Community Building, the original courthouse (above). The paving of Highway 158 through downtown Mocksville meant the controversial removal of the courthouse. Destruction of the old building began around 3:00 a.m. on the appointed day to minimize any possible disruption.

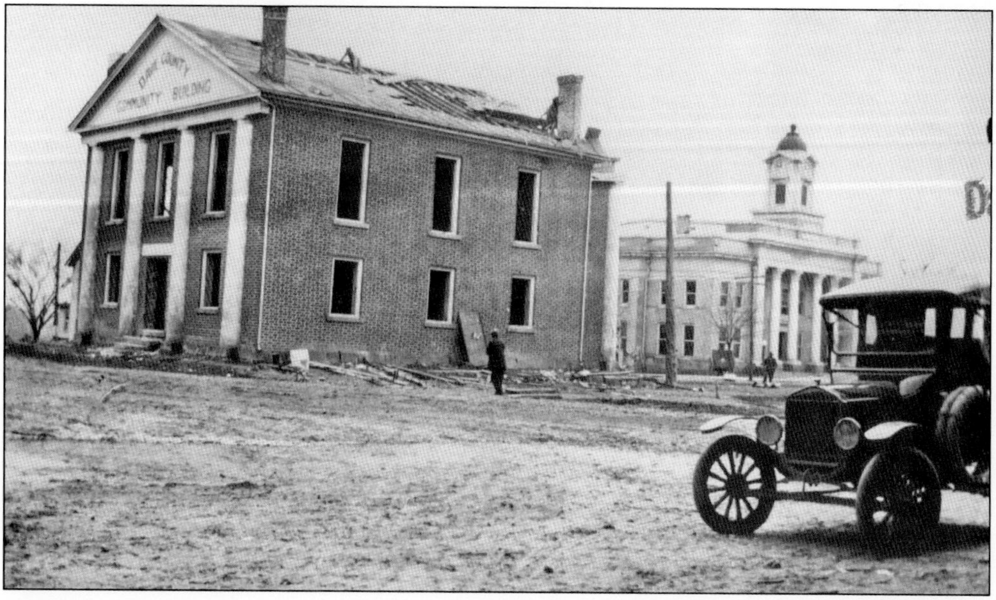

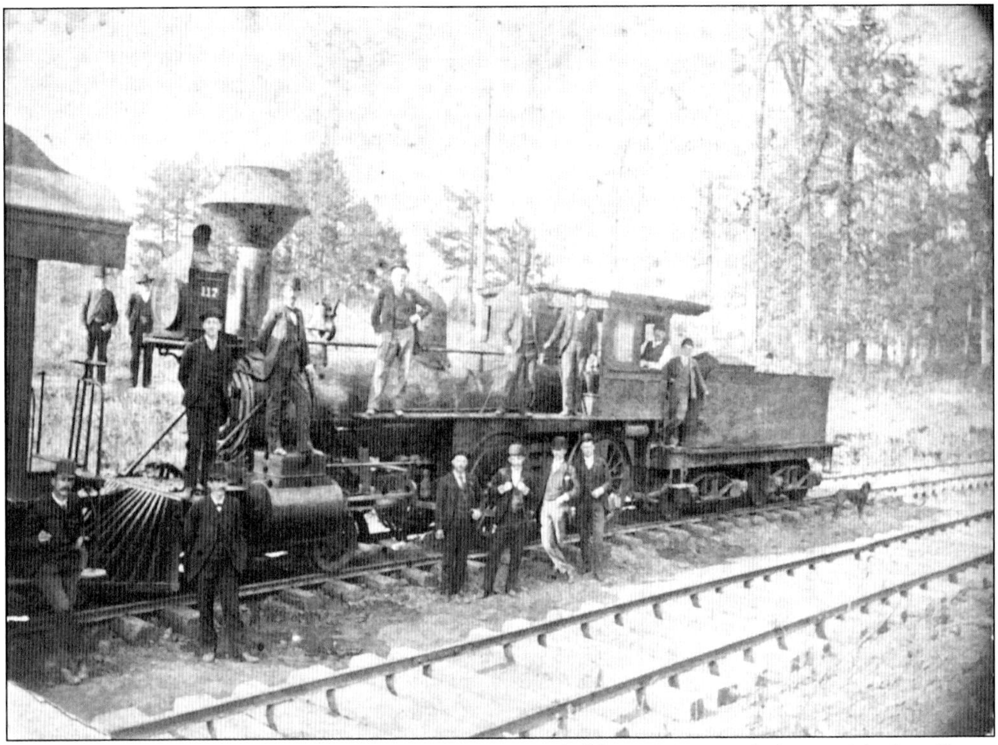

The Railroad. The first train in Davie County traveled from Winston-Salem to Mocksville on November 1, 1891. A. M. McGlamery served as the first agent of the depot station. The rail line was extended west to Mooresville in 1899.

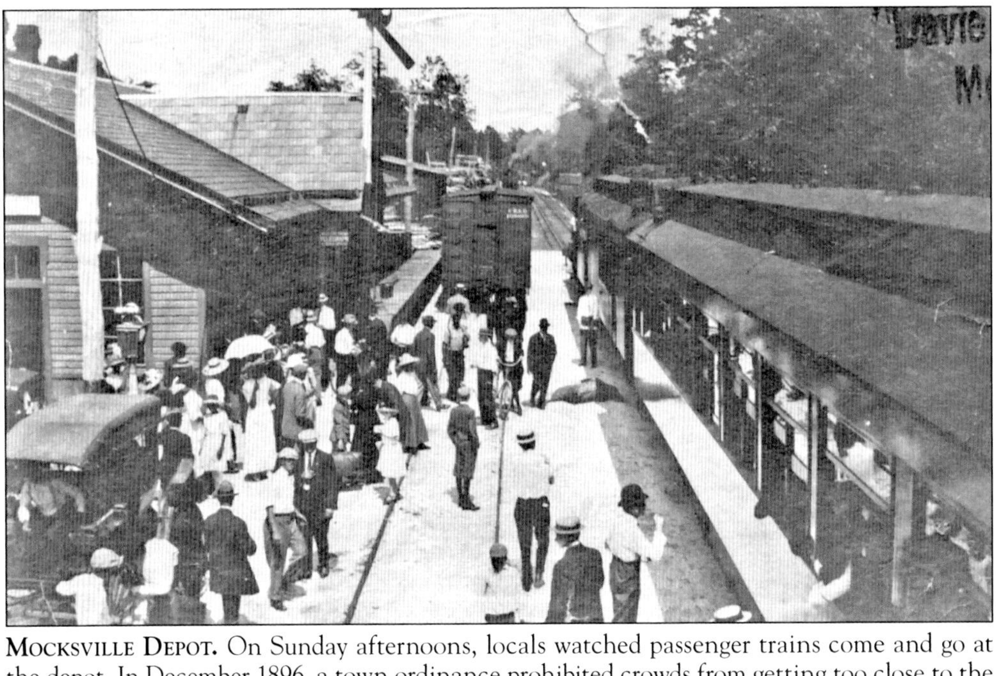

Mocksville Depot. On Sunday afternoons, locals watched passenger trains come and go at the depot. In December 1896, a town ordinance prohibited crowds from getting too close to the trains. A year later, the town appointed a special policeman to keep order.

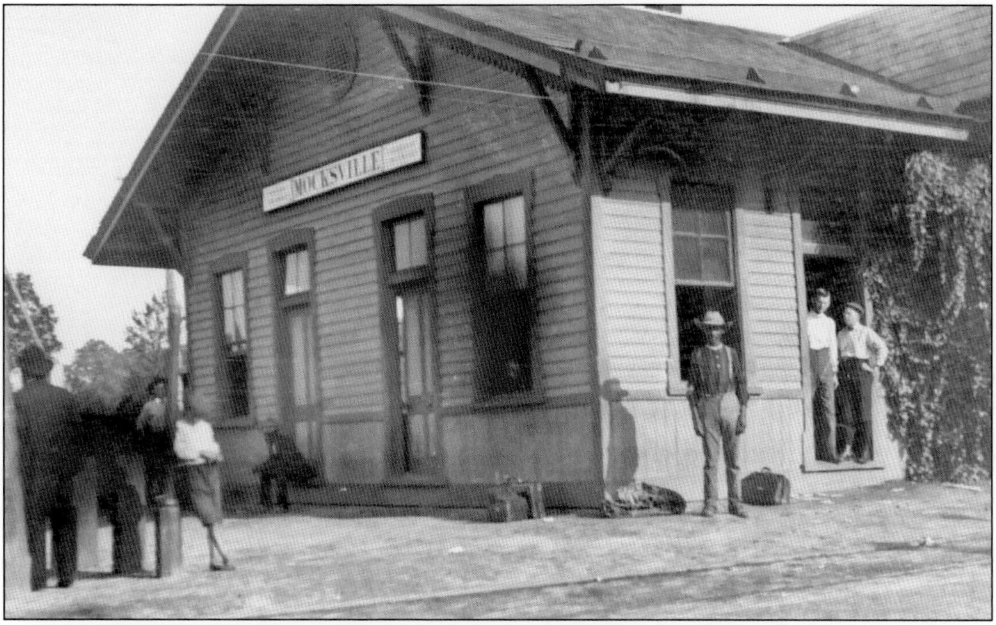

RAILROAD DEPOT STATION. One train, carrying both passengers and freight, arrived daily from Winston-Salem at 8:00 p.m. and returned at 7:00 the following morning. The engine pulled the train to Mocksville and pushed the train back to Winston-Salem after being turned by hand on a turntable near the depot. Both passenger and mail service ceased in 1967.

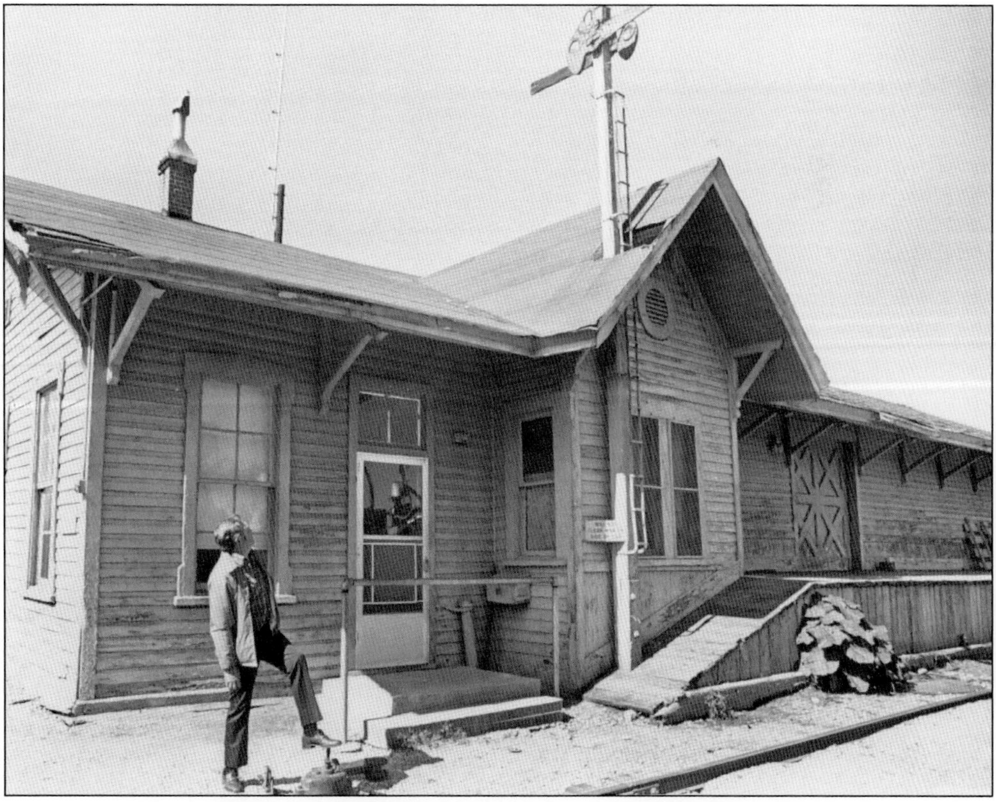

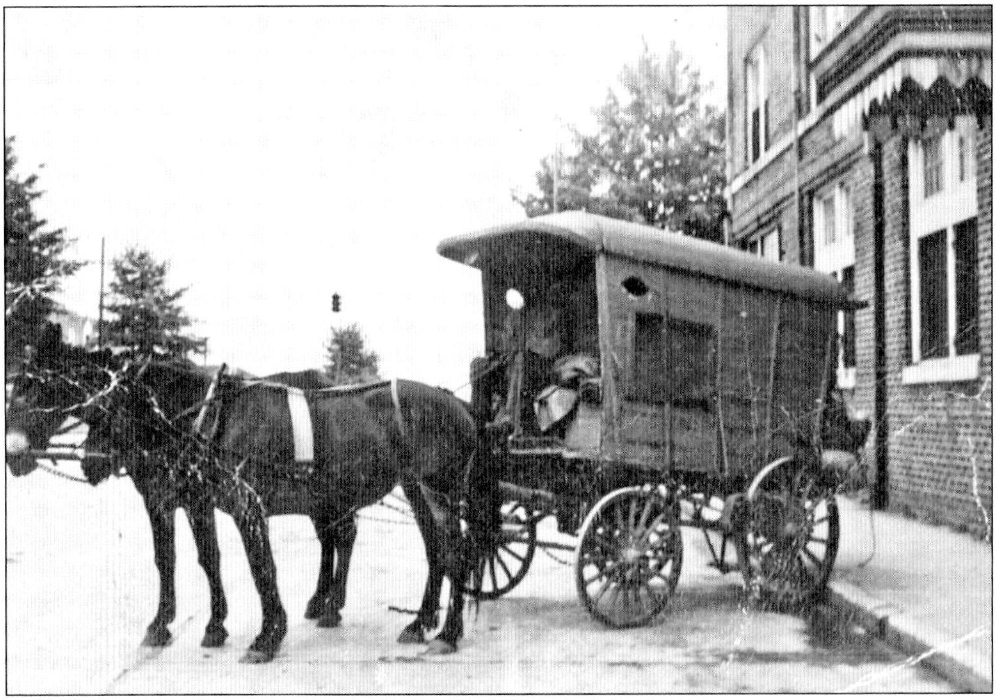

MAIL WAGON. Perry Arnold hauled the mail from the train depot to the post office in the 1930s.

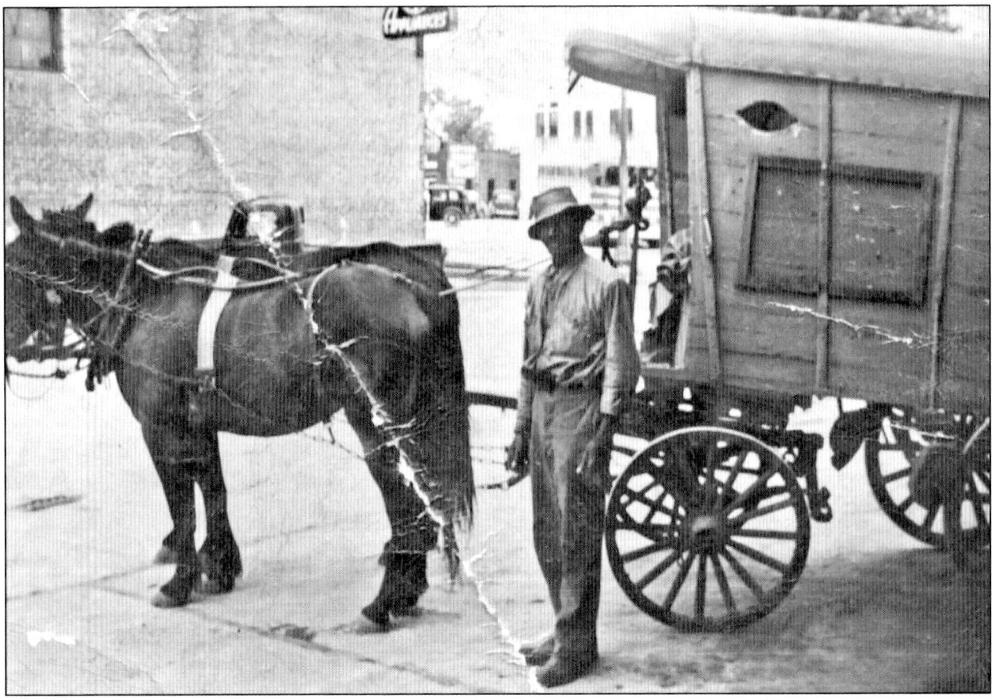

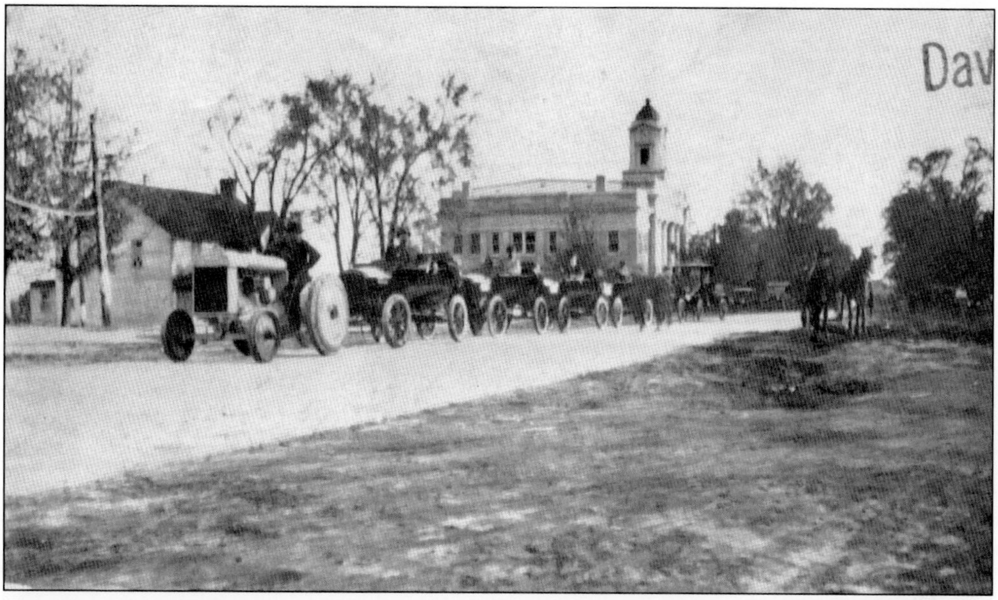

New Ford Model Ts. A tractor pulls a line of new cars through the Mocksville square. Ford Motor Company shipped the unassembled Model Ts by train. Sanford Motor Company workers then unloaded the cars at the train depot, placed the bodies on the chassis, hooked the cars together, and pulled them by tractor to the motor company to complete assembly. The March House (left) and the courthouse appear in the background.

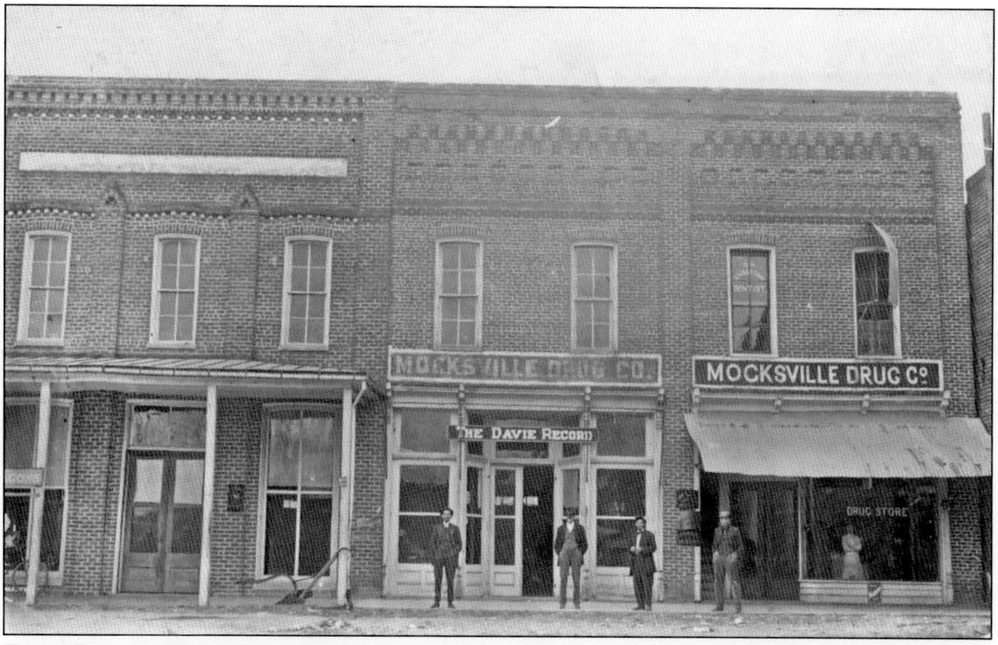

Davie Record Newspaper Office. From left to right stand editor and owner C. Frank Stroud, police chief W. P. Etchison, Armit Sheek, and an unidentified man. The newspaper's original owner, E. H. Morris, printed its first edition on April 1, 1899. C. Frank Stroud bought the newspaper in 1908. The C. C. Sanford and Sons Company appears to the left and the Mocksville Drug Company to the right. Dr. R. P. Anderson practiced dentistry on the second floor over the drugstore.

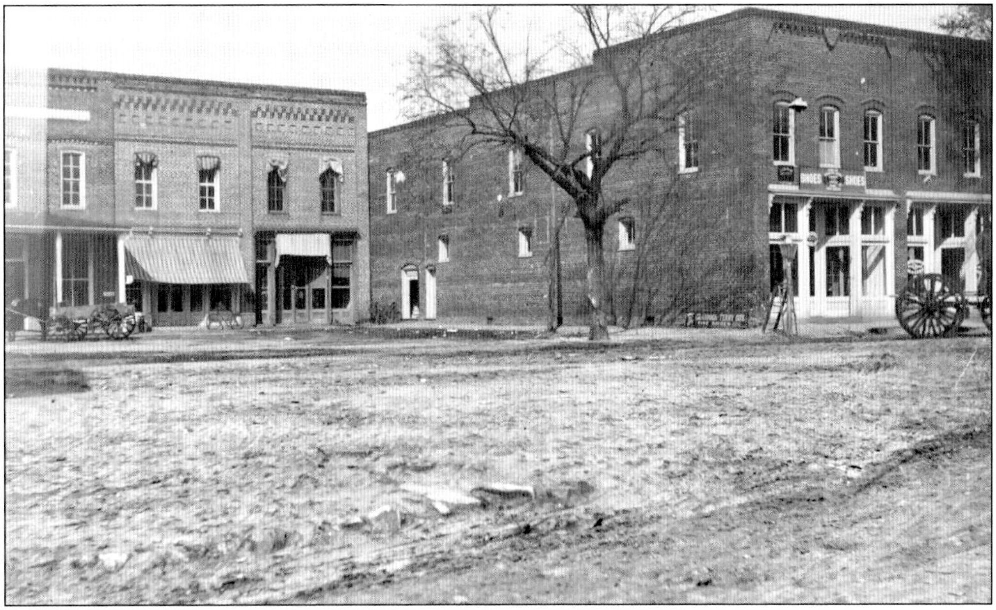

West Side of Square. Two views of the west side of the square show the Mocksville Drug Store (left) and the A. M. McGlamery and Company, a retailer of shoes, clothing, dry goods, and notions, before and after signage and power lines. The drugstore opened in July 1908, "prepared to dispense ice cream, crushed fruits, and all the soft drinks. A complete line of drugs and sundries will be carried, and prescriptions filled," according to the *Davie Record*. Electric lights illuminated about 200 homes in Mocksville on January 26, 1924. A public celebration marked the event on the square with music by the Cooleemee Band.

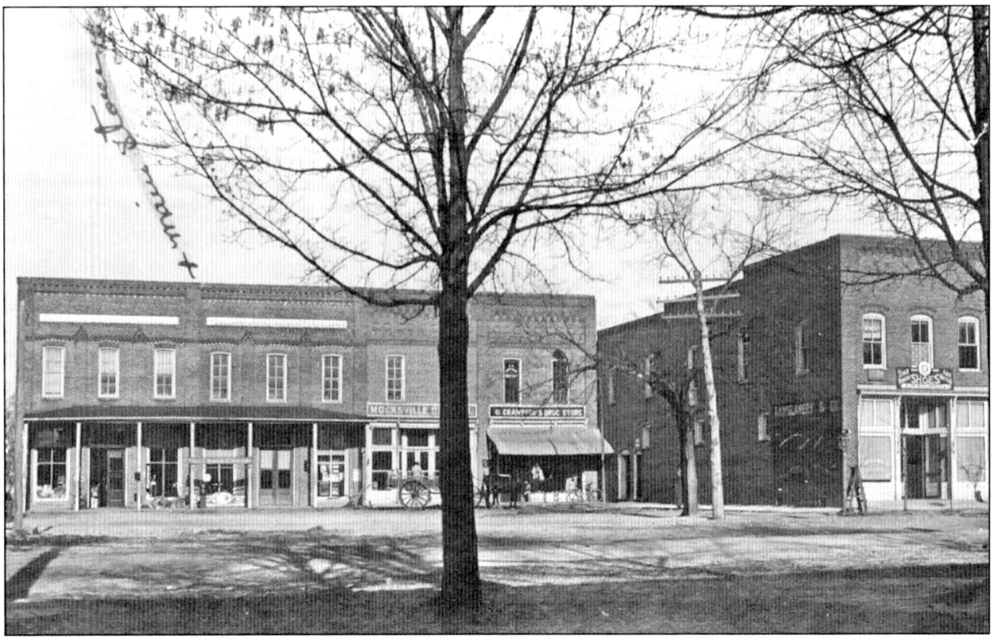

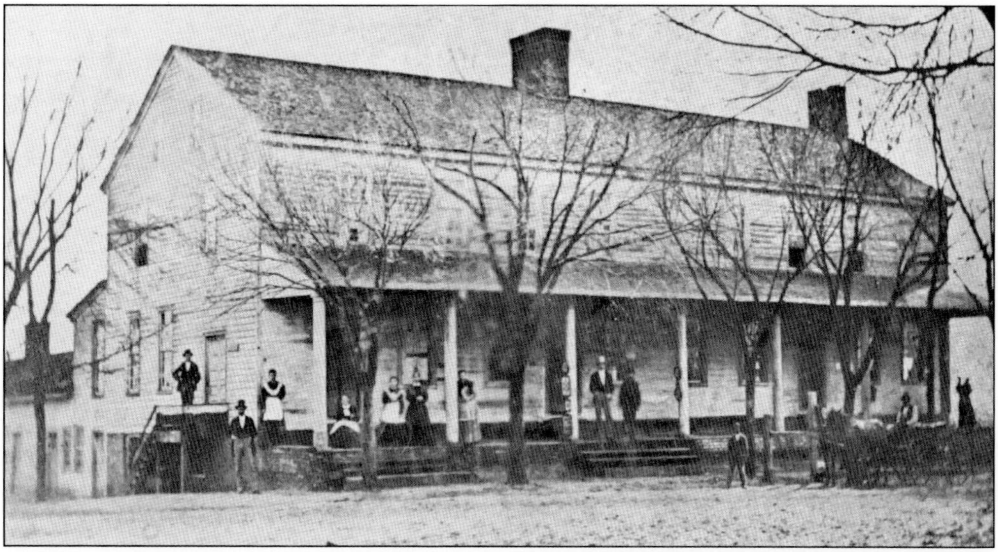

KELLY OR DAVIE HOTEL. The hotel stood on the site of today's Mocksville Courthouse. For 70 years, the hotel represented the hub of social activity in Mocksville, hosting many balls, dances, skating parties, and receptions. The *Western Carolinian* first advertised the hotel on February 14, 1839: "New Establishment in Mocksville, Davie County. Thomas Foster informs the public that he has removed from his former stand to his new building on the public square in the town of Mocksville where he will continue to keep a House of Entertainment. His house is roomy and commodious, attached to which are six comfortable offices for gentlemen of the Bar, all convenient to the Court House. The subscriber pledges himself to the most diligent exertions to give satisfaction to such as may call on him. His Table, Bar and Stables are provided in the best manner that the country will afford, and his servants are faithful and prompt." On December 14, 1904, the hotel went up in flames. Fortunately, the fire only cost the life of Holloway Pass's bird dog.

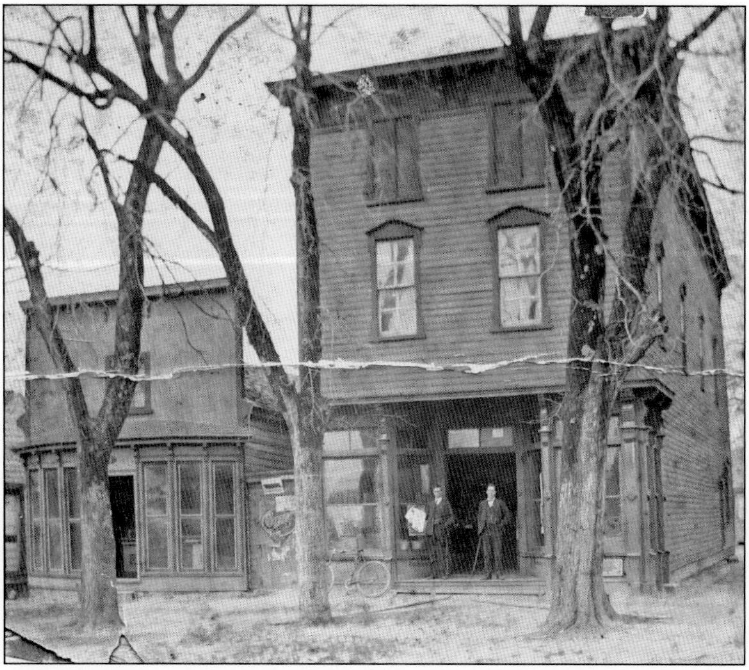

WILLIAMS AND ANDERSON GENERAL STORE, C. 1905. Clerk Arthur Daniel (left) and proprietor Zollicofer Anderson stand in the doorway of the general store owned by Anderson and O. L. Williams. Thomas Young owned the building. The structure to the left housed the P. K. Manos café.

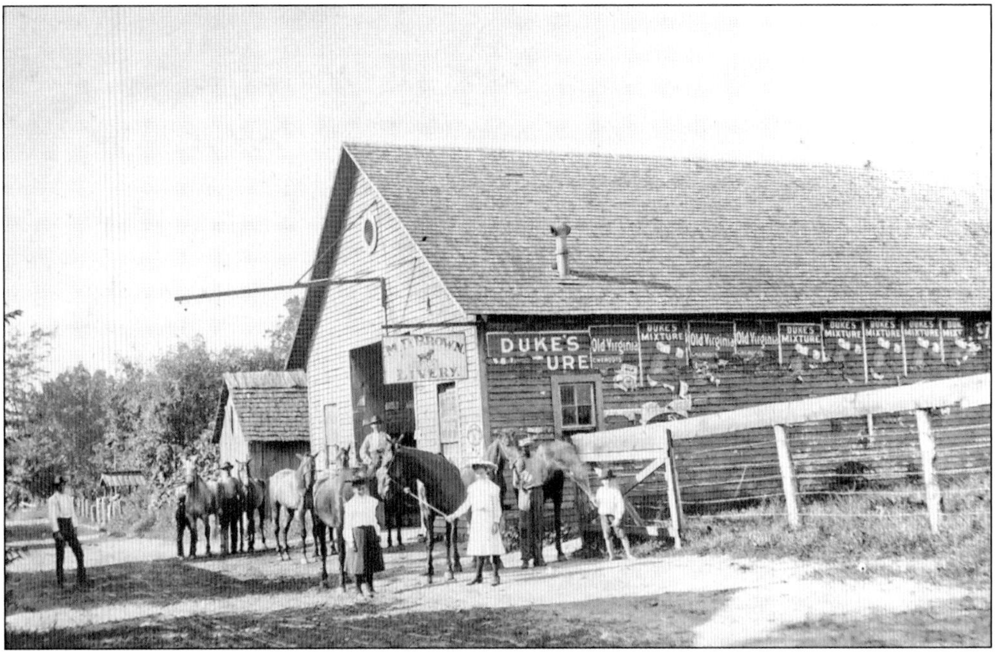

Mack Brown Livery Stable. The livery stable stood on the site of the present-day Mocksville Town Hall between Salisbury and Clement Streets. Salesmen arriving on the train from Winston-Salem rented buggies to make their rounds within the county.

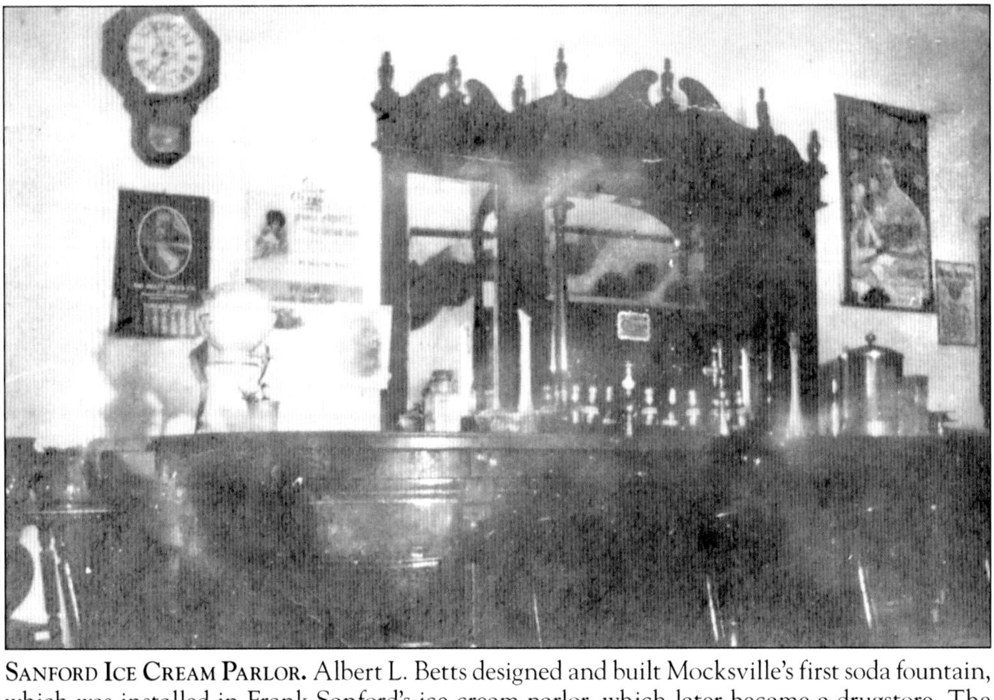

Sanford Ice Cream Parlor. Albert L. Betts designed and built Mocksville's first soda fountain, which was installed in Frank Sanford's ice cream parlor, which later became a drugstore. The cabinet featured hand-carved woodwork. Sanford's later became Wilkins Drug Store.

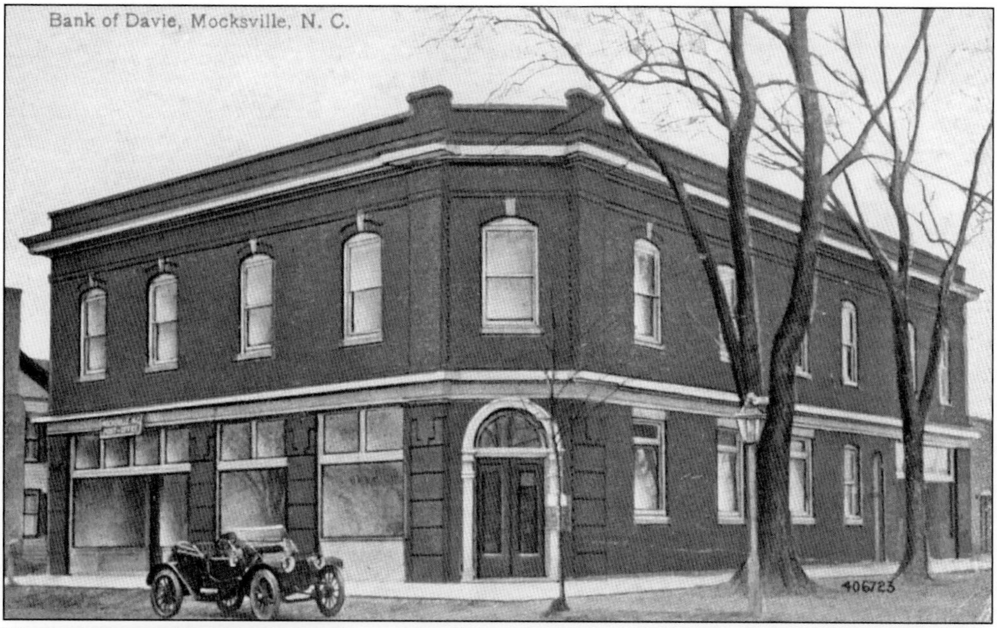

BANK OF DAVIE. The first Davie County bank, established in 1901, appointed as officers president W. A. Bailey, vice presidents T. B. Bailey and James McGuire Jr., cashier T. J. Byerly, and attorney E. L. Gaither; and as directors J. F. Hanes, H. Clement, James McGuire, E. M. Armfield, W. F. Byerly, Z. N. Anderson, C. C. Sanford, W. A. Bailey, A. M. McGlamery, E. E. Hunt, O. L. Williams, W. J. Armfield, and H. T. Smithdeal. The bank operated out of the first floor of the Masonic Building. On January 26, 1903, T. J. Byerly and James McGuire Jr. prevented a bank robbery. Byerly, who roomed near the bank, heard two explosions and roused McGuire. Arming themselves with shotguns, they found the bank door blown open with nitroglycerine and exchanged a dozen or more shots with the burglars, who escaped. Authorities later arrested the four bank robbers—James Lang, Walter Wood, Charles Rogers, and H. B. Wilson—near Monroe, North Carolina.

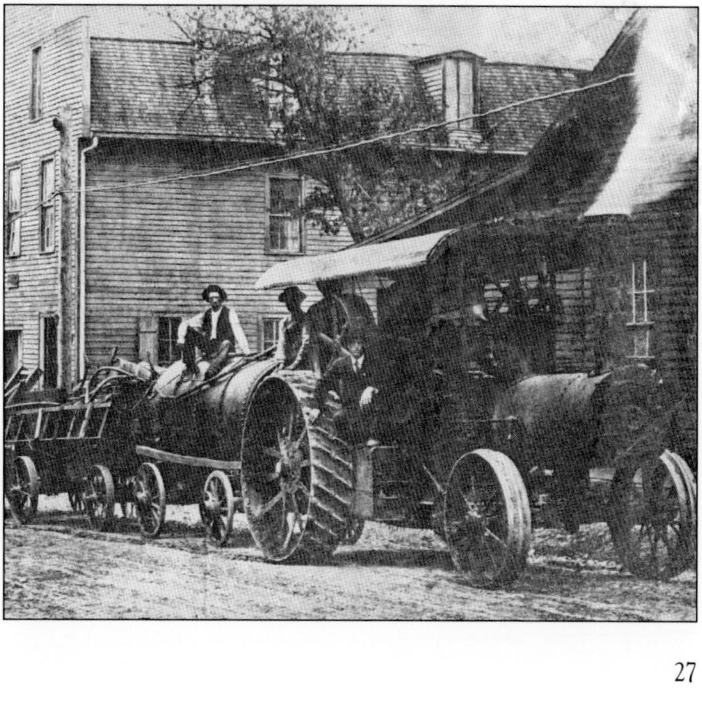

STEAM-POWERED WAGON TRAIN. On September 14, 1912, W. S. Boyd of Ijames Crossroads and Tom Gaither of Sheffield moved their sawmill from Stony Point to Mocksville. A 60-horsepower steam engine pulls the wagon train down Water Street by the Monkey Cigar Factory, which burned in 1951. Boyd sits on the water wagon, Jim Mason sits on the water tank of the steam boiler, and Guy, Tom, and Allen Gaither stand in the shadows.

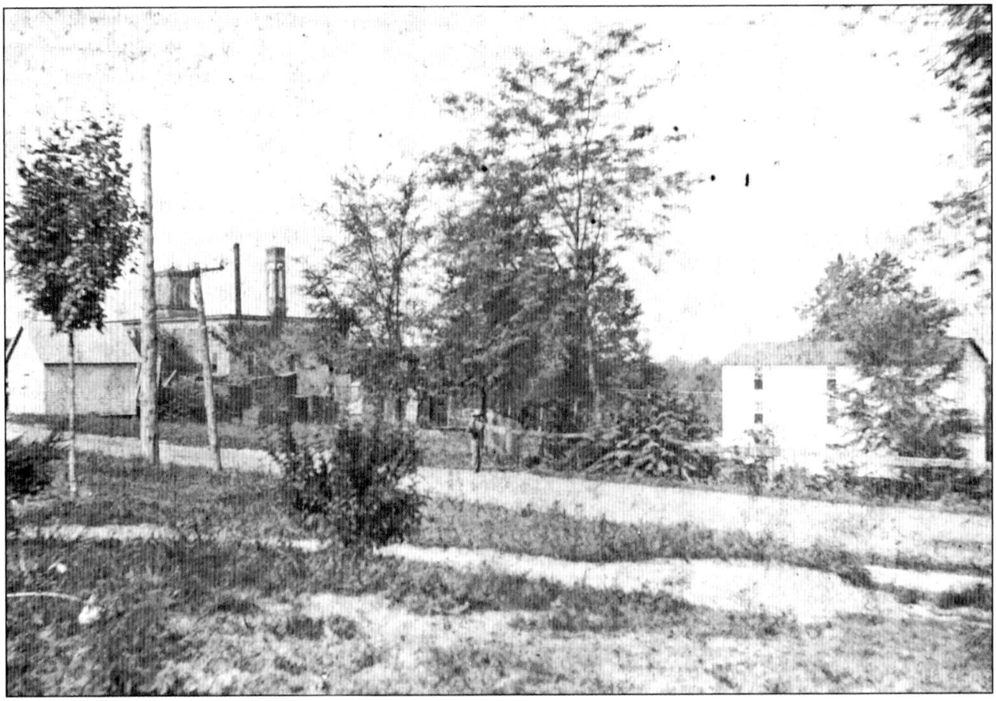

Mocksville Chair Factory. This company produced thousands of chairs from 1901 to 1917 in the old Brown Brothers Tobacco Factory at the corner of West Maple and Salisbury Streets. The factory operated by steam boilers fired with excess wood from production. Gaston Horn organized the company and supervised the plant. Company officials included Pres. E. L. Gaither, Vice Pres. C. C. Sanford, and secretary-treasurer James McGuire. Rufus Fry's photograph (above) shows the factory in July 1905. The image of factory employees (below) features night watchman Chal Brown holding a lantern.

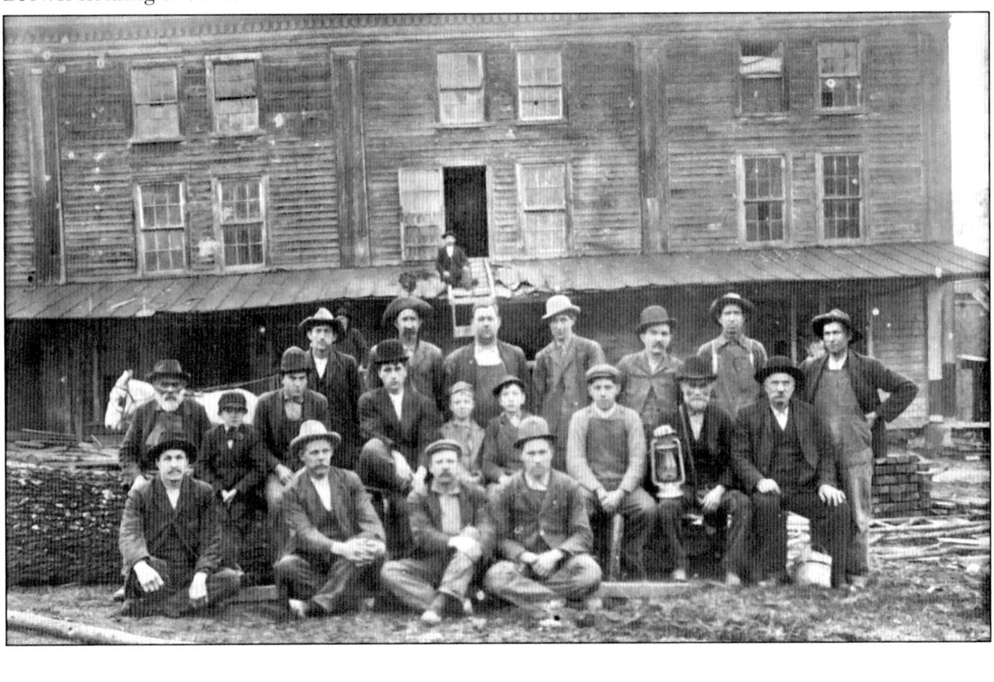

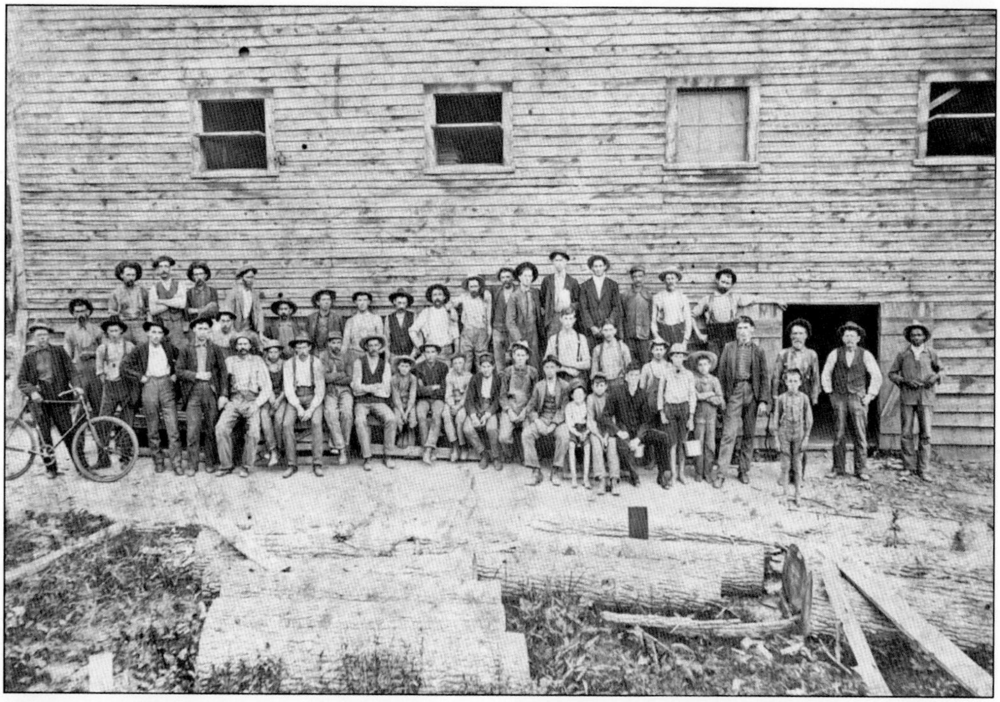

Mocksville Chair Factory Employees. The employees pose in front of the factory between 1906 and 1910. In the image below, only three workers are identified: W. H. Smith (first row, third from the left), Whitt Austin (third row, third from the left), and Giles Howard (second row, far right, with the long white beard).

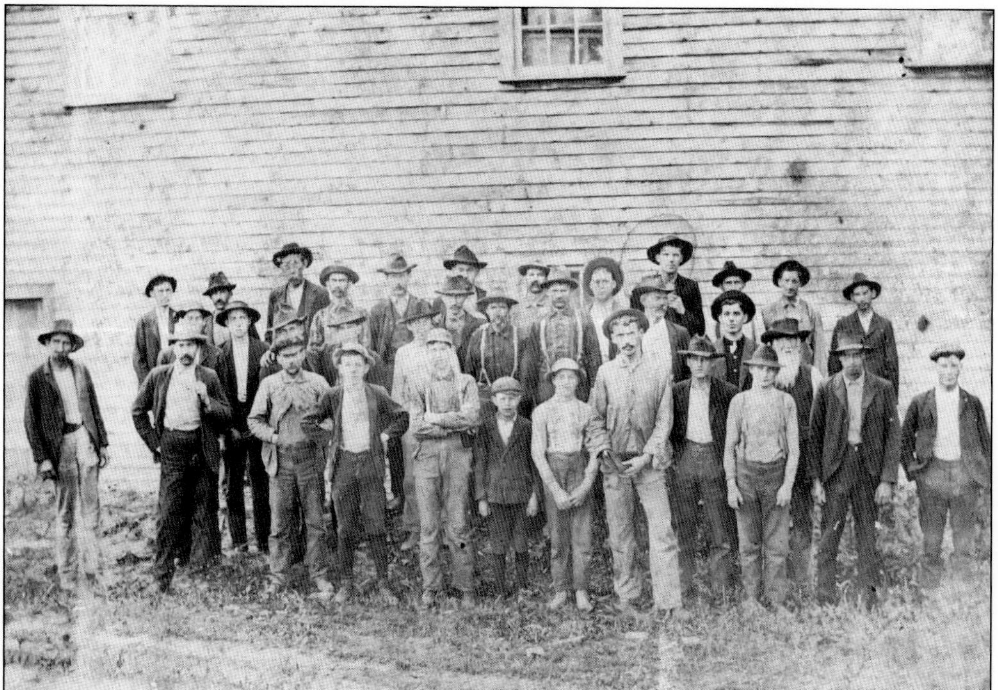

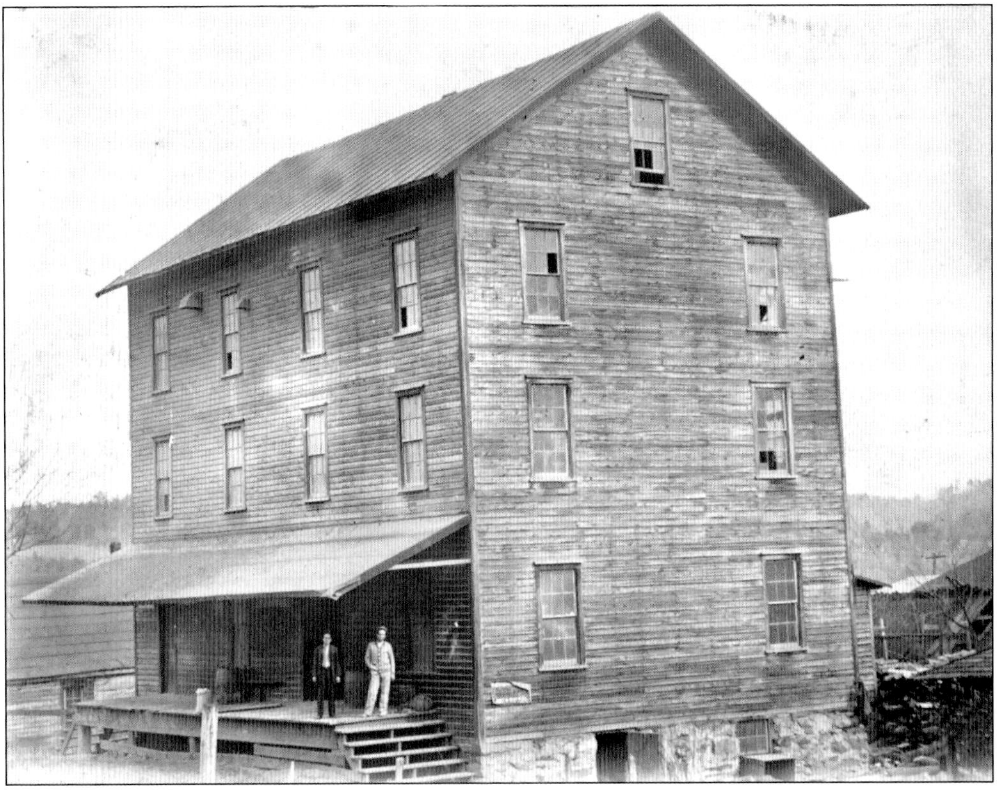

BROWN'S MILL, 1907. Brown's Grist Mill, the forerunner of the J. P. Green Milling Company, operated on Dutchman's Creek at the Salem Road crossing, below the present bridge on Highway 158. J. P. Green bought the mill in 1911 and moved the building to its present location on Depot Street.

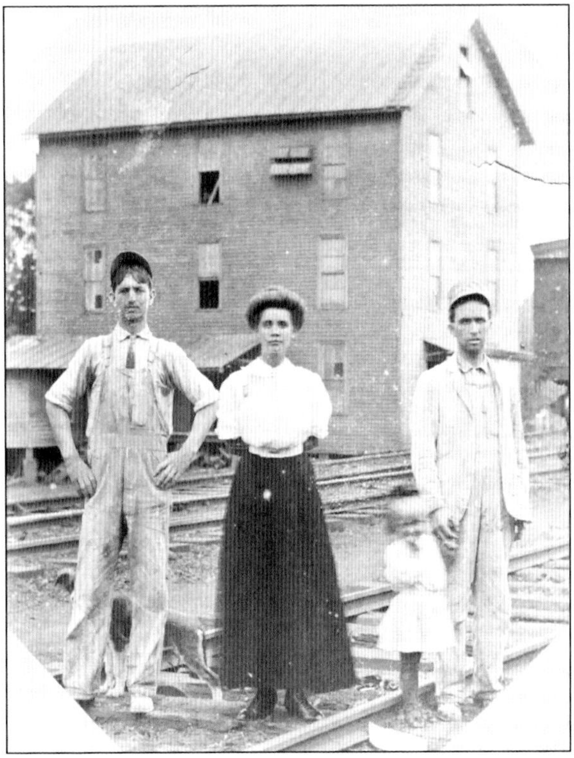

J. P. GREEN MILLING COMPANY. Frank McCubbins, Henrietta Wilson, F. K. Benson, and J. F. Naylor stand in front of the mill, the oldest manufacturing company in Davie County still operating under its original name.

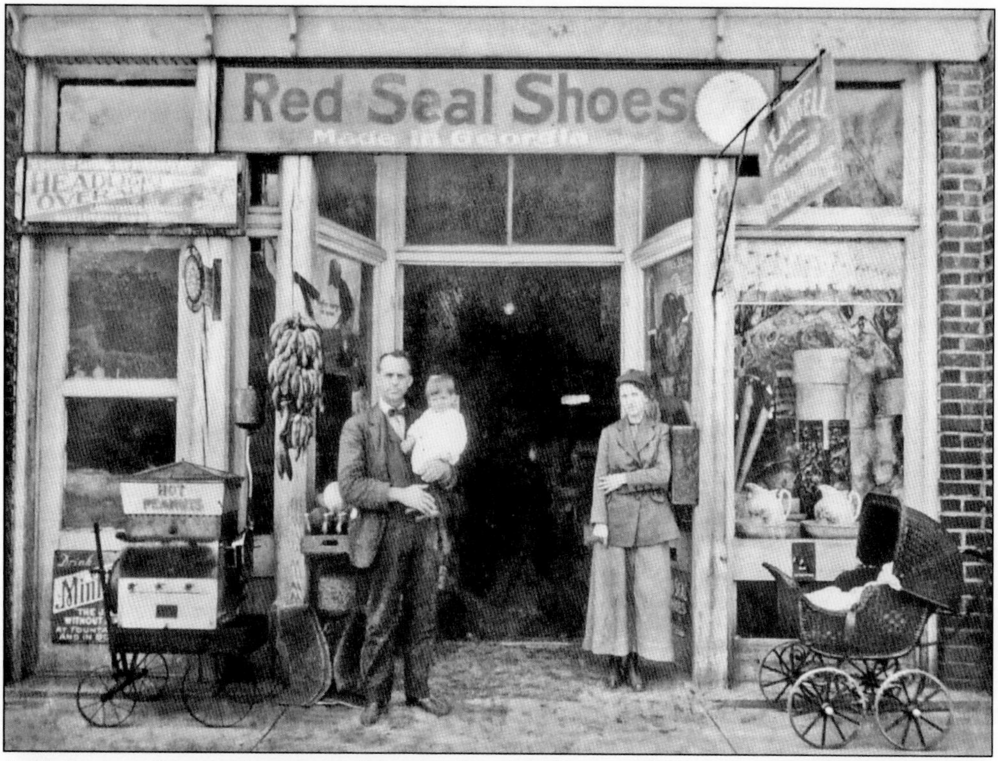

J. T. ANGELL STORE (EXTERIOR). John Tilden Angell entered the mercantile business in Oak Grove around 1897, later moved his store to Fork Church, in April 1908 relocated to Mocksville, and in 1910 erected the brick building on Main Street shown in the above photograph. Spending 33 years in the mercantile business, Angell operated under the slogan "Pay Less and Tote."

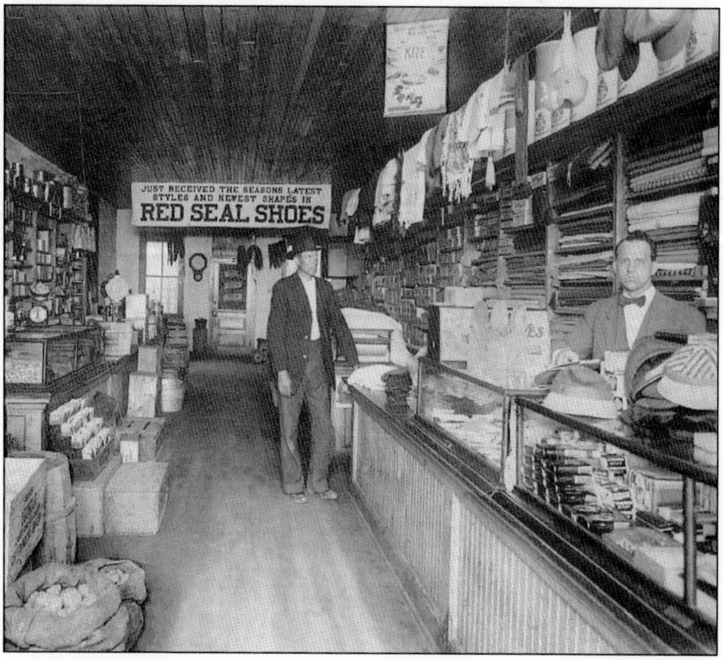

J. T. ANGELL STORE (INTERIOR). The November 5, 1915, *Davie Record* newspaper advertised, "Don't Forget Angell's this week. Try me for good prices. Try Angell for just a short time, say eight or twelve months. I will sell at a cut price. When in town come to see me. If you don't buy, let me see you any way." The store sold Good and Sweet Candy, Sea Island Sheeting, Arbuckle's Coffee, buckets, clothing, oats, cottonseed meal, and sweet feed.

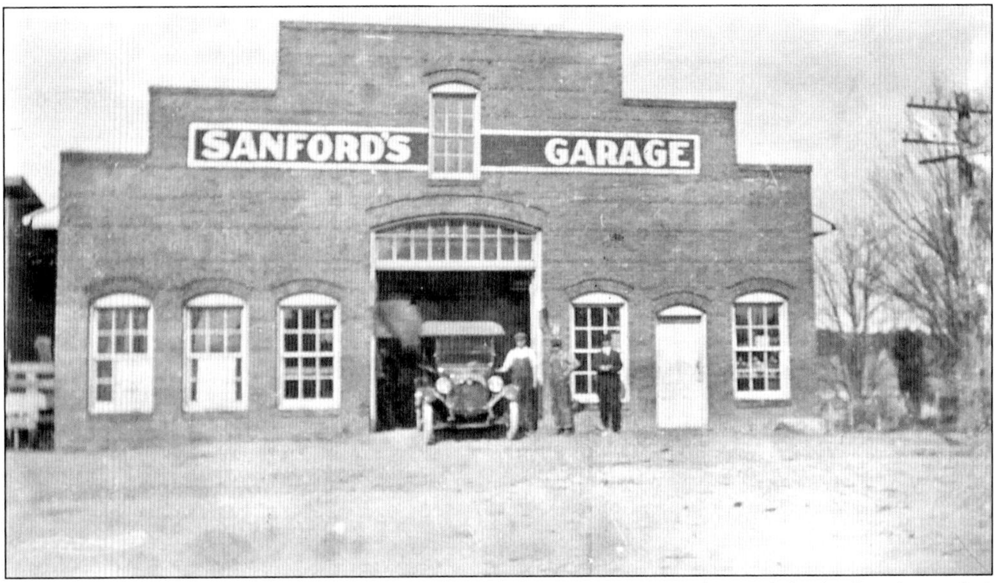

SANFORD'S GARAGE. The C. C. Sanford and Sons Company operated a Ford dealership from 1913 to 1960, when the local franchise was transferred to Reavis Ford. Sanford advertised in 1915, "A Car of Fords received today. Two sold. If you want one better put in your order at once. Runabout $480; Touring Car $530."

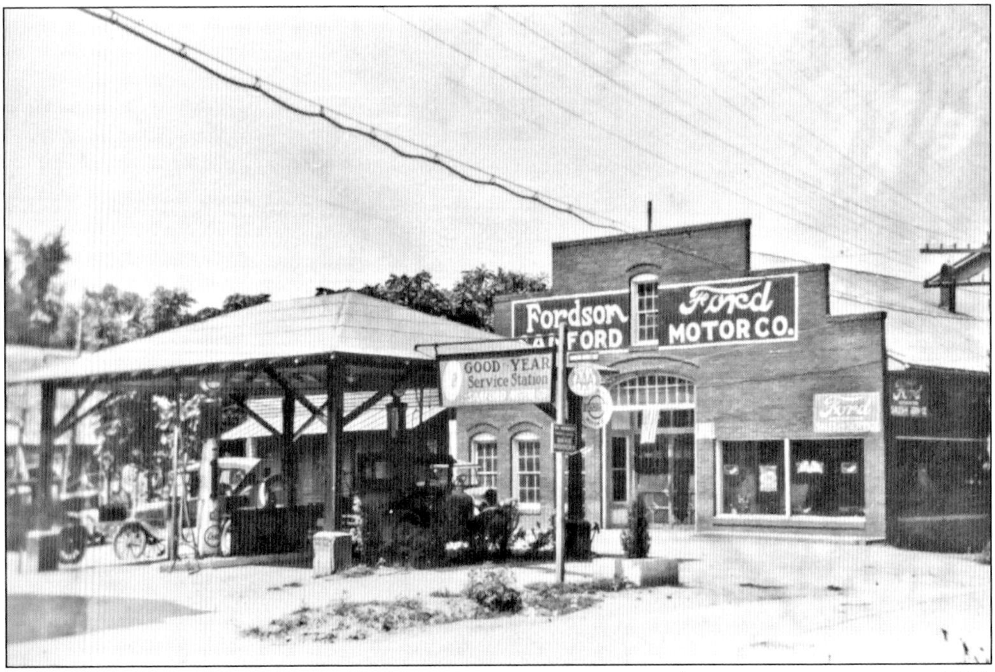

SANFORD MOTOR COMPANY. Sanford Motor Company organized as a separate entity in 1924. Construction of the current Mocksville Town Hall led to the razing of the building in 1977. The Sanfords also opened one of the earliest service stations in the area across Clement Street from the motor company. Esso recognized the business as one of the oldest continuously operating Standard Oil service stations in the country in 1956, including the tenure of gasoline pumps situated in front of the motor company. (Courtesy of Gwynn Meroney.)

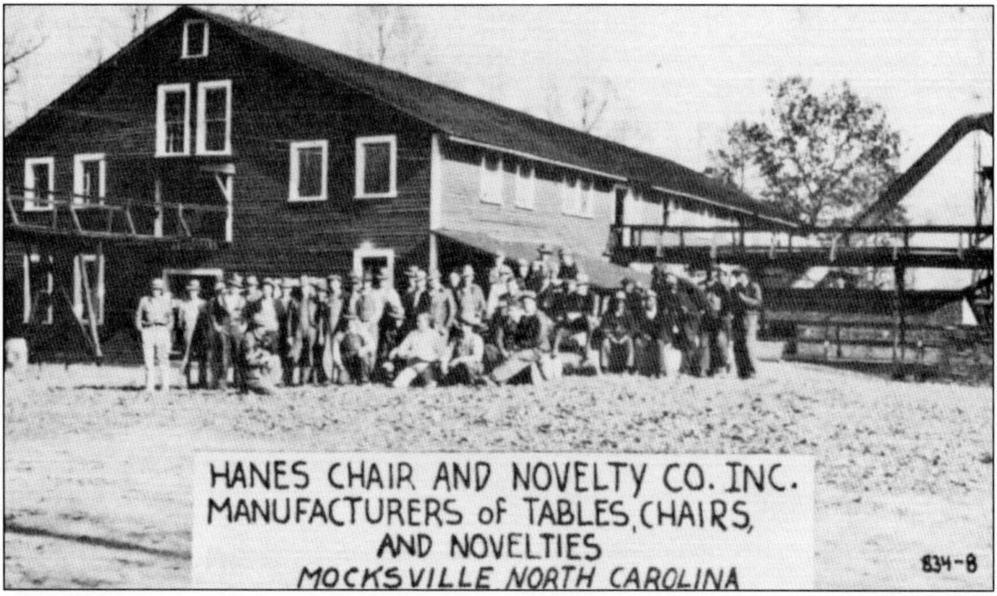

Hanes Chair and Novelty Company, Inc. J. B. Johnstone and J. F. Hanes founded Hanes Chair and Table, located on the east side of the railroad, north of the train depot. R. D. Bayless of Athens, Tennessee, and J. W. Harris of Charlotte bought and renamed the factory Hanes Chair and Novelty Company in 1937. Fire destroyed the building in 1945, but production resumed later that year. D. E. Headen of High Point purchased and renamed the company Hanes Chair and Furniture in 1947.

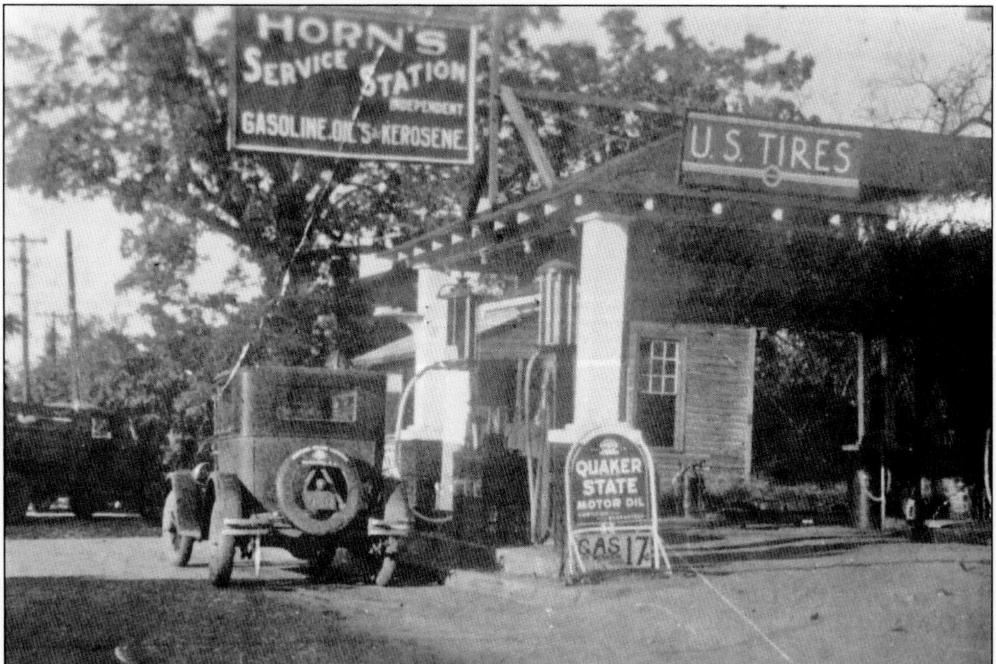

Horn's Service Station. Claude Horn Sr. owned and operated the service station on Main Street. The photograph, taken in the 1920s or 1930s, also shows the office of attorney Jacob Stewart in the background. (Courtesy of Gwynn Meroney.)

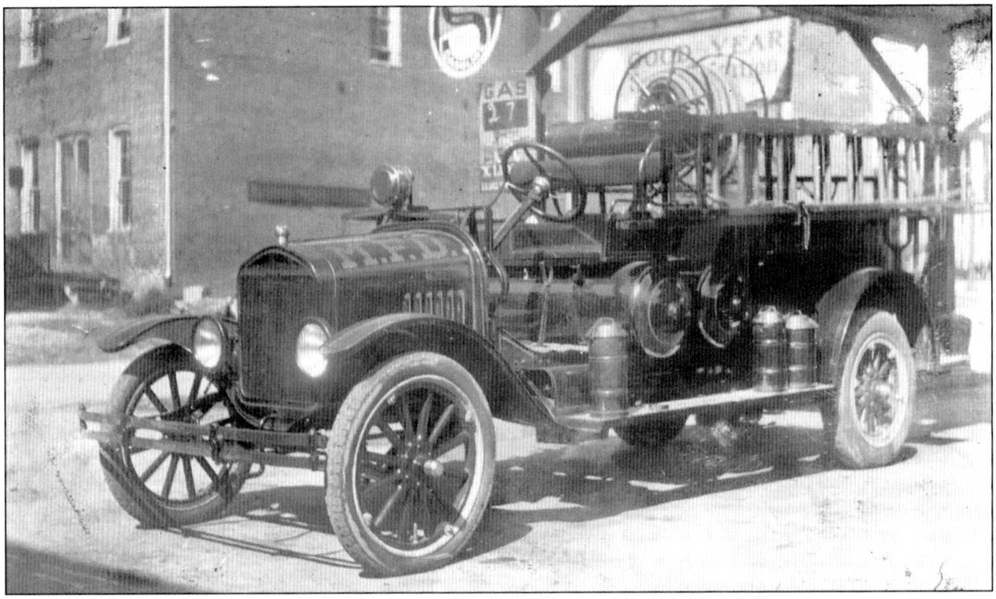

MOCKSVILLE'S FIRST FIRE TRUCK. The truck, built on a Model T chassis and purchased by the town in 1925, featured a 20-horsepower motor and a speed of 35 miles per hour. Equipment included two 30-gallon soda-acid tanks, four 2.5-gallon portable tanks, and 400 feet of 2.5-inch hose. Prior to the fire truck, firemen hand-pulled a cart with a hose mounted on a reel.

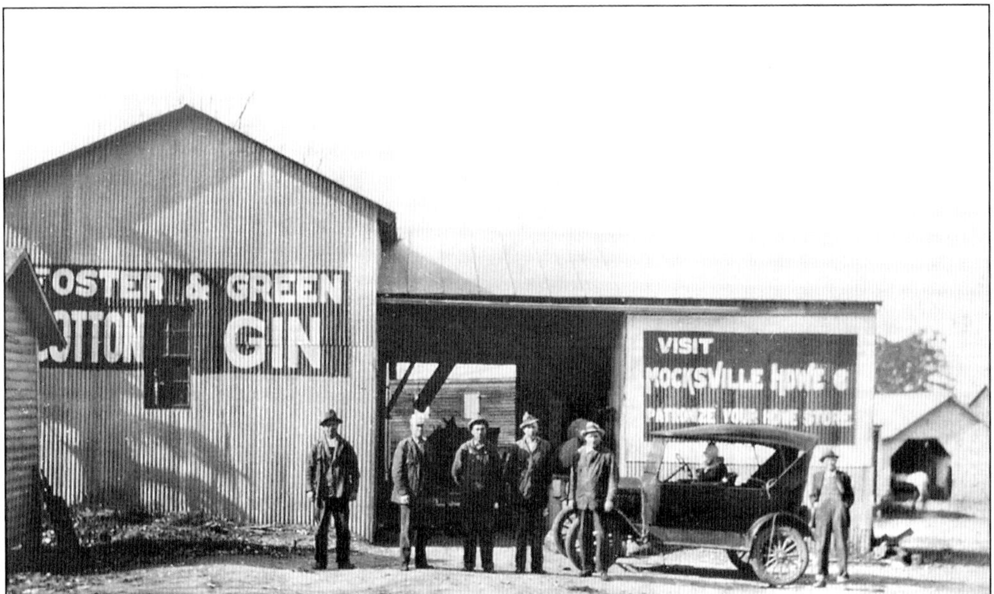

FOSTER AND GREEN COTTON GIN. In 1928, E. Pierce Foster and J. P. Green established a cotton gin on Salisbury Street on property originally belonging to the Clement estate. During the first year of operation, the site ginned 1,200 bales of cotton, increasing to 2,200 bales over the next three to four years. At the death of J. P. Green, Pierce Foster purchased full interest in the operation. In 1950, the Foster Cotton Gin moved from its location in town to the Salisbury highway. The photograph above shows six men standing, from left to right, unidentified, J. P. Green, unidentified, Grady Sain, E. Pierce Foster, and unidentified.

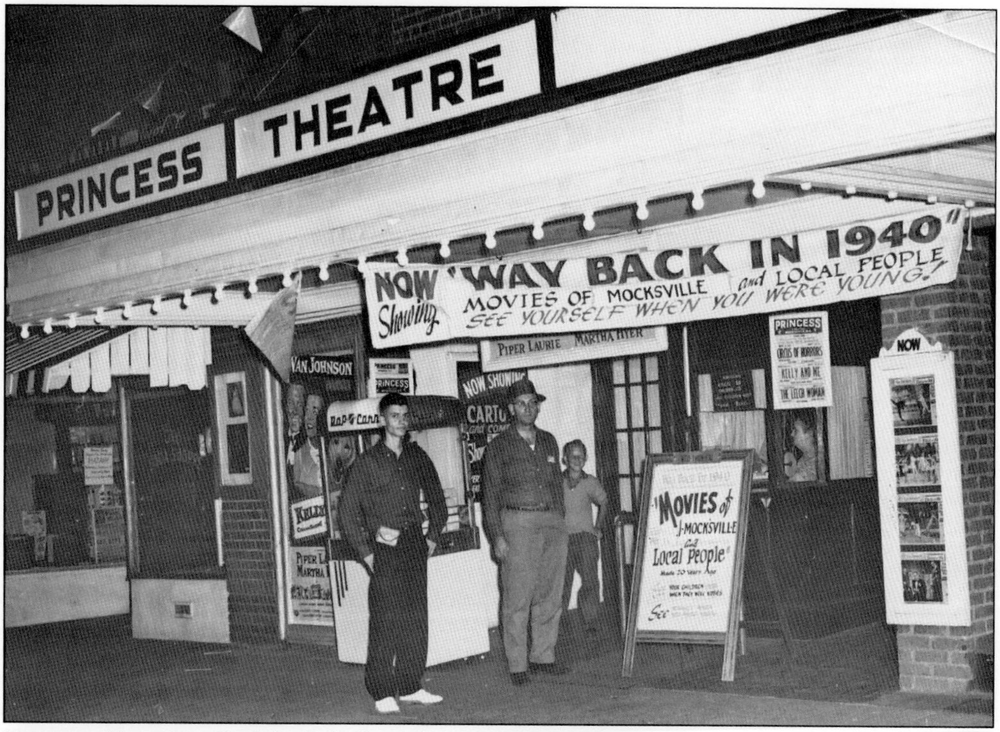

Princess Theatre. Built by J. A. Daniel in 1927, Frank Fowler took over the operation in 1937. The theater closed in 1963 after 36 years in business. Lee Waters of Lexington, who made a series of films in Davie County in the 1930s and 1940s, took the above photograph about 1957, picturing from left to right Gwynn Meroney, Otis Hendrix, Freddie Young, and Ethel Fowler. (Courtesy of Gwynn Meroney.)

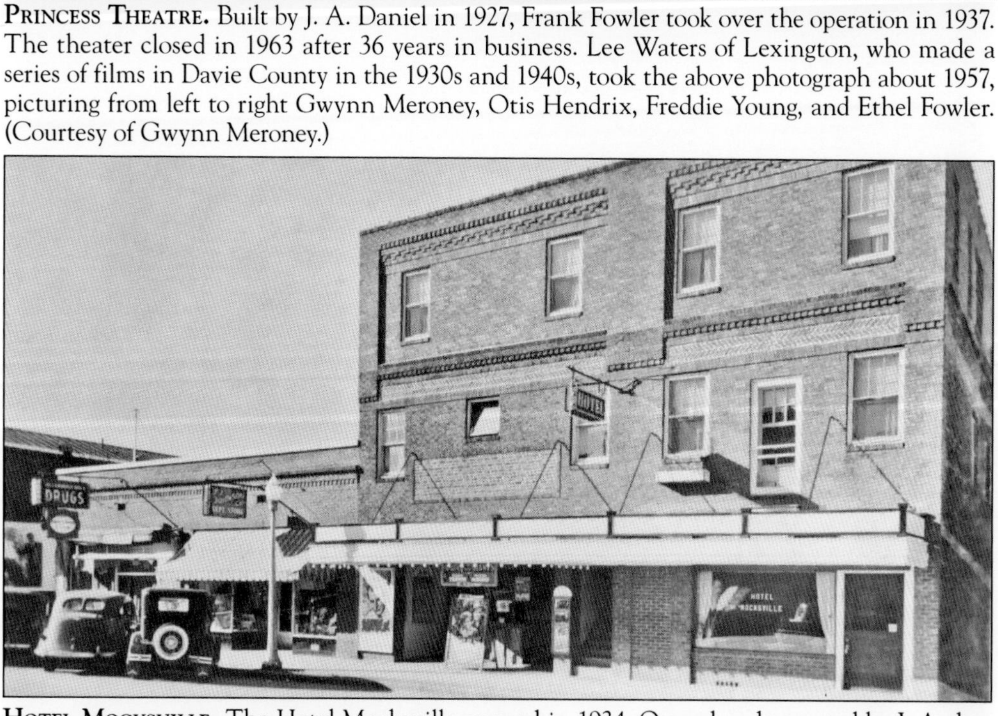

Hotel Mocksville. The Hotel Mocksville opened in 1934. Owned and operated by J. Arthur Daniel, the only hotel in town had 22 rooms. With business strong, Daniel added a third floor in 1935. Traveling salesmen chose to stay at the hotel because of its good food. Chairs lined the sidewalk, allowing guests to enjoy the cooling evening air before retiring to their rooms at night.

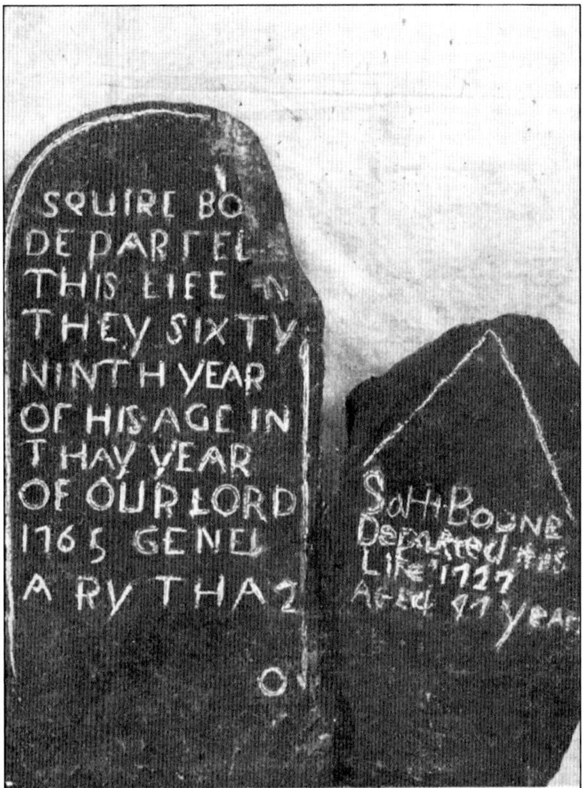

The Graves of the Father and Mother of Daniel Boone, Mocksville N. C.

7769-MANUFACTURED FOR MOCKSVILLE DRUG CO., MOCKSVILLE, N. C.

Joppa Burying Ground. Organized in 1767, Joppa Presbyterian Church began as a wooden frame structure with a door at each end in the southeast section of a graveyard. Squire Boone and Sarah Morgan Boone, the parents of Daniel Boone, lie buried in the cemetery, then known as Burying Ground Ridge. Squire Boone died in January 1765. His tombstone is the oldest known in Joppa Cemetery. Sarah died in 1777. The church moved to the town of Mocksville in 1834, leaving the cemetery neglected for many years. Preservation of the cemetery fell under the auspices of Joppa Cemetery, Inc., when the church deeded the cemetery to the organization in 1951. The cemetery continues as an important historical destination for many visitors to Mocksville.

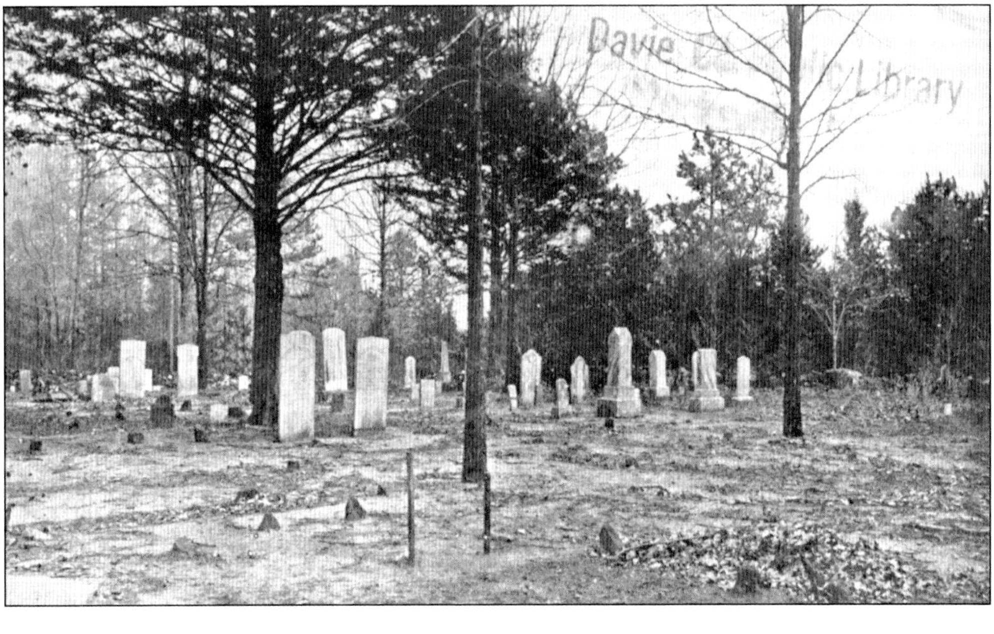

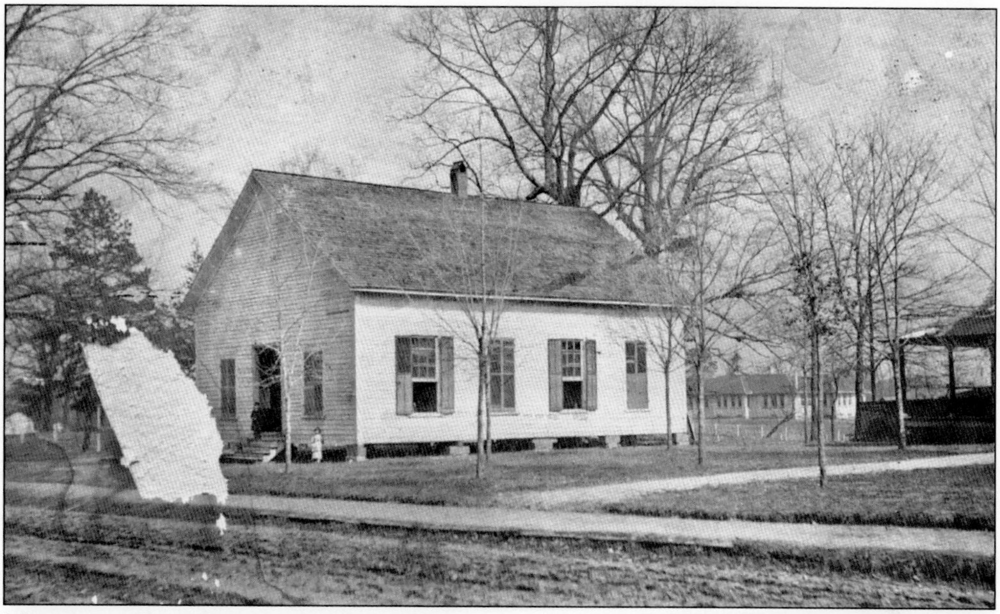

Mocksville First Baptist Church. The First Baptist Church of Mocksville organized in 1864 with 10 charter members and Moses Baldwin as the first pastor. The original white frame church, taking the congregation more than two years to build, had a front door, four windows on each side, and two windows on each end. A woodstove and kerosene lamps in wall brackets provided heating and light. The sparse interior consisted of three sections of pews divided by two side aisles, two amen corners facing the pulpit, a table and a horsehair-upholstered sofa donated by Martha Martin, and the organ. The first decade saw services conducted on a monthly basis since the preacher served several area churches. A Sunday school commenced in the courthouse in 1872.

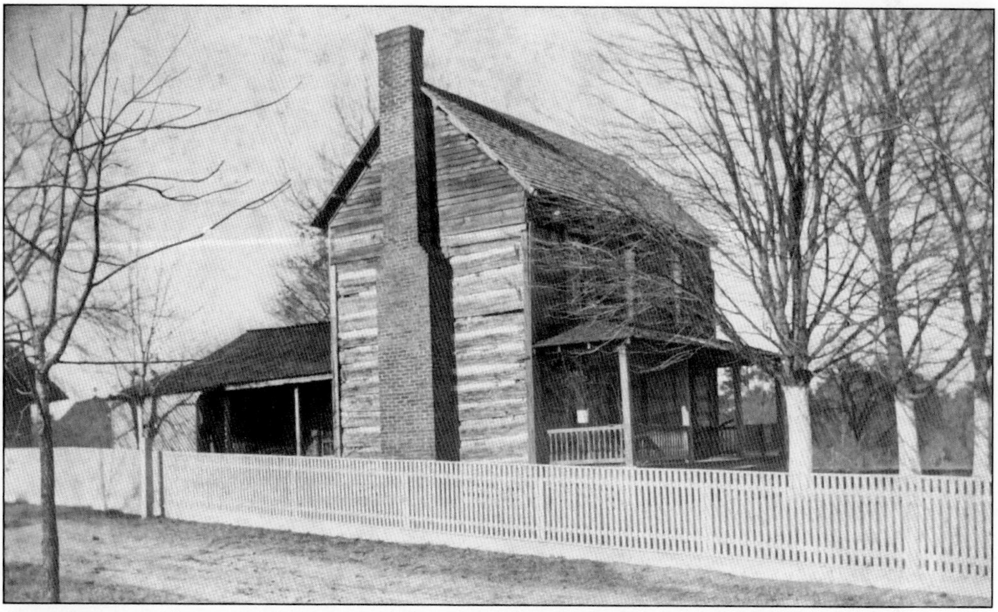

First Baptist Church Parsonage. The original parsonage stood on Salisbury Street.

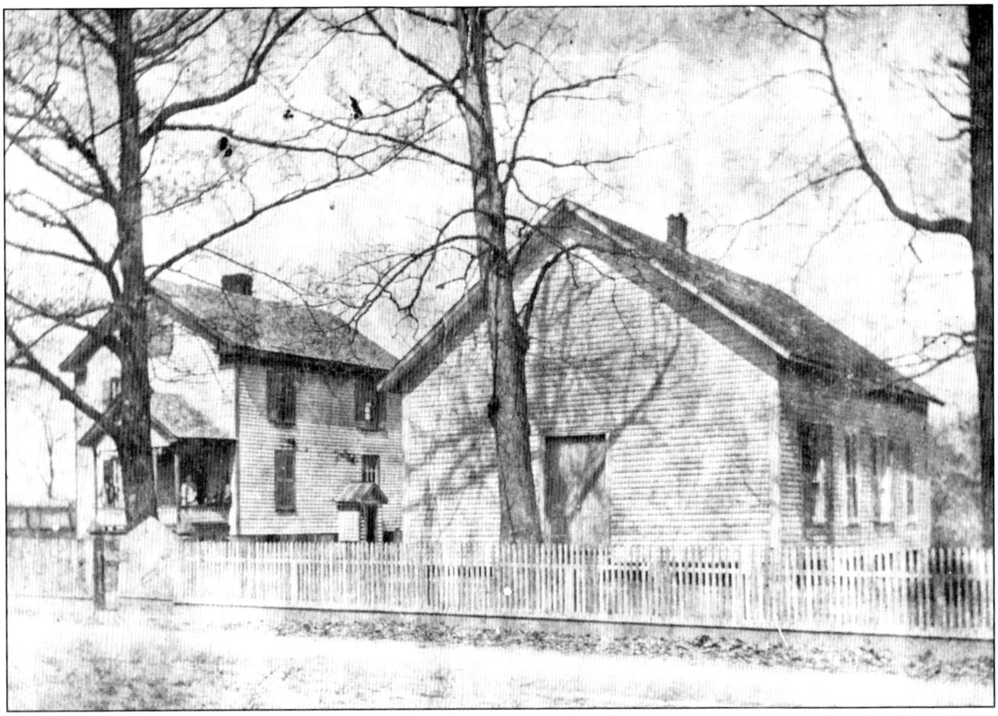

FIRST BAPTIST CHURCH AND SECOND PARSONAGE. Church construction was finished in 1875, with the second parsonage built adjacent to the church around 1883. Baptisms in the late 1880s occurred at the site of a spring down the hill behind the church. Water filled a wooden baptismal pool constructed there to a necessary depth for immersions.

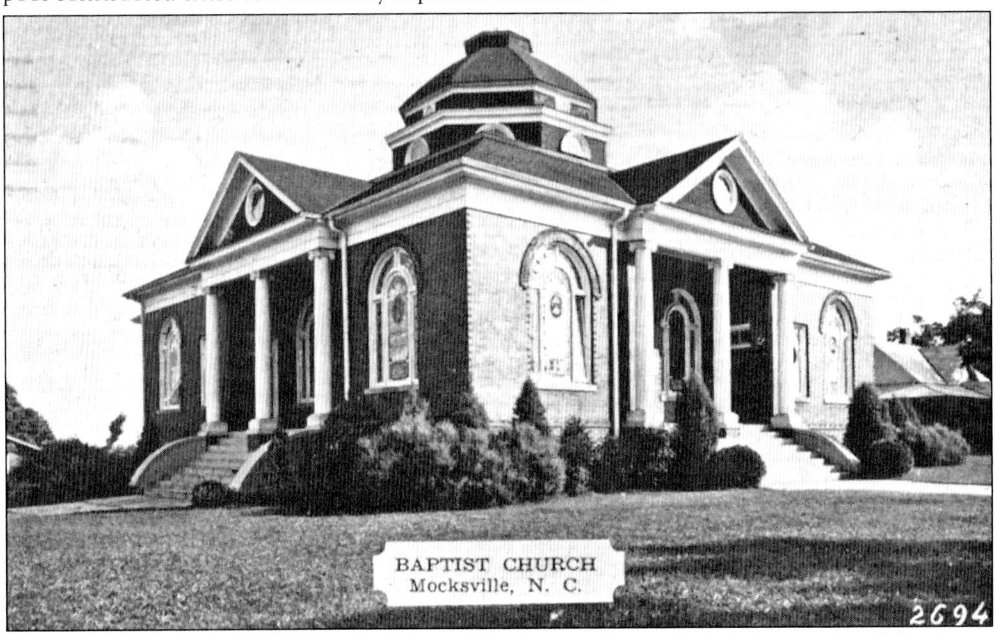

NEW FIRST BAPTIST CHURCH. The first church building stood on the current site of the Davie County Public Library. In September 1905, the church moved across the street, dedicating this new building on September 1, 1918. The church constructed the present-day sanctuary in 1967.

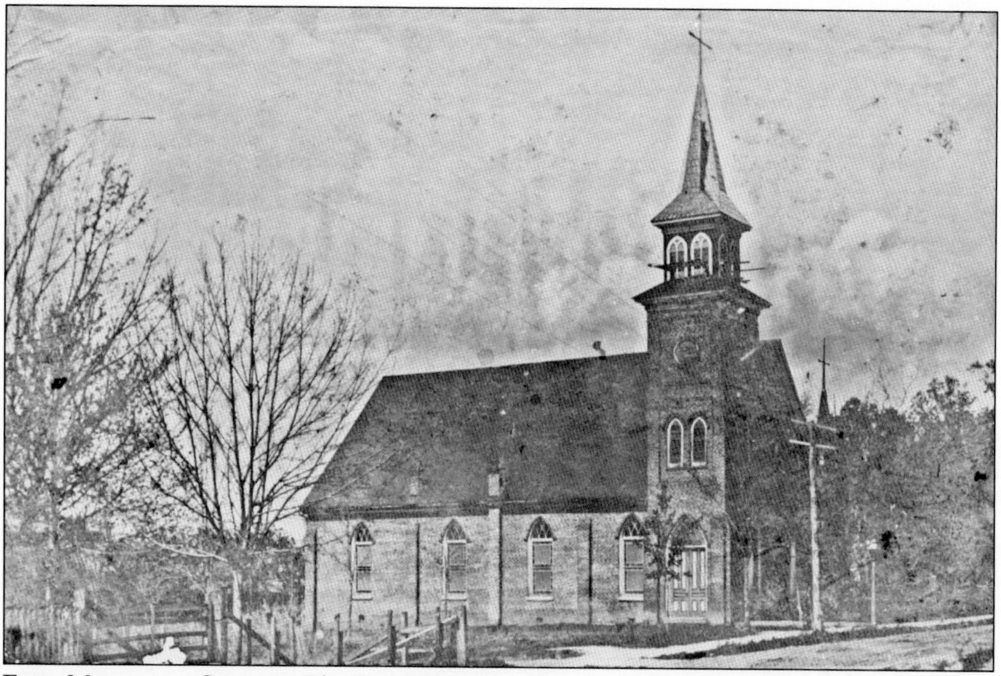

First Methodist Church. The First Methodist Church organized in 1833 with the Reverend Charles P. Moorman as the first pastor. Built in 1895, the present church was enlarged in 1918 and again in 1930. Early church leaders included Jesse A. Clement, Mark D. Armfield, Braxton Bailey, John McRorie, Baxter Clegg, Jacob Eaton, A. G. Carter, Shadrack Fitzgerald, and Henry R. Call. The church housed the first sessions of the Davie County Court from 1837 to 1839 during construction of the courthouse.

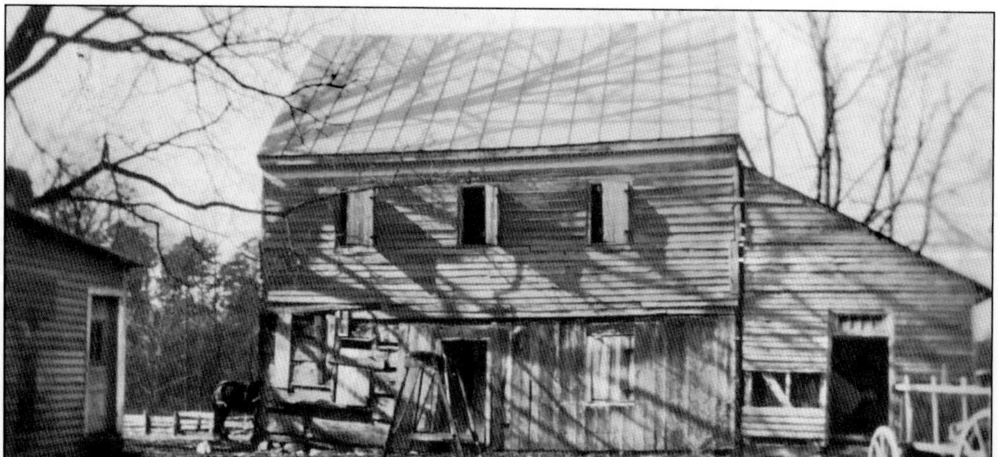

White House. Hugh Wilson, a pioneer settler of Mocksville, built the house in the original community of Mocks Old Field. Among the town's oldest landmarks, this first painted home stood on Salisbury Street facing Depot Street until its destruction in 1963.

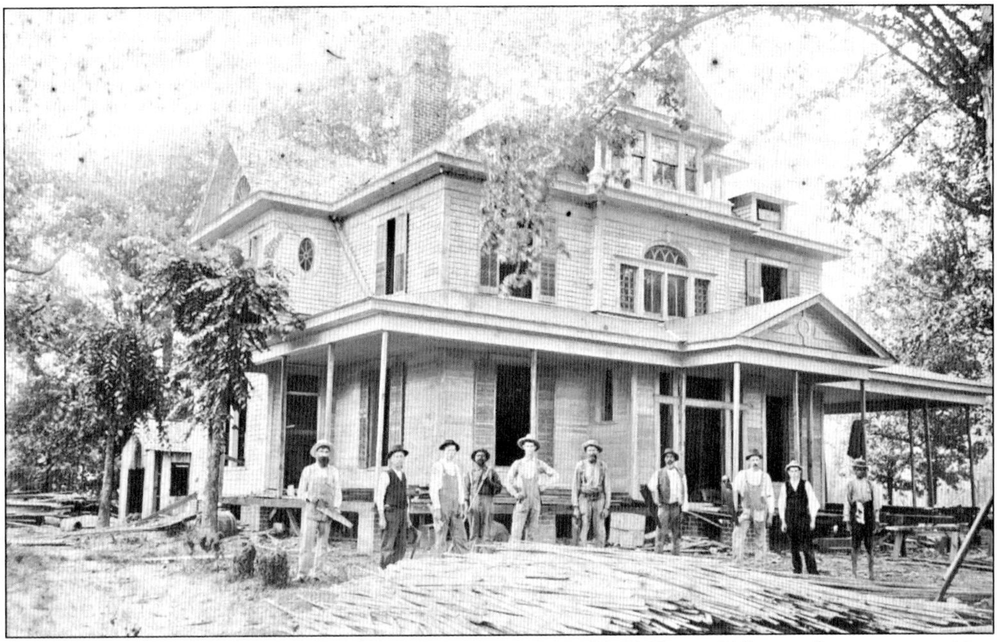

Philip Hanes House. In 1902, Philip Hanes, co-owner of B. F. Hanes Tobacco Company, and his wife, Sallie Clement Booe, built this house on property inherited from Sallie's father, Alexander Booe. The house, built on the outskirts of Mocksville at that time, still stands at the corner of North Main Street and Milling Road. Shortly after completion of the construction, Philip died from injuries sustained in an accident. His widow continued living in the home until her death in late 1927. (Courtesy of John and Susan Stowers.)

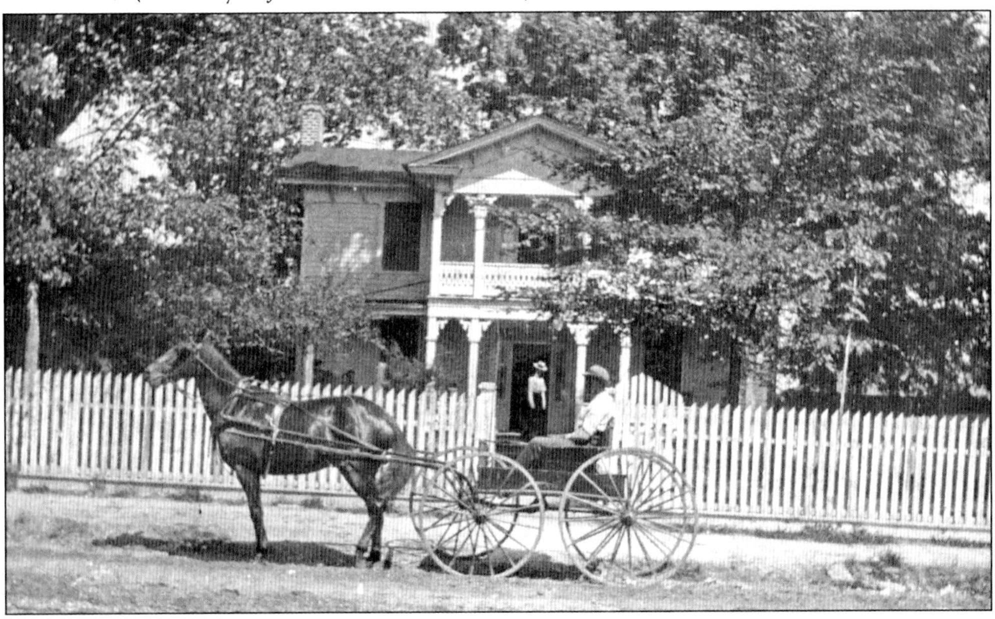

Home of Dr. James McGuire. The Philip Hanes family rented the house, built by Dr. James McGuire in the 1880s, in 1901 before A. Turner Grant's purchase in 1910. In the photograph, Philip and Sallie Hanes's daughter Sadie emerges from the house toward the buggy. The now-demolished structure stood on the site of the First Baptist Church's current parking lot.

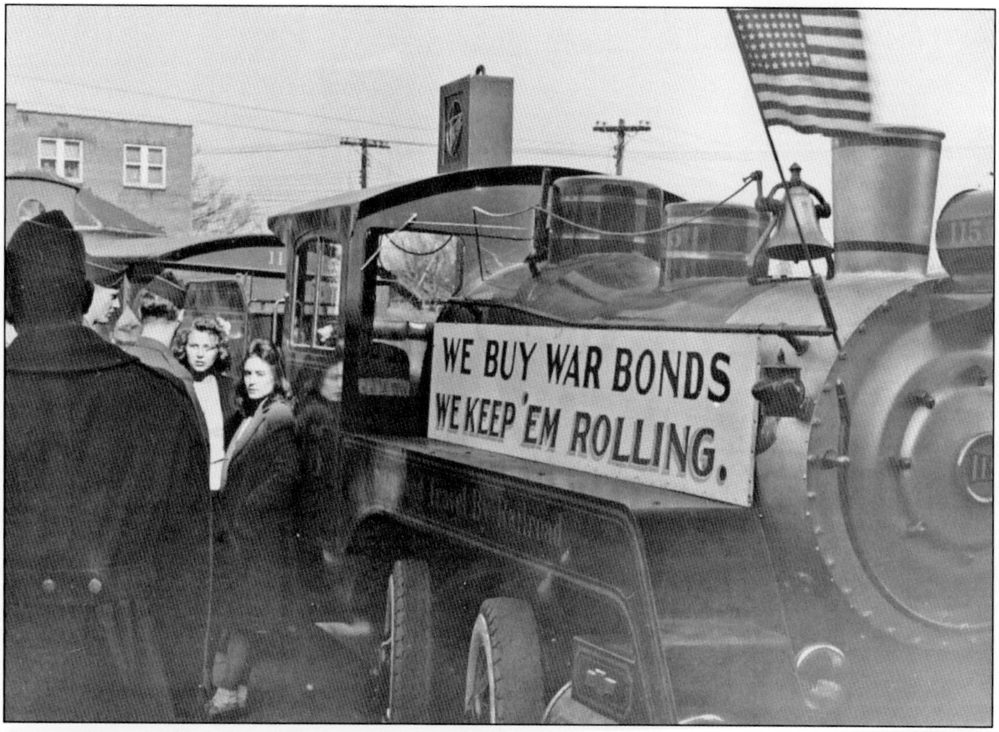

Court Square War Bond Rally. War bond rallies during World War II raised money to support the war effort.

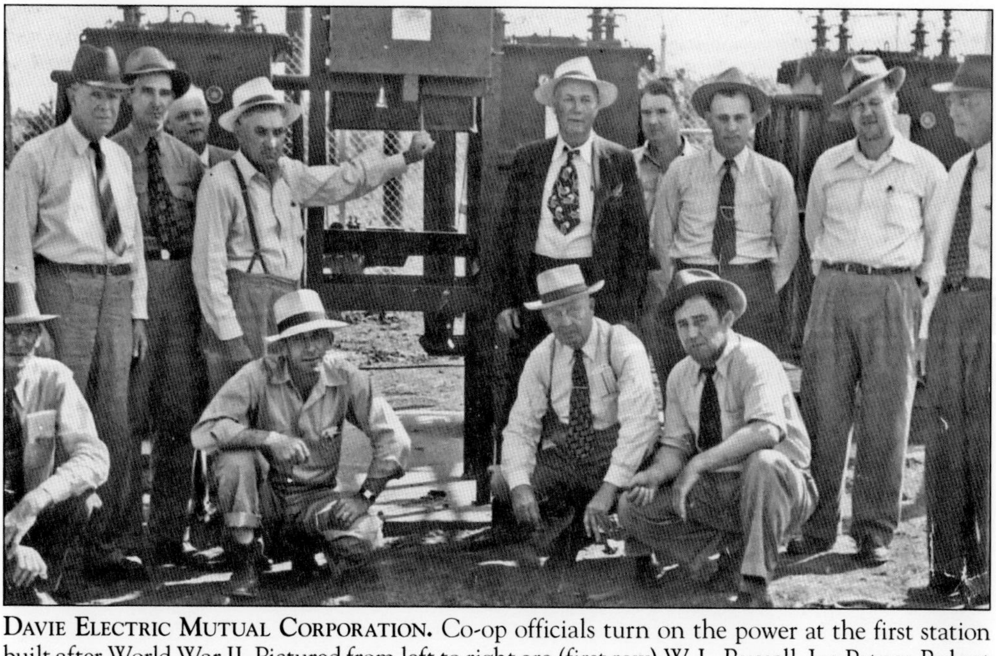

Davie Electric Mutual Corporation. Co-op officials turn on the power at the first station built after World War II. Pictured from left to right are (first row) W. L. Russell, Joe Patner, Robert Shoemaker, and J. C. Jones; (second row) Gwynn Roberts, R. L. Seaford, E. R. Crater, Charlie Smoot, Grover Chatham, T. N. Crawford, W. B. Renegar, Rufus Sanford, and W. F. Barnes. (Courtesy of Gwynn Meroney.)

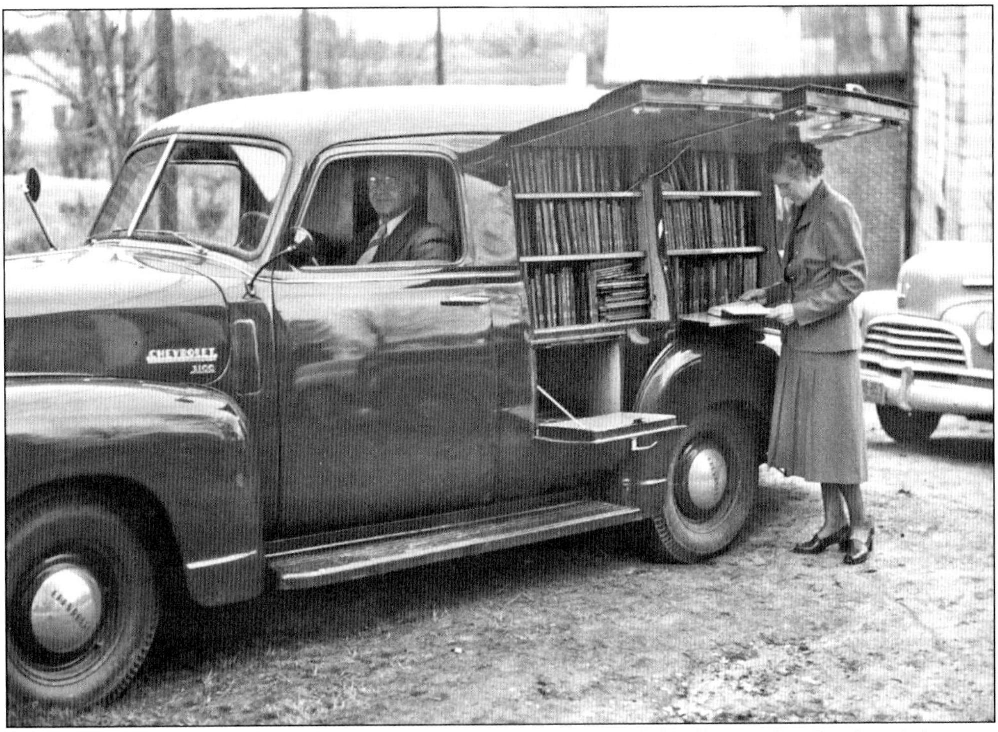

Davie County Library Bookmobile. The library board decided to buy its first bookmobile, seen here with librarian Blanche Hanes Clement and driver Richard Brinegar, on December 10, 1948. The bookmobile, constructed on a pickup truck, carried about 700 books. Lola Etchison served as the bookmobile librarian for $10 per Wednesday.

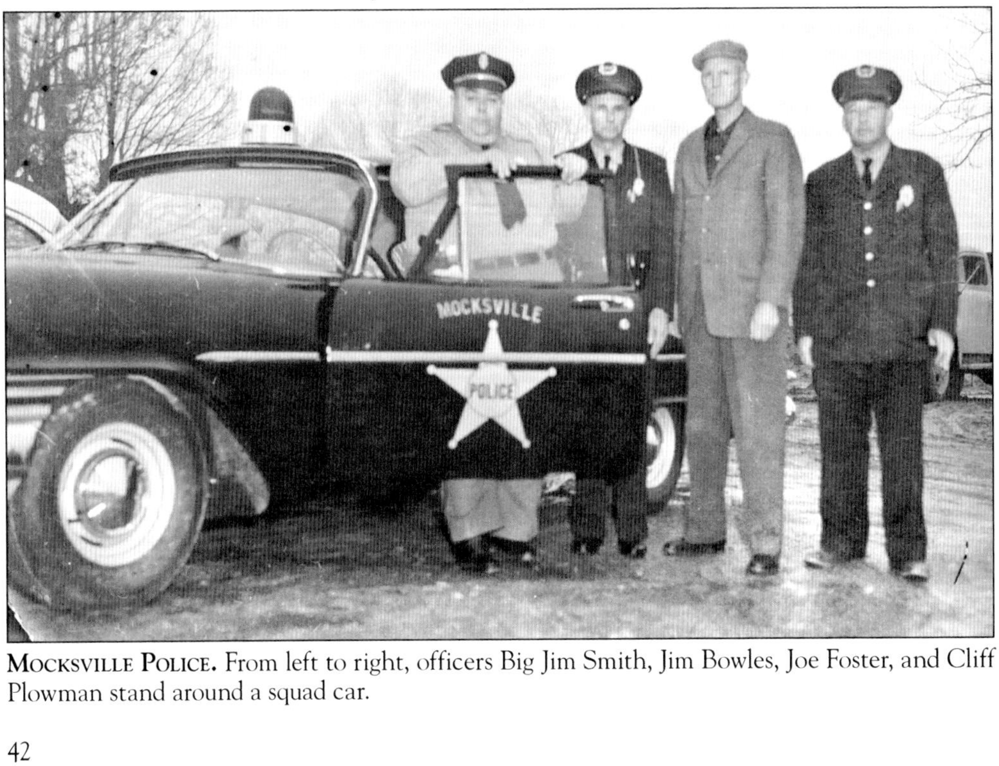

Mocksville Police. From left to right, officers Big Jim Smith, Jim Bowles, Joe Foster, and Cliff Plowman stand around a squad car.

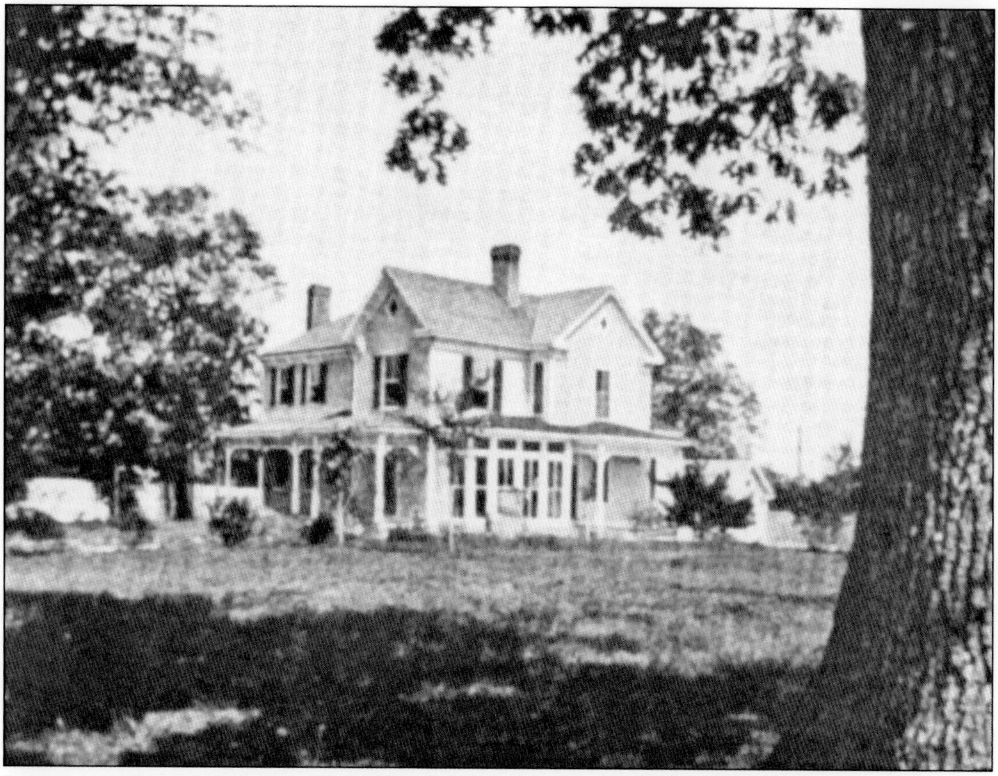

Ingleside Hunting Lodge. Judge Richmond Pearson built the original house in the early 1800s. Later owners added Victorian architecture and porches. Will Sanford and Junius Bailey purchased and operated the home as the Ingleside Lodge around 1900. The lodge's season ran from November 1st to March 15th, with access to 8,000 acres of hunting grounds in the county.

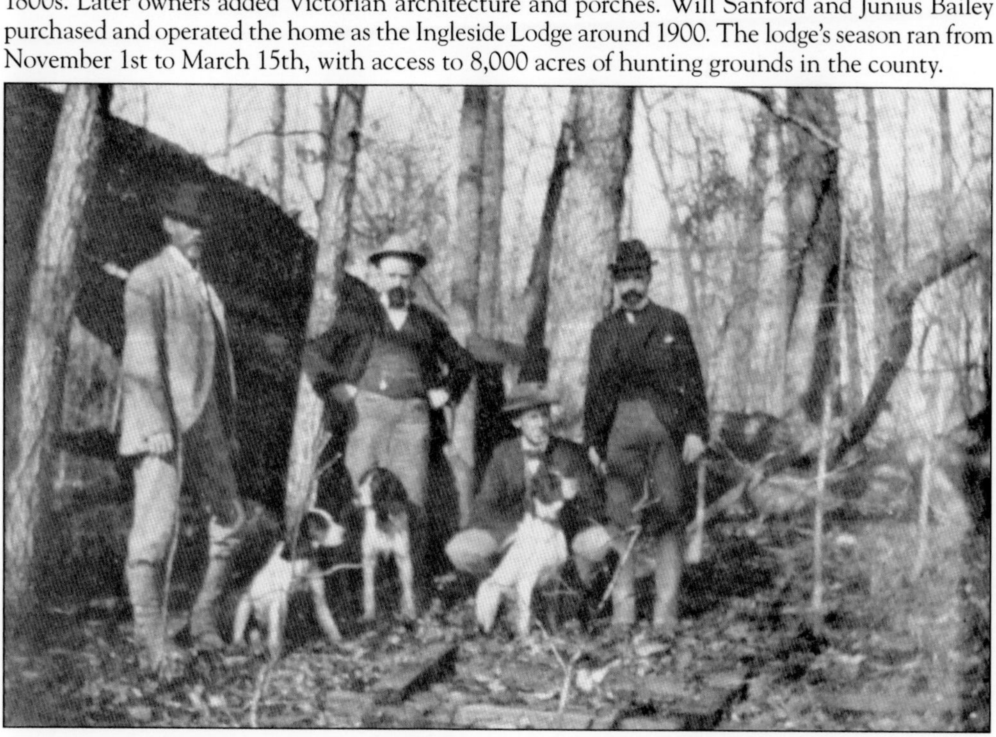

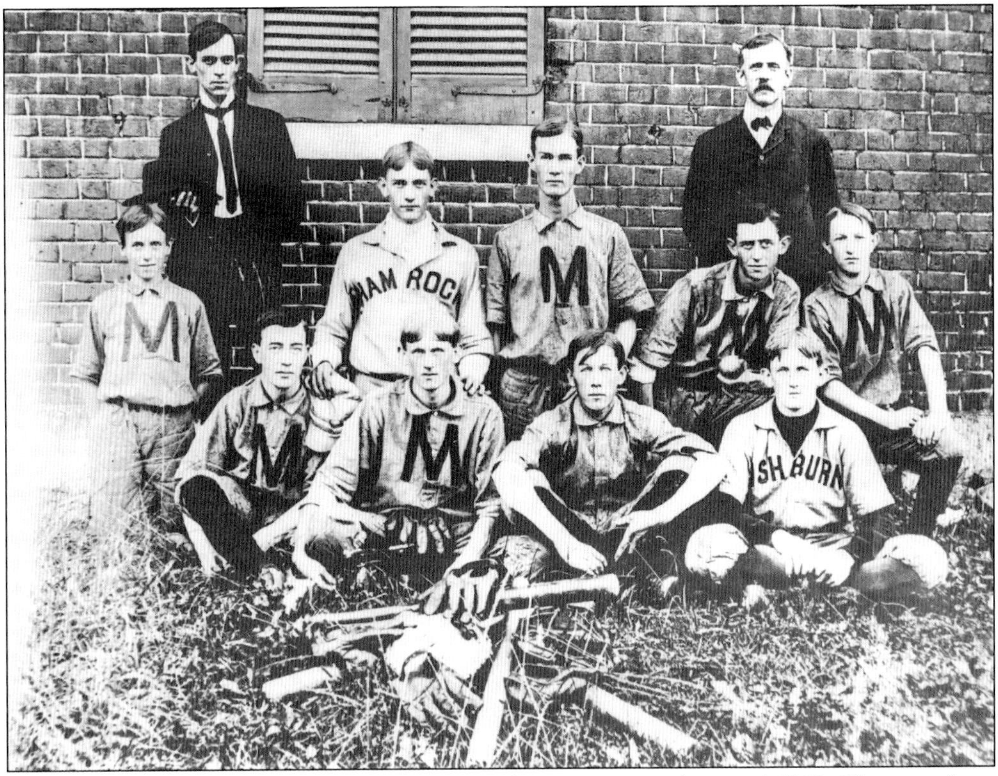

MOCKSVILLE MEN'S BASEBALL TEAM. Team members are pictured around 1902. They are, from left to right, (first row) Henry Kelly, Hugh Sanford, Arch Early, and John Sanford; (second row) Tommie Stone, Spencer Hanes, Frank Early, Frank Clement, and Walter Call; (third row) A. Turner Grant and Hartley Trundle.

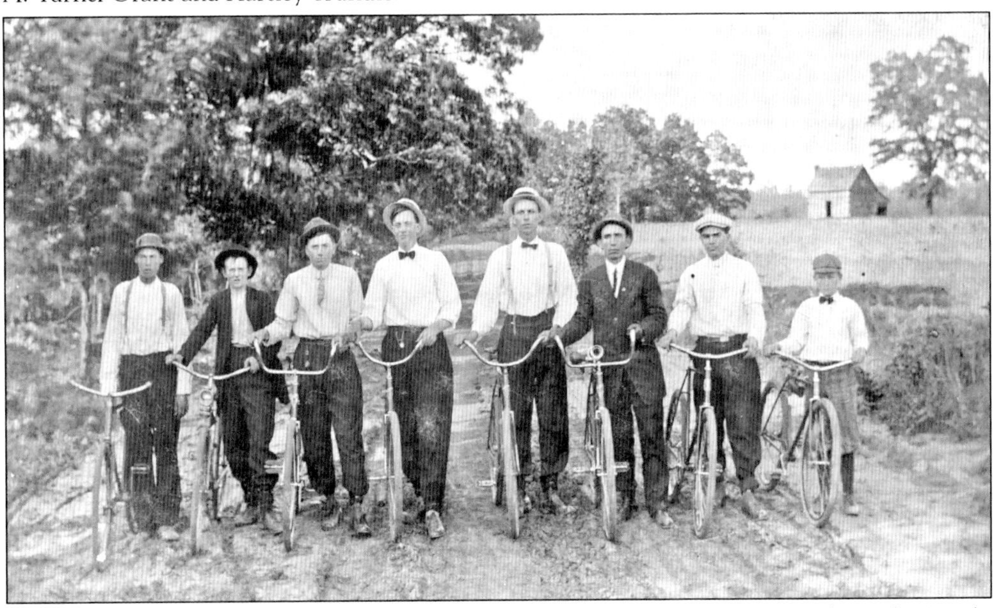

MOCKSVILLE BICYCLING CLUB. These 1910 bicyclists are, from left to right, Boss Mickey, John Leach, Roy Holthouser, Will Leach, Sam Binkley, Frank Stroud, John Kerr Foster, and Swift Hooper.

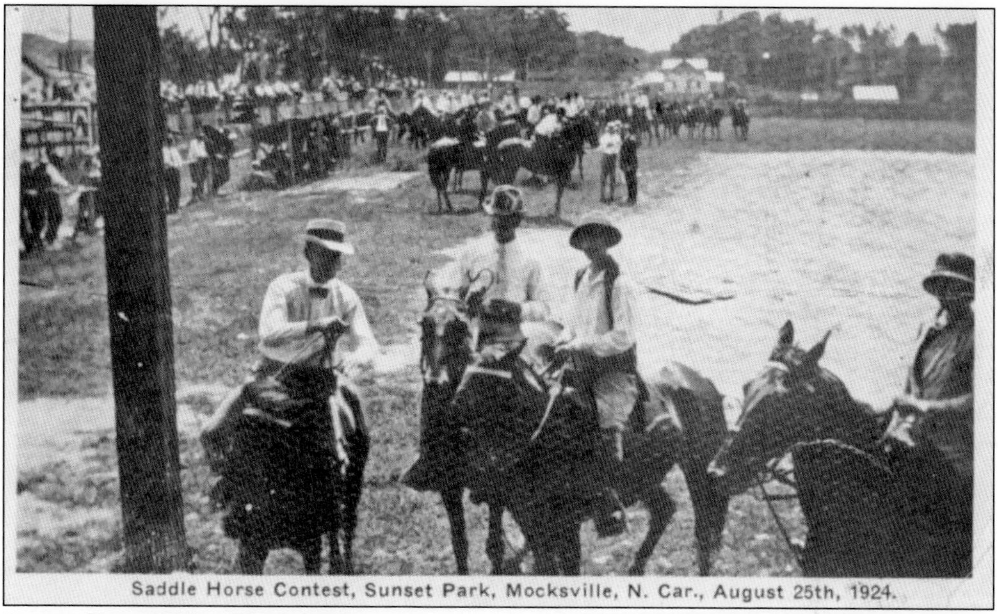

SUNSET PARK. Walter Clement donated land for Sunset Park near the present-day Davie County Hospital. The photograph shows a saddle horse contest on August 25, 1924. The August 27th edition of the *Davie Record* referenced the horse races at Sunset Park, along with a large horse traders' convention, parade, and sale of stock in Mocksville. The park later included a baseball field. (Courtesy of Gwynn Meroney.)

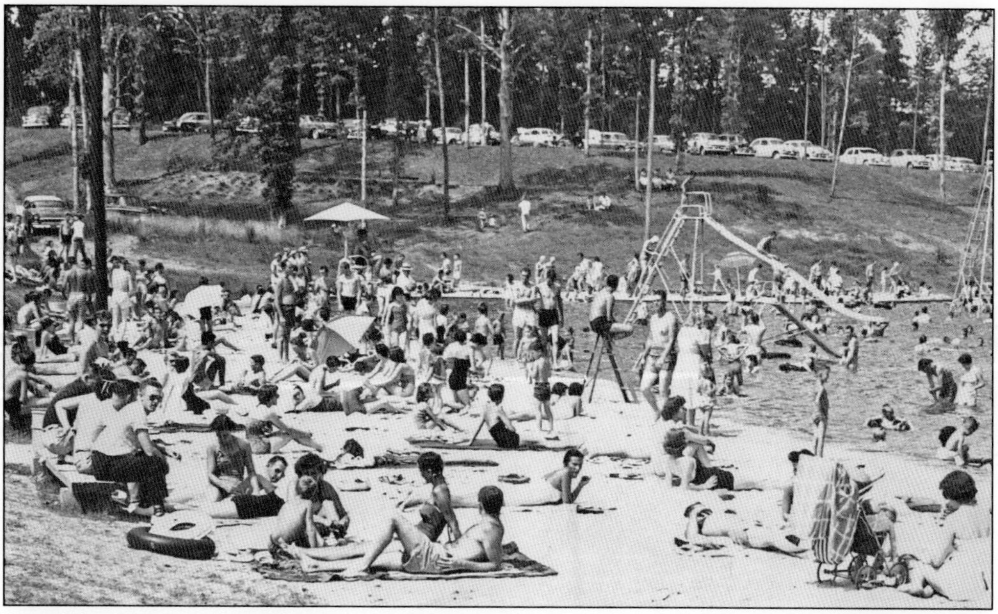

LAKE HIDE-AWAY. Lake Hide-Away, designed and built by Theodore "Dock" Brown of Mocksville, opened on June 12, 1954. The lake, one of the hottest social spots in the 1950s, attracted crowds of up to 250 people. The facility closed in 1968 but was reopened in 1978, when it was owned by Gene Plott of Clemmons. The updated grounds included a bathhouse, a concession stand, a lounge area with a jukebox, and an 18-hole miniature golf course. White sand imported from the eastern part of the state provided a beach experience.

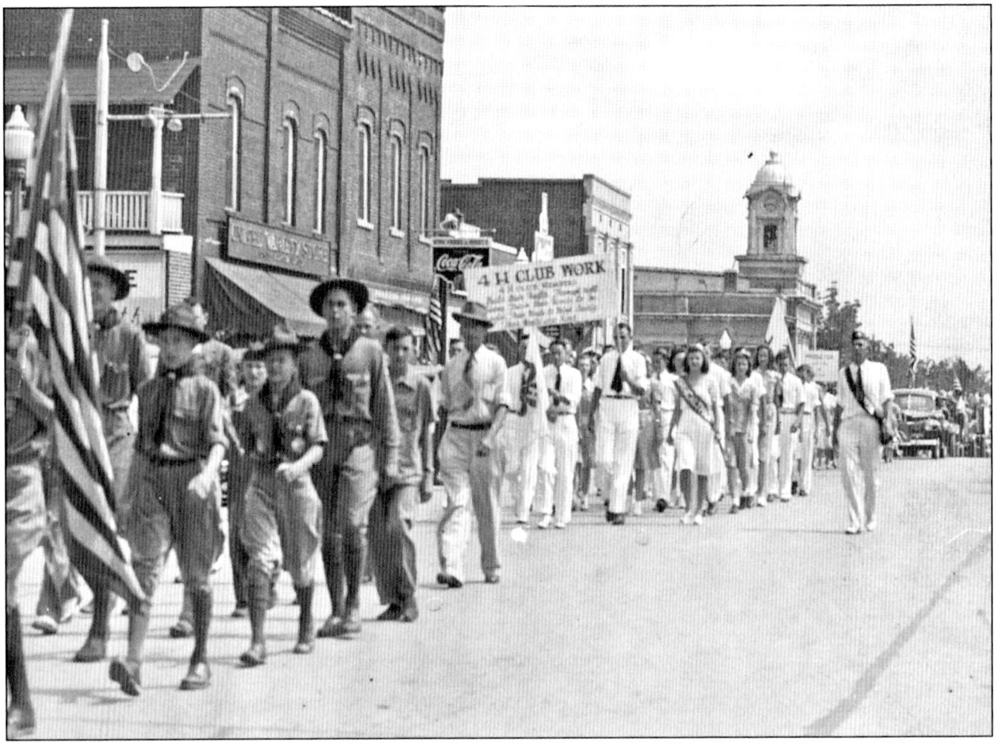

Main Street Parades. Two traditional community parades continue today: the Fourth of July parade (pictured above, with Boy Scouts and the 4-H Club) and the Christmas parade (shown below).

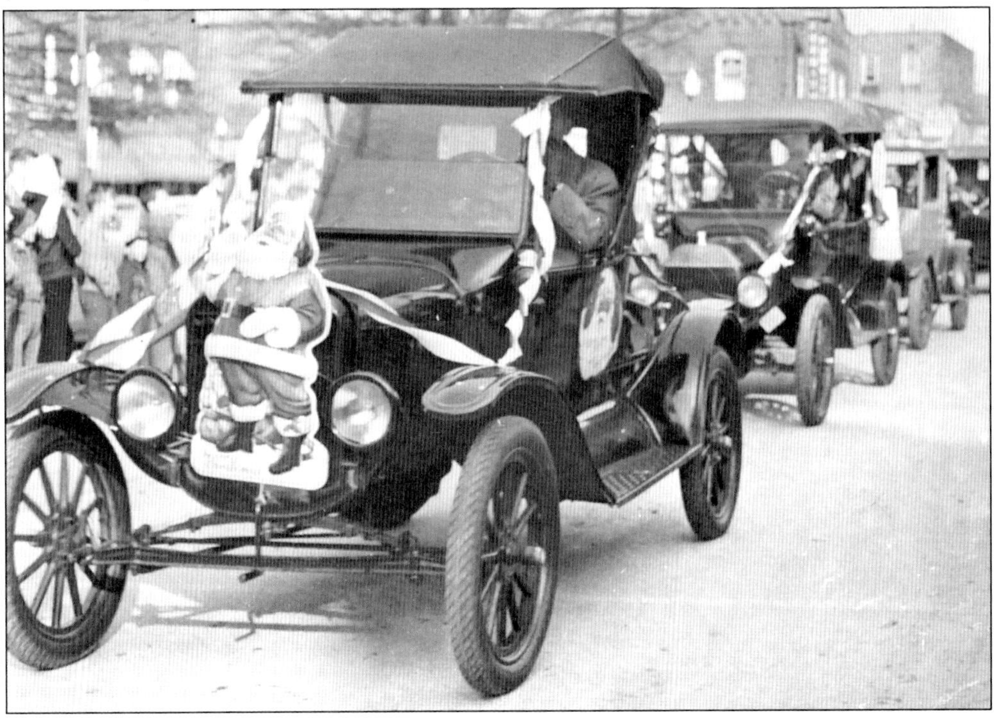

Two

MASONIC PICNIC

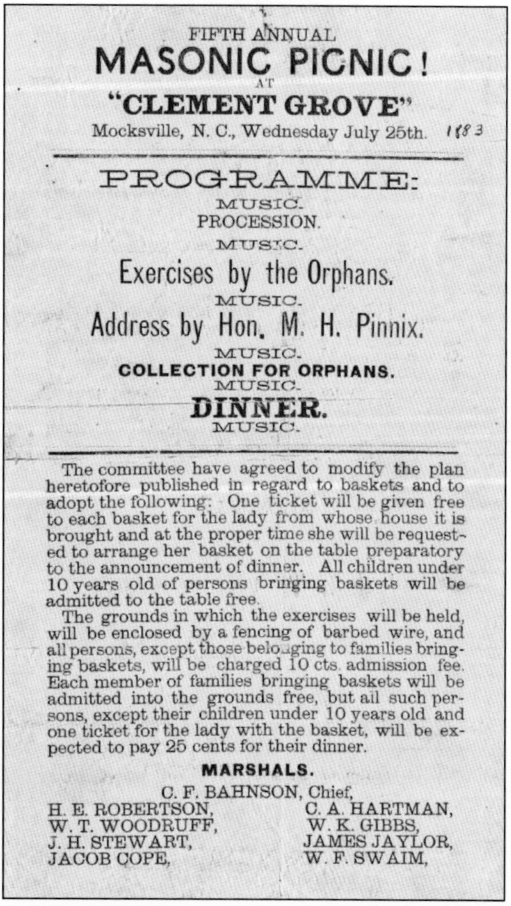
FIFTH ANNUAL
MASONIC PICNIC!
AT
"CLEMENT GROVE"
Mocksville, N. C., Wednesday July 25th. 1883

PROGRAMME:
MUSIC.
PROCESSION.
MUSIC.
Exercises by the Orphans.
MUSIC.
Address by Hon. M. H. Pinnix.
MUSIC.
COLLECTION FOR ORPHANS.
MUSIC.
DINNER.
MUSIC.

The committee have agreed to modify the plan heretofore published in regard to baskets and to adopt the following: One ticket will be given free to each basket for the lady from whose house it is brought and at the proper time she will be requested to arrange her basket on the table preparatory to the announcement of dinner. All children under 10 years old of persons bringing baskets will be admitted to the table free.

The grounds in which the exercises will be held, will be enclosed by a fencing of barbed wire, and all persons, except those belonging to families bringing baskets, will be charged 10 cts. admission fee. Each member of families bringing baskets will be admitted into the grounds free, but all such persons, except their children under 10 years old and one ticket for the lady with the basket, will be expected to pay 25 cents for their dinner.

MARSHALS.
C. F. BAHNSON, Chief,

H. E. ROBERTSON,	C. A. HARTMAN,
W. T. WOODRUFF,	W. K. GIBBS,
J. H. STEWART,	JAMES JAYLOR,
JACOB COPE,	W. F. SWAIM,

MASONIC PICNIC ADVERTISEMENT, 1883. On May 11, 1877, Capt. W. A. Clement proposed an annual picnic sponsored by the Mocksville Masonic Lodge, with proceeds going to the Oxford Orphanage. The Shoals in Cooleemee hosted the first five Masonic Picnics (from 1878 to 1882) with entertainment consisting of boating, swimming, fishing, ball games, and dinners. The first year collected $35 for the orphanage. In 1883, the picnic was moved to Clement Grove in Mocksville.

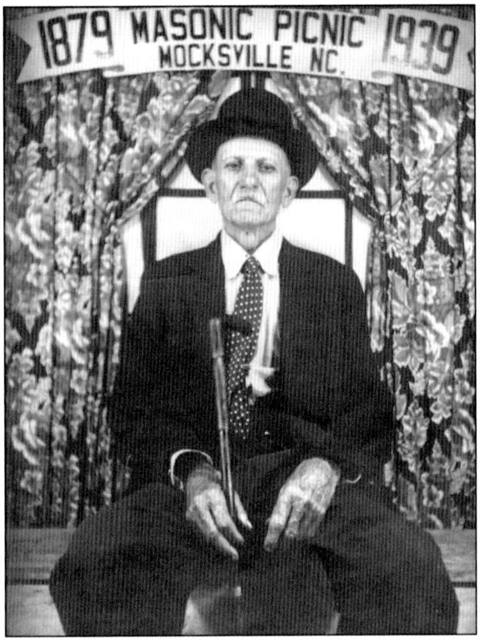

MASONIC PICNIC 1939 SOUVENIR. Andrew Shermer took advantage of the photographer's booth at the Masonic Picnic of 1939, while wearing his best suit. Born on May 21, 1866, Shermer died on December 1, 1942. He had three daughters: Ada Shermer Roberson, Mae Shermer Faircloth, and Paulina Shermer Barney. (Courtesy of Lucy Barney.)

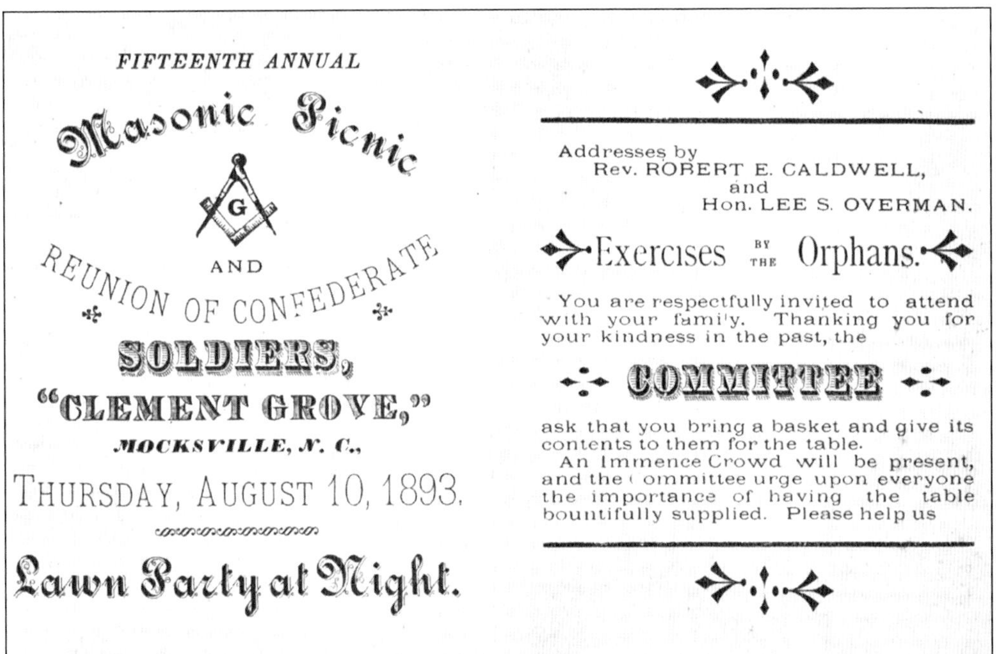

FIFTEENTH ANNUAL

Masonic Picnic

AND

REUNION OF CONFEDERATE

SOLDIERS,

"CLEMENT GROVE,"

MOCKSVILLE, N. C.,

THURSDAY, AUGUST 10, 1893.

Lawn Party at Night.

Addresses by
Rev. ROBERT E. CALDWELL,
and
Hon. LEE S. OVERMAN.

Exercises BY THE Orphans.

You are respectfully invited to attend with your family. Thanking you for your kindness in the past, the

COMMITTEE

ask that you bring a basket and give its contents to them for the table.

An Immence Crowd will be present, and the Committee urge upon everyone the importance of having the table bountifully supplied. Please help us

MASONIC PICNIC ANNOUNCEMENT, 1893. Until about 1900, picnic announcements identified the event as the Masonic Picnic and Reunion of Confederate Soldiers. Veterans continued on the program as late as 1904. Children from the orphanage sang and performed skits, and area bands played concerts. Speakers have addressed the picnic since 1879. For about 30 years beginning in 1892, an excursion train delivered attendees from Winston-Salem. The *Davie Record* estimated attendance in 1916 at 10,000 people, with only half choosing to purchase the gate or dinner tickets. The others congregated in the woods along the railroad line outside the fenced arbor and visited with friends and family, spreading their picnic dinners on the ground.

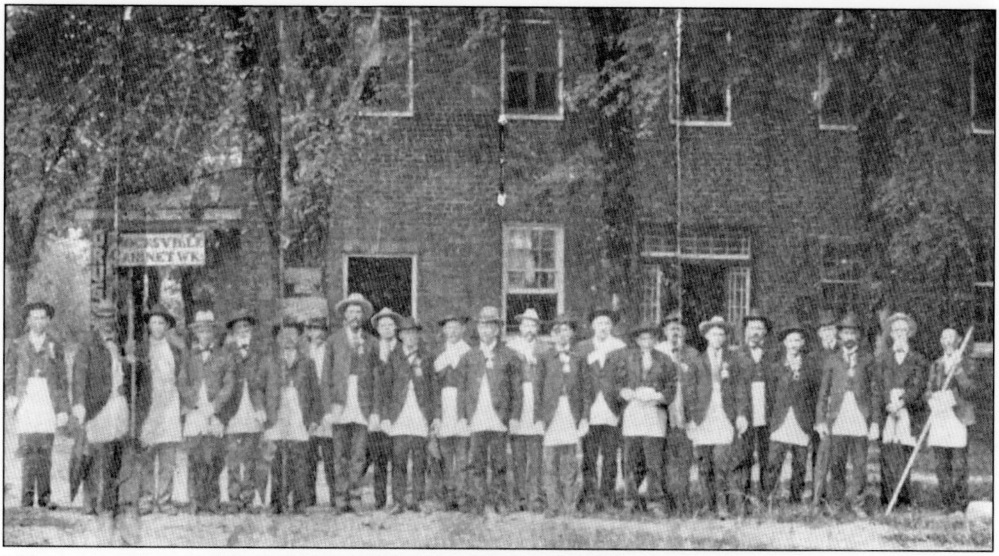

Mocksville Lodge No. 134 in 1905. The Mocksville Masonic Lodge was organized in 1850. Here Masons pose before their lodge hall. From left to right are J. H. Coley, F. M. Johnson, D. L. Dyson, J. D. Frost, W. A. Owens, O. L. Williams, M. Waters, J. B. Campbell, Jerry Wellman, W. C. Denny, S. A. Woodruff, O. C. Austin, T. B. Bailey, D. W. Granger, W. T. Woodruff, C. L. Granger, J. A. Current, W. T. Starrett, F. T. Poindexter, E. H. Pass, J. L. Sheek, Z. N. Anderson, B. O. Morris, and V. E. Swain. (Courtesy of Jack Pennington.)

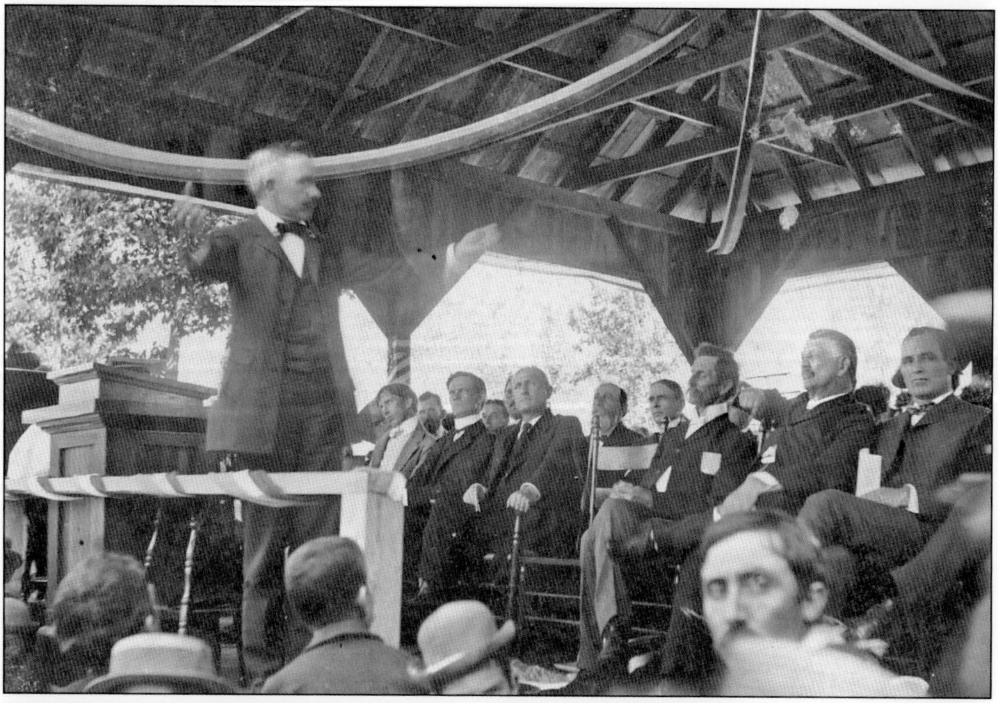

Gov. Charles Brantley Aycock. Governor Aycock addresses the crowd under the arbor at the annual Mocksville Masonic Picnic in the early 1900s. Masons constructed the arbor in 1899 to seat 1,200 people under its roof. A raised stage at the front accommodates the performers and speakers.

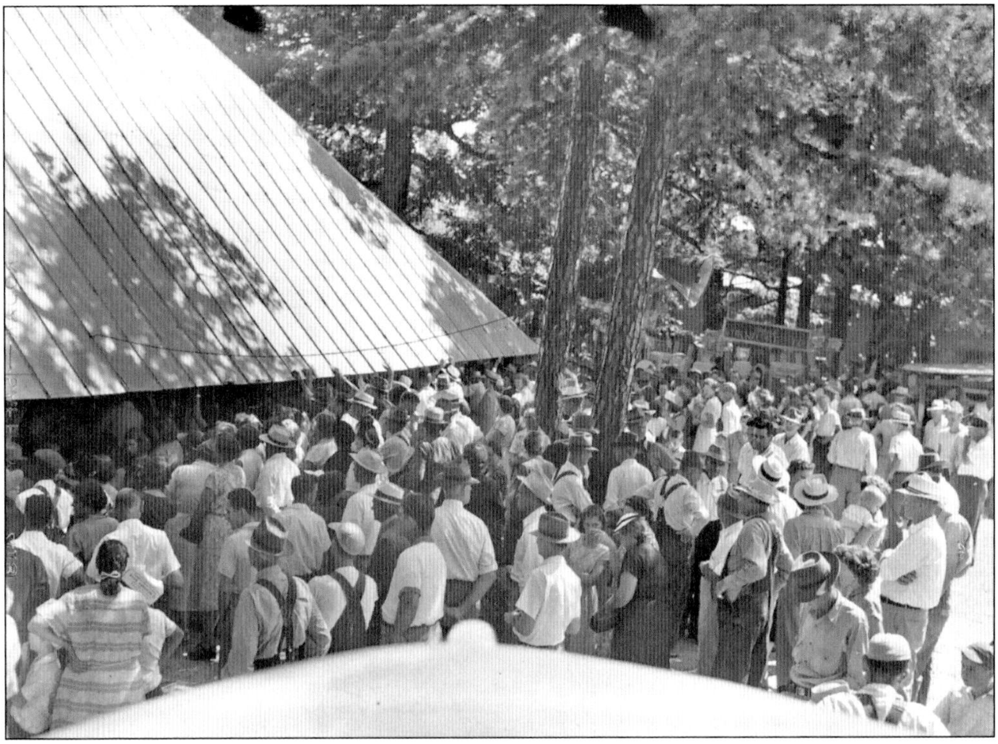

Masonic Picnic. Many county women contributed to the picnic meal, traditionally held on the second Thursday in August. The women brought country ham biscuits, fried chicken, potato salad, garden green beans, butter beans, peas, corn on the cob, summer tomatoes, pickles right out of the crock, lemon tarts, pecan pie, and a variety of cakes. The noon meal cost 75¢ in 1914; in 1919, Masons sold 1,000 dinner tickets. Before a covered picnic shelter in the 1920s protected against rain, one county resident in 1912 had to turn "a chess pie upside down to drain off the water."

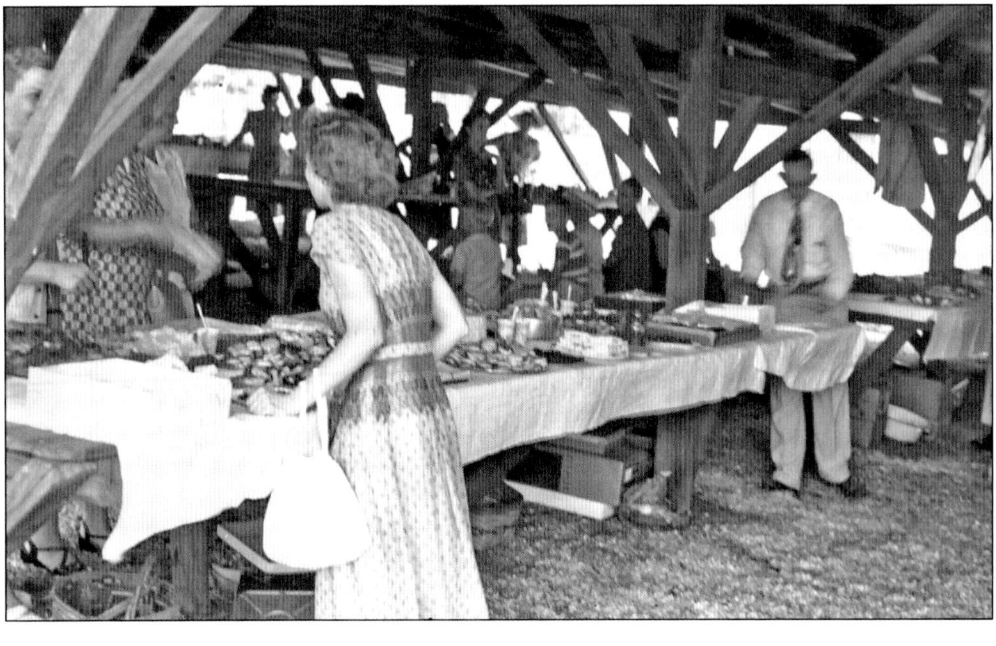

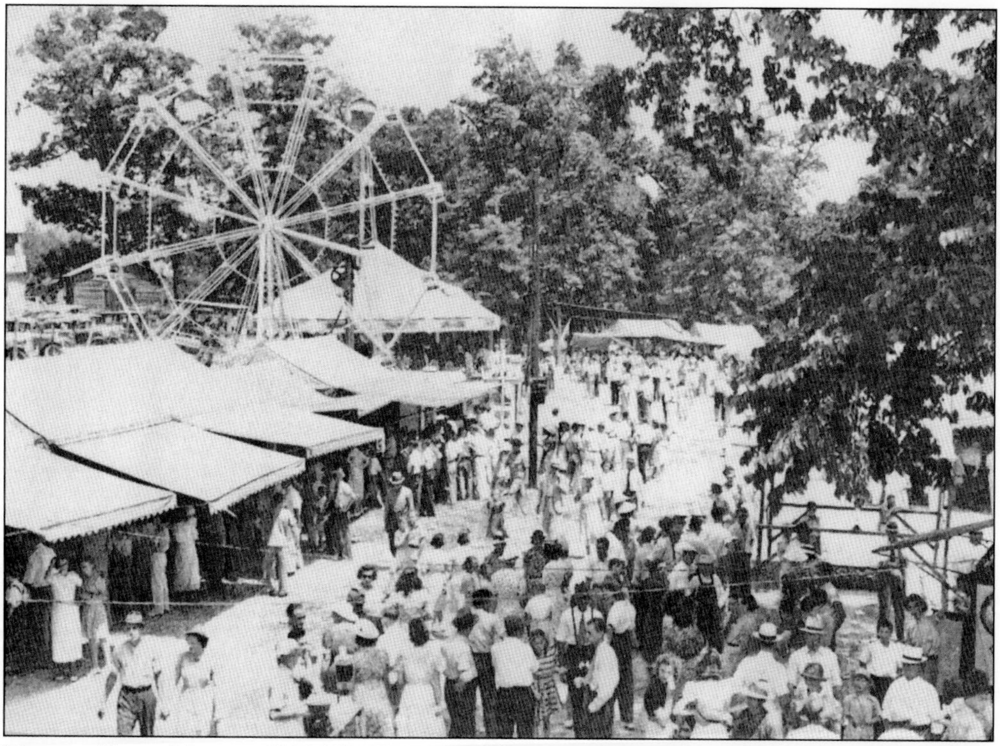

Masonic Picnic Midway, 1939. The Ferris wheel features prominently on the midway each year, with the merry-go-round behind it. (Courtesy of Forsyth County Public Library Photo Collection.)

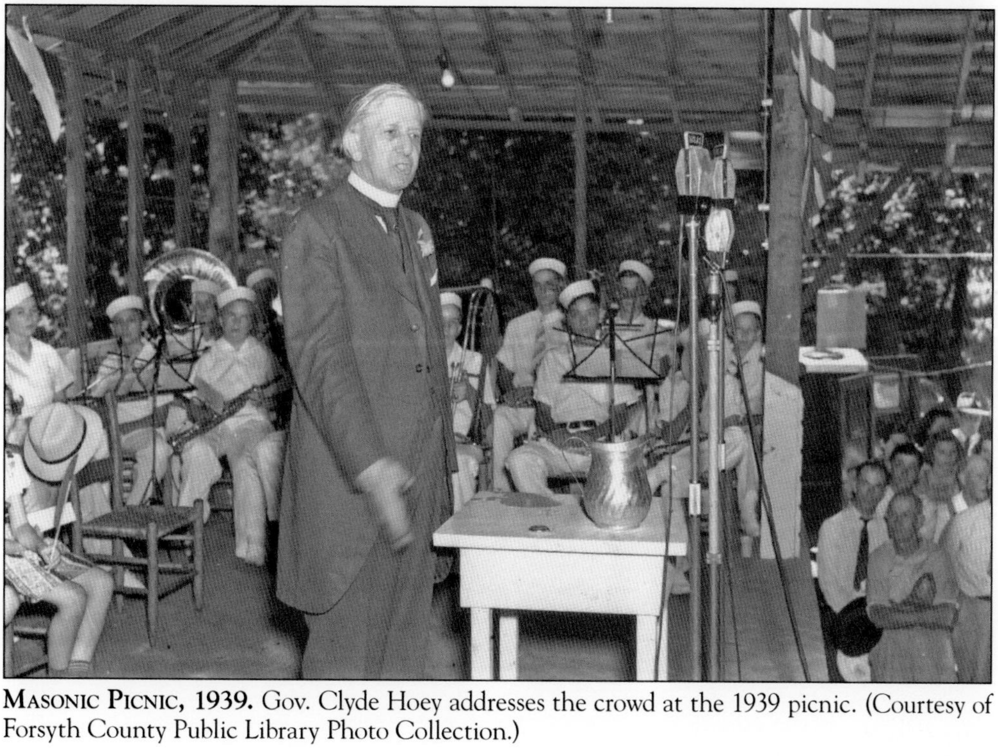

Masonic Picnic, 1939. Gov. Clyde Hoey addresses the crowd at the 1939 picnic. (Courtesy of Forsyth County Public Library Photo Collection.)

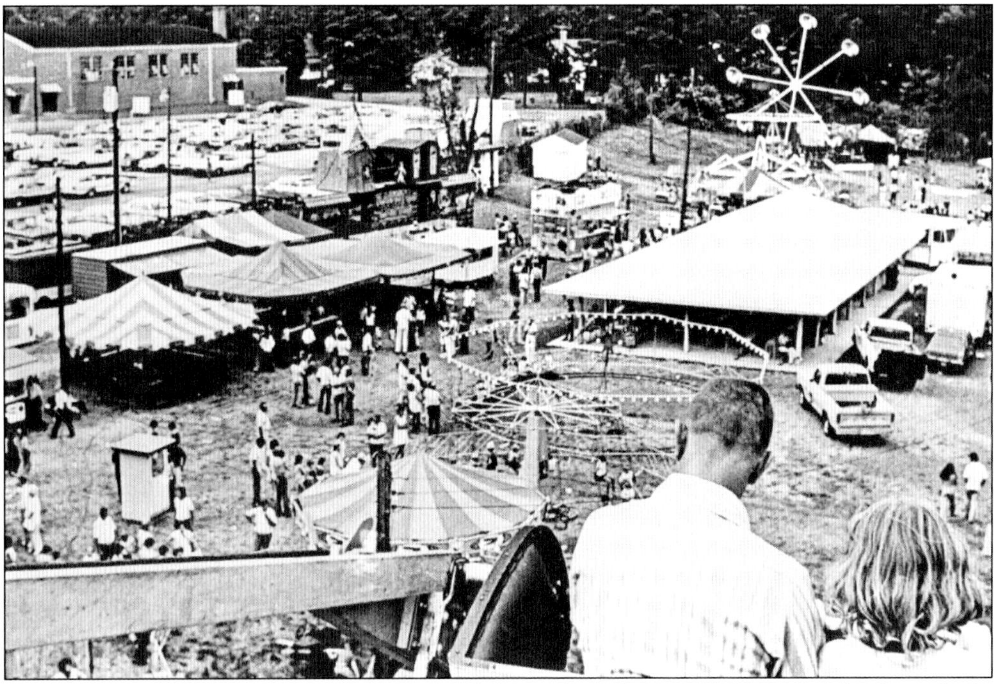

Masonic Picnic Midway, c. 1970. A view of the midway from atop the Ferris wheel overlooks the picnic grounds. Corinthian Masonic Lodge No. 17, the oldest fraternal organization for black men in Mocksville, celebrated its 100th anniversary in 1974. The lodge sponsors the annual Masonic and Davie Educational Union Picnic on the Saturday after the second Thursday in August to benefit the Oxford Orphanage and provide financial assistance to college students, needy families, and other worthy causes.

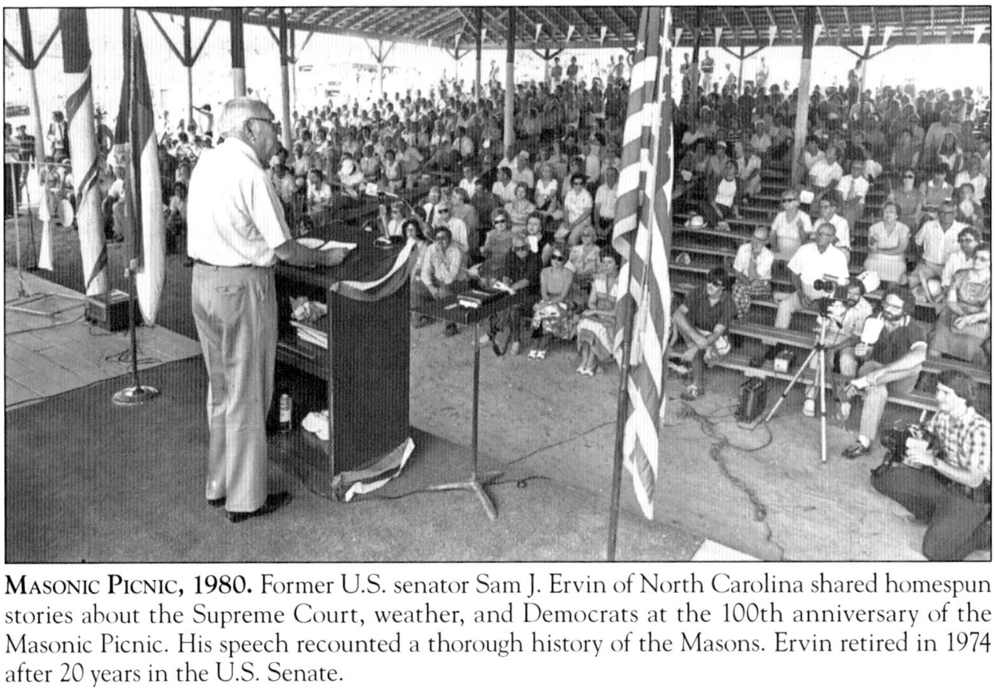

Masonic Picnic, 1980. Former U.S. senator Sam J. Ervin of North Carolina shared homespun stories about the Supreme Court, weather, and Democrats at the 100th anniversary of the Masonic Picnic. His speech recounted a thorough history of the Masons. Ervin retired in 1974 after 20 years in the U.S. Senate.

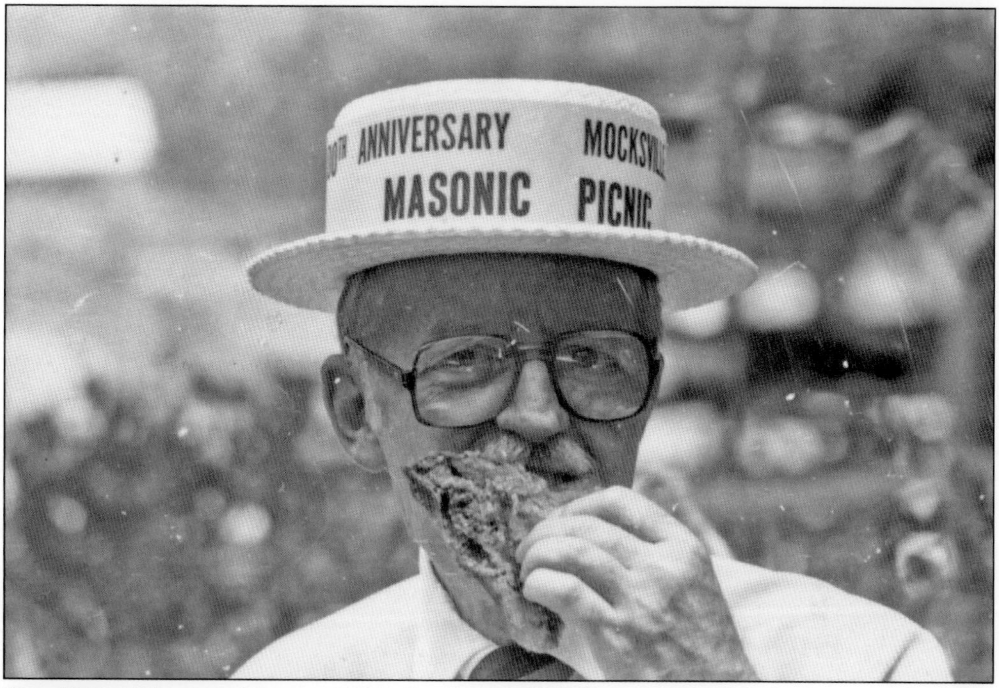

THE 100TH MASONIC PICNIC, 1980. Dr. Francis W. Slate enjoys fried chicken at the annual picnic. Polio epidemics caused the cancellation of the picnic in 1935 and 1944.

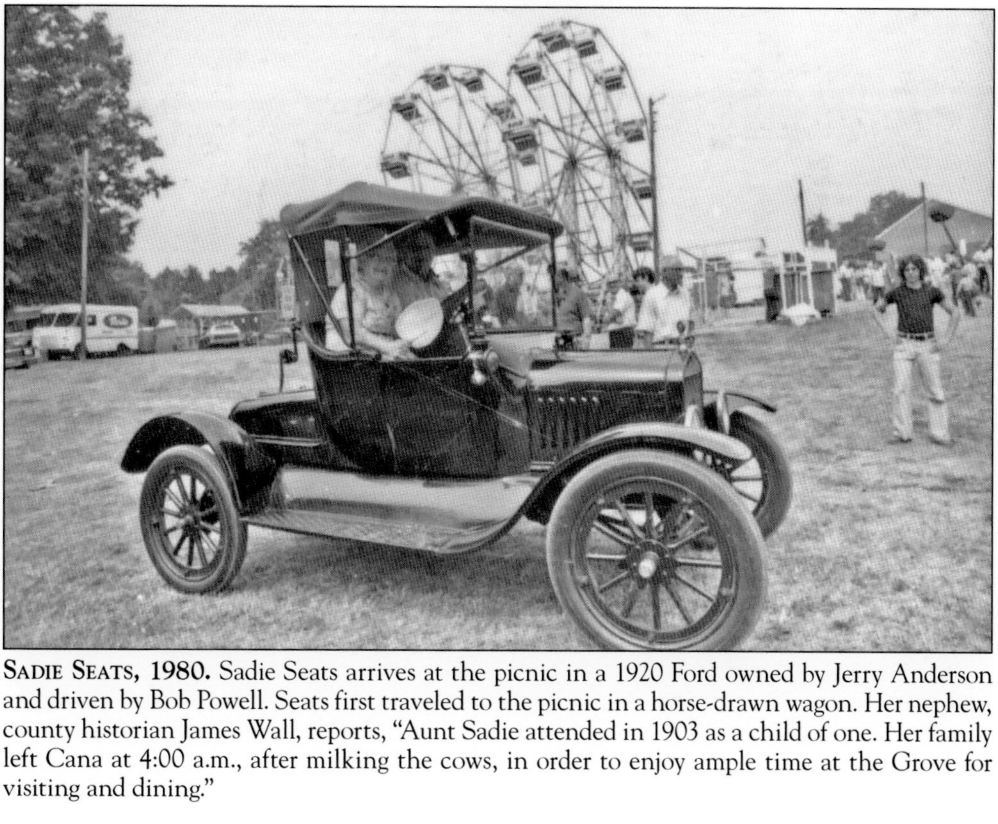

SADIE SEATS, 1980. Sadie Seats arrives at the picnic in a 1920 Ford owned by Jerry Anderson and driven by Bob Powell. Seats first traveled to the picnic in a horse-drawn wagon. Her nephew, county historian James Wall, reports, "Aunt Sadie attended in 1903 as a child of one. Her family left Cana at 4:00 a.m., after milking the cows, in order to enjoy ample time at the Grove for visiting and dining."

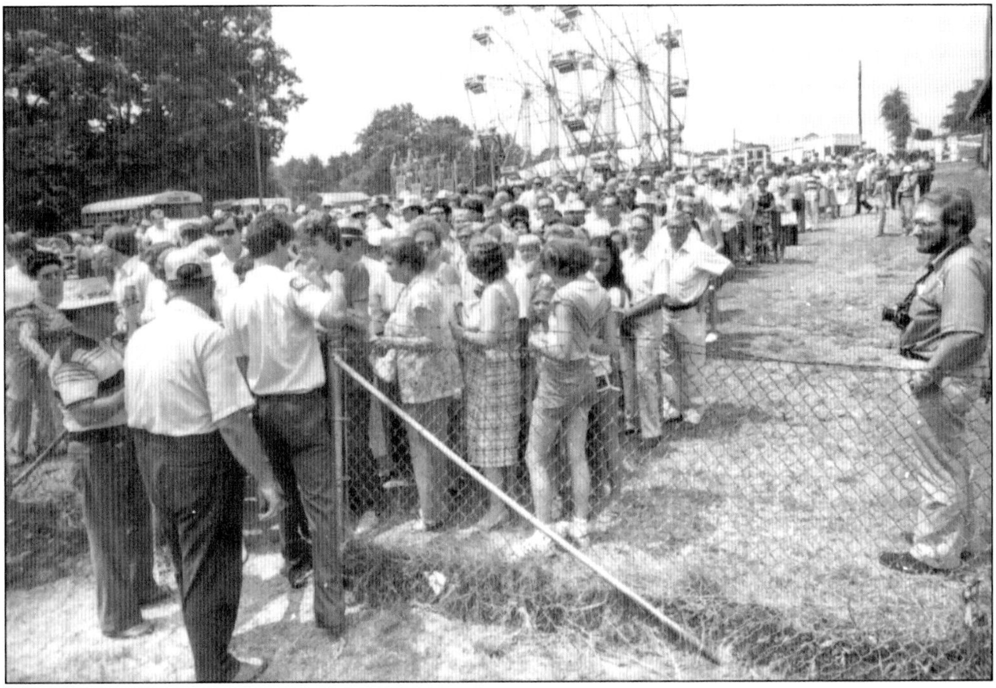

PICNIC LINE, 1980. Hungry picnic attendees line up for the grub.

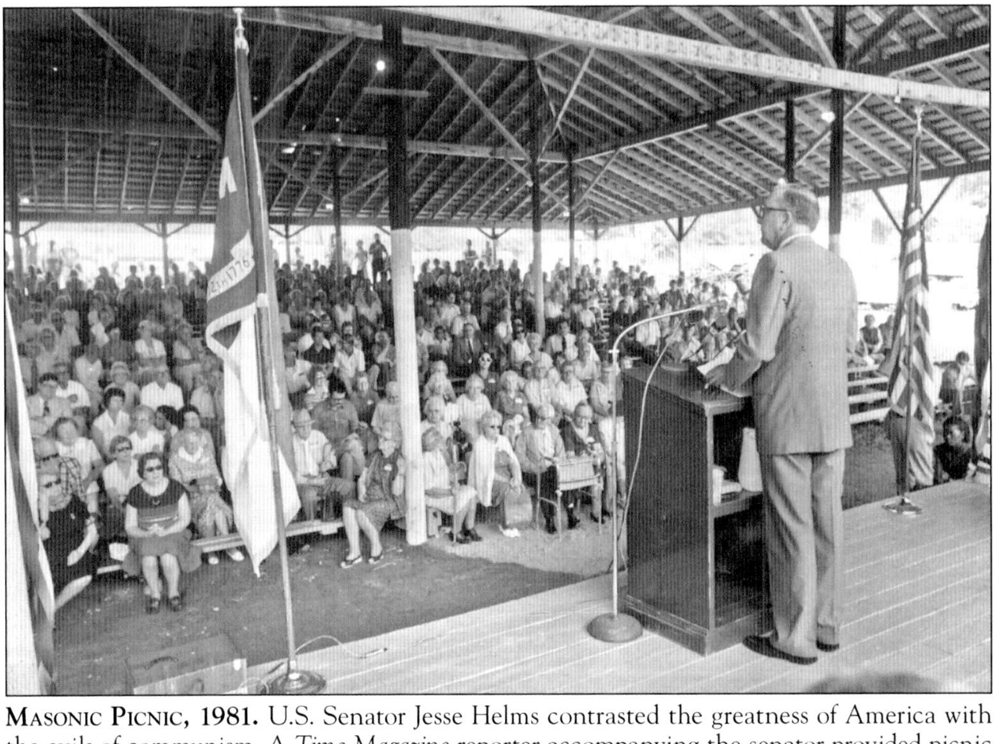

MASONIC PICNIC, 1981. U.S. Senator Jesse Helms contrasted the greatness of America with the evils of communism. A *Time Magazine* reporter accompanying the senator provided picnic photographs for the September 14, 1981, issue on Helms.

Three

COOLEEMEE

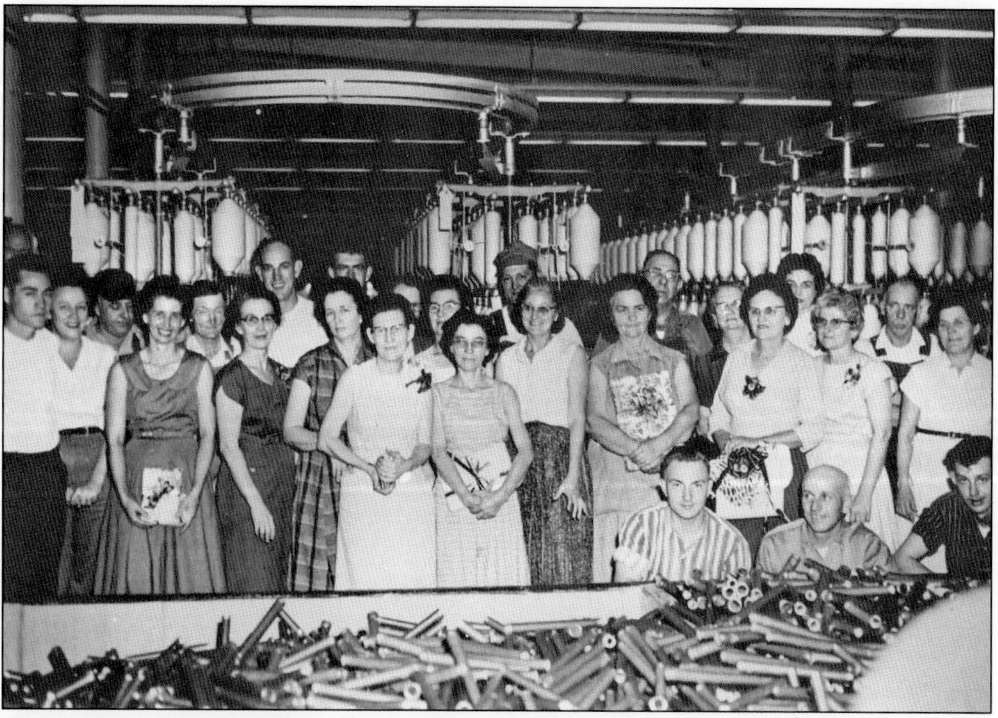

ERWIN MILLS SPINNING ROOM, LATE 1940S. Modern living and weekly pay brought farmers to the South Yadkin River banks to build a new cotton mill and town. The farmers brought their country ways: big families, faith in God, neighborly obligation, and self-reliance. The town population rose to nearly 3,000, with a workforce of almost 1,400. Erwin Mills ranked as Davie County's largest payroll and taxpayer. The mill closed in 1969, but the town lived on. (Courtesy of Textile Heritage Center at Cooleemee.)

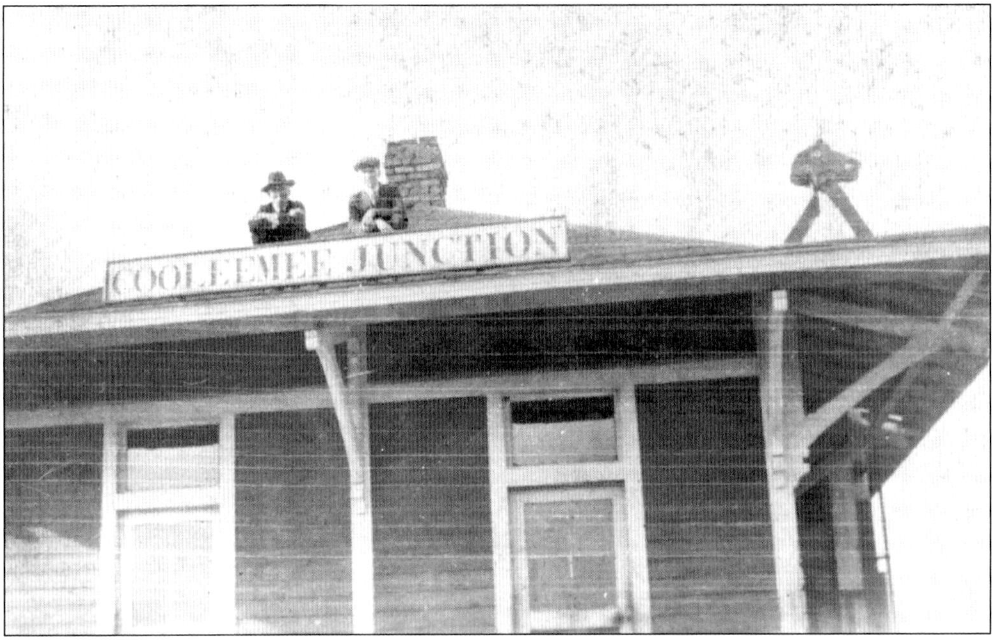

COOLEEMEE JUNCTION DEPOT. The railroad depot stood along the main track of the Winston-to-Charlotte line that later became part of the Southern Railroad. With early roads little more than rutted dirt wagon trails, a modern cotton mill could not bring in materials or ship out finished cloth without trains. A spur line that ran parallel to the river connected the junction to the mill. When needed, locomotives pulled cars, including large coal shipments. (Courtesy of Textile Heritage Center at Cooleemee.)

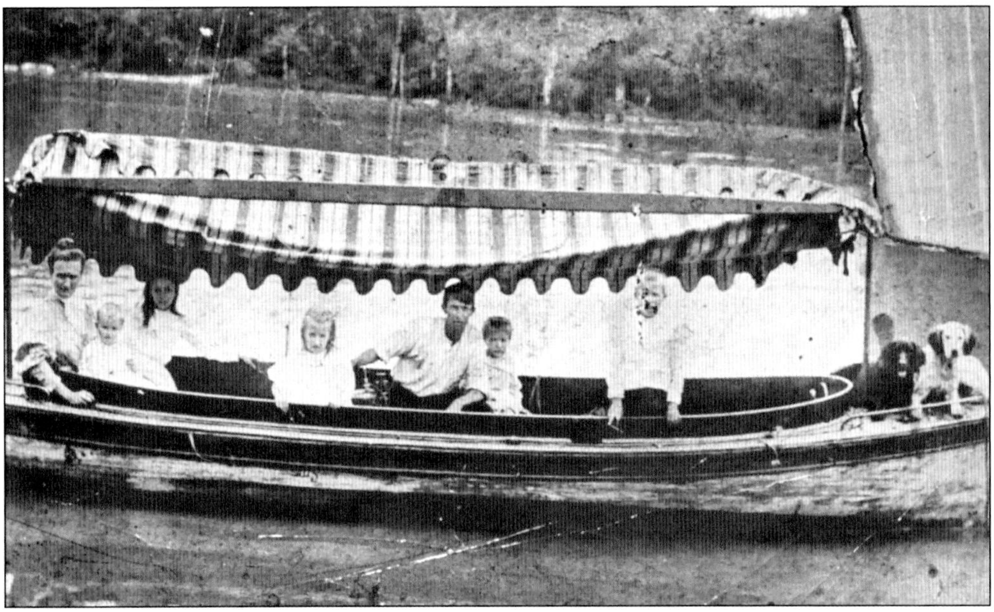

CHARLIE CARTER'S RIVERBOAT. Charlie Carter's riverboat, *The City of Cooleemee*, made the 2-mile trip on the South Yadkin River between the town and Cooleemee Junction. Mail and passengers met the north and southbound trains that made four stops daily. (Courtesy of Textile Heritage Center at Cooleemee.)

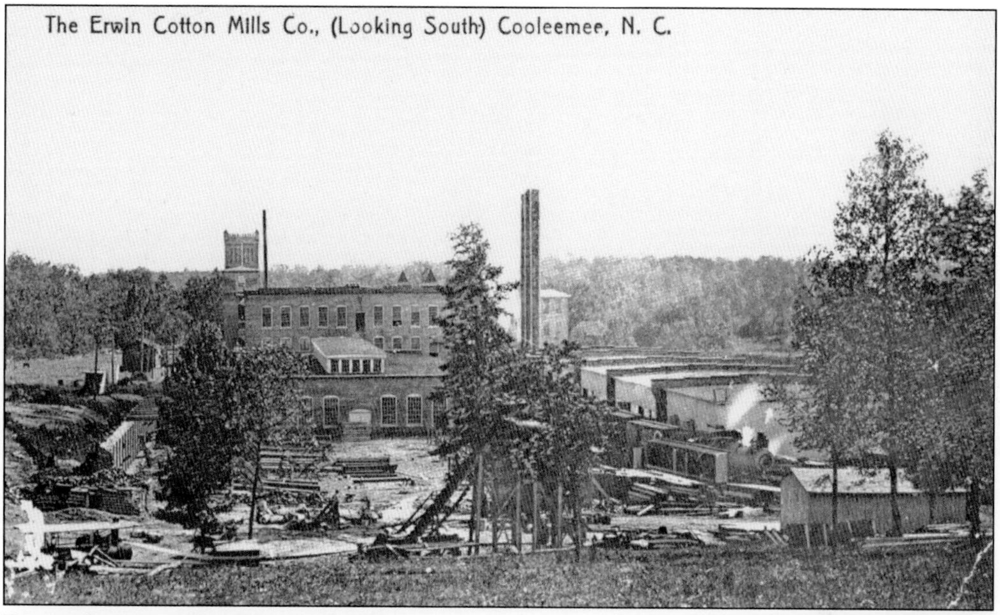

Erwin Cotton Mill No. 3. By 1901, production at the cotton mill commenced in the main departments of opening, carding, spinning, and weaving. The three main floors each contained 56,000 square feet of space. A water turbine turning large wheels transferred power to shafts, belts, and machines until the installation of new models with electric motors in the 1930s. The mill produced and dyed a large variety of fabrics. (Courtesy of Textile Heritage Center at Cooleemee.)

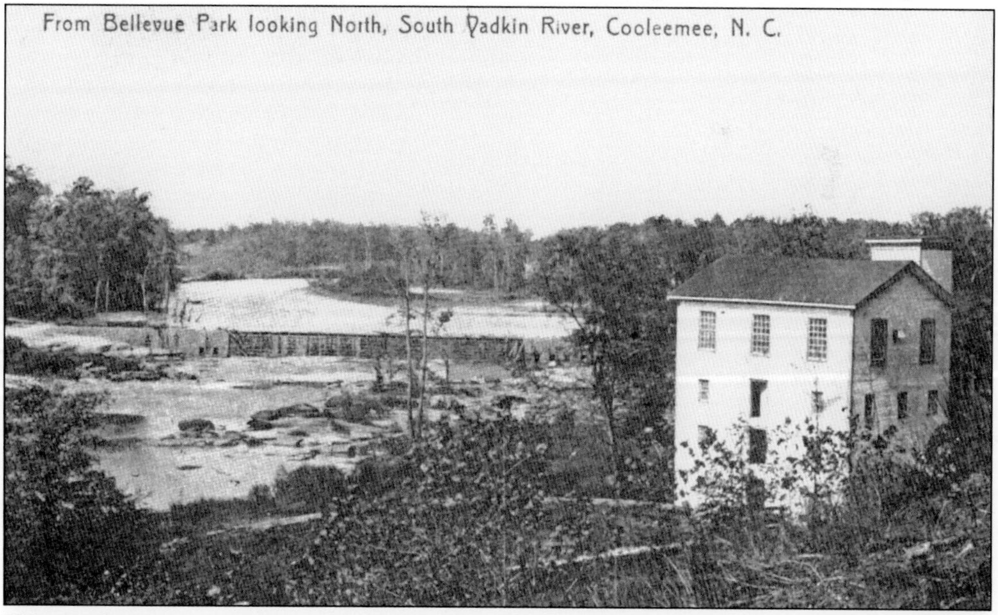

View of Gristmill and Dam from Park. The South Yadkin River, descending 18 feet at Pearson Falls at Cooleemee, powered an antebellum rural industrial complex that included a gristmill, a sawmill, and an iron foundry that manufactured textile machinery. Later a 12-foot stone dam helped power the cotton mill, while a modern roller mill replaced the gristmill. In 2005, a power company bulldozed the stone foundation of the roller mill. (Courtesy of Textile Heritage Center at Cooleemee.)

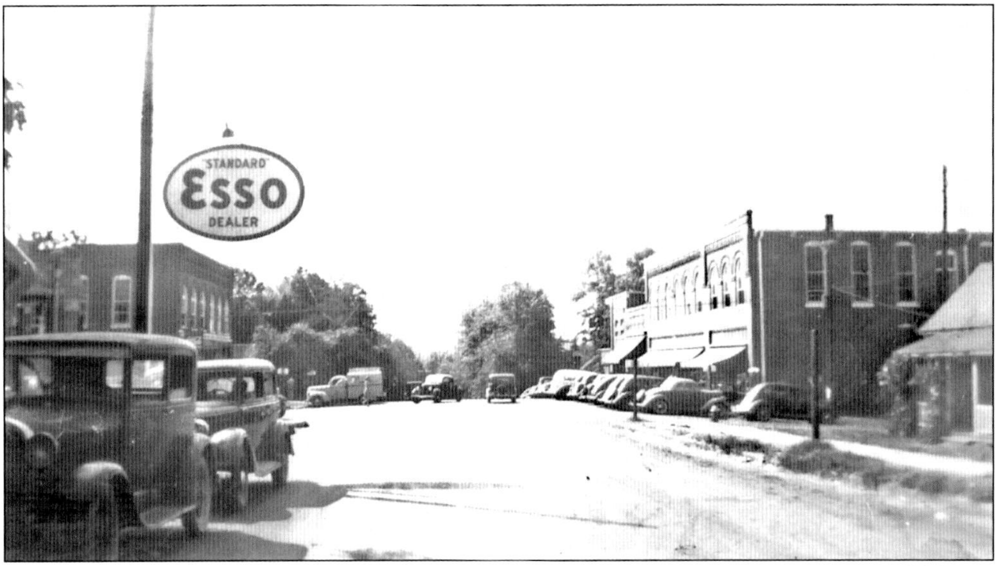

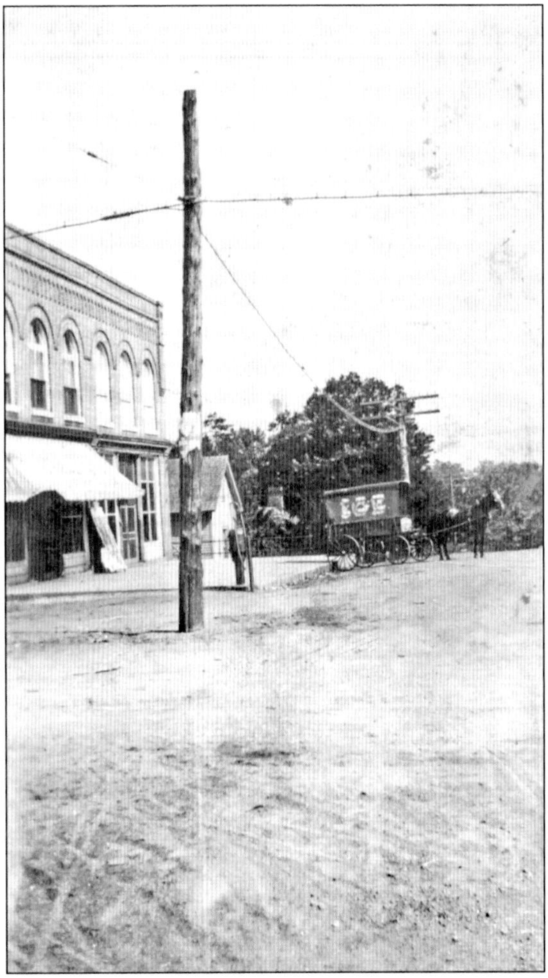

COOLEEMEE OLD SQUARE. Social life centered on Cooleemee's downtown square at the top of a hill overlooking the mill. At the J. N. Ledford Company store, customers could purchase anything from diapers to coffins. Also on the west side of the square stood the Bank of Cooleemee, the show house, and the post office. The square's east side housed Hoyle's Drug Store and the café and meat market, with Dr. Andrew Byerly's office and the fraternal meeting hall upstairs. Dick Everhart's service station dispensed gasoline and repaired a growing stock of automobiles. (Both, courtesy of Textile Heritage Center at Cooleemee.)

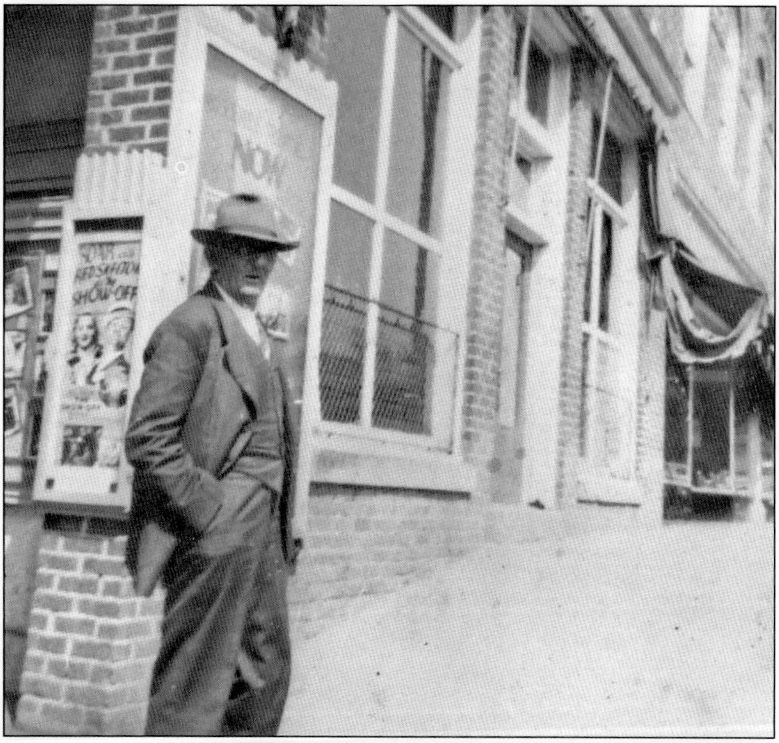

MOVIE THEATER. The new movie theater, one of the early "talkies" in the state, replaced an old silent picture show house on Bridge Street in 1927. (Courtesy of Textile Heritage Center at Cooleemee.)

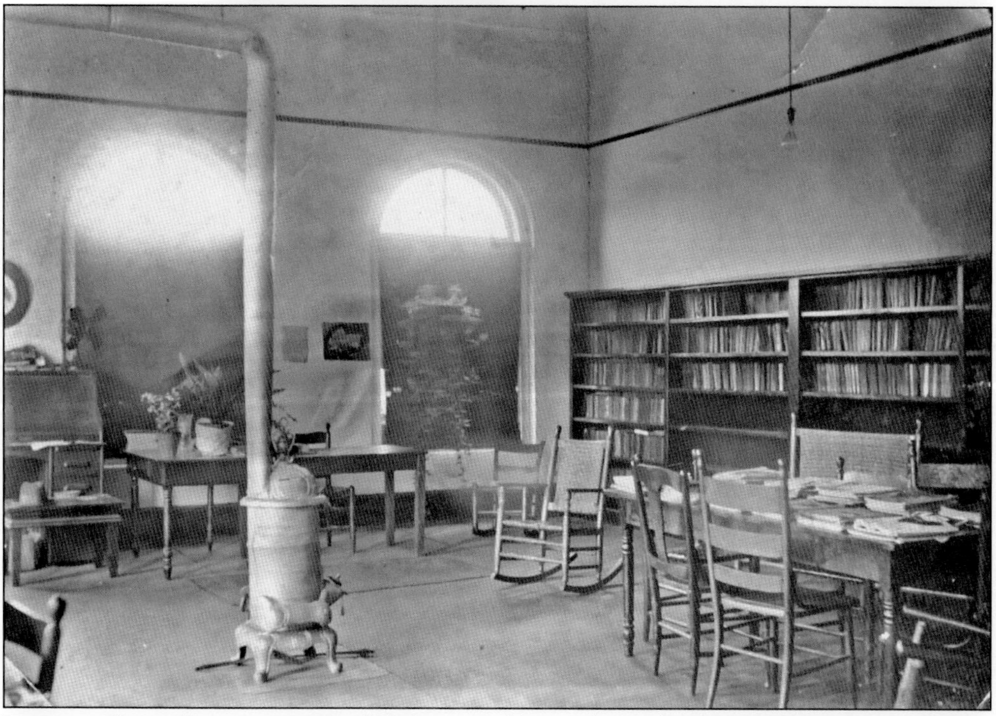

LIBRARY. The mill company provided the town library above the J. N. Ledford store. Later the library relocated to the Recreation Center in the old Zachary House. (Courtesy of Textile Heritage Center at Cooleemee.)

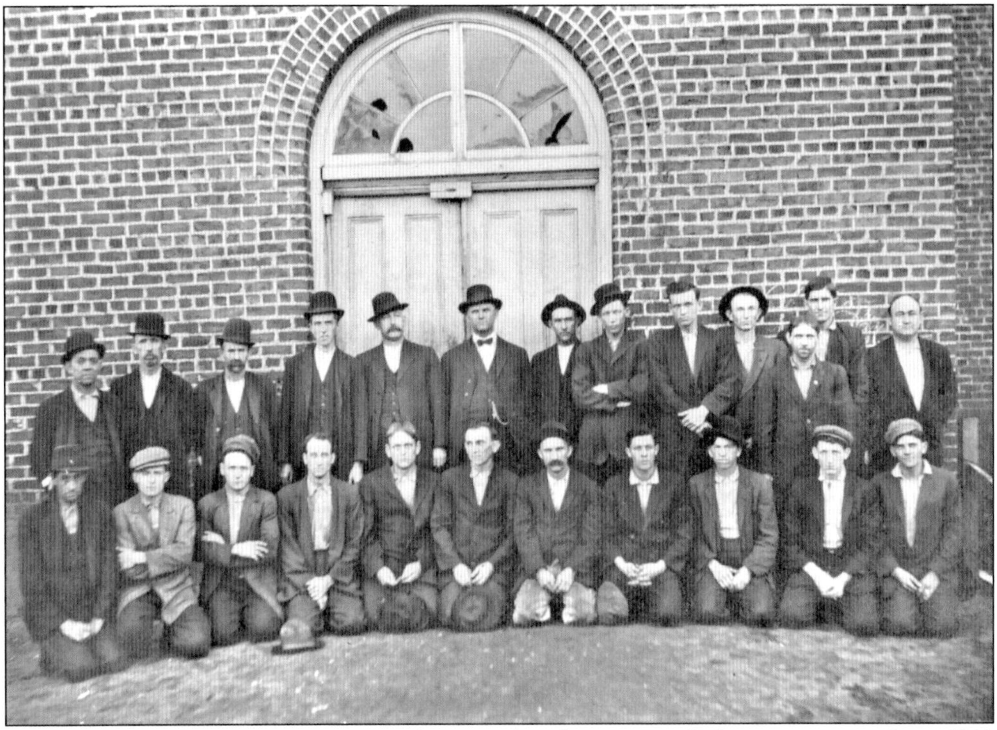

WARPER AND SLASHER ROOM, 1911. Photographs of various mill departments made in 1911 included the Warper and Slasher Room hands wearing their bowler hats and wool caps. (Courtesy of Textile Heritage Center at Cooleemee.)

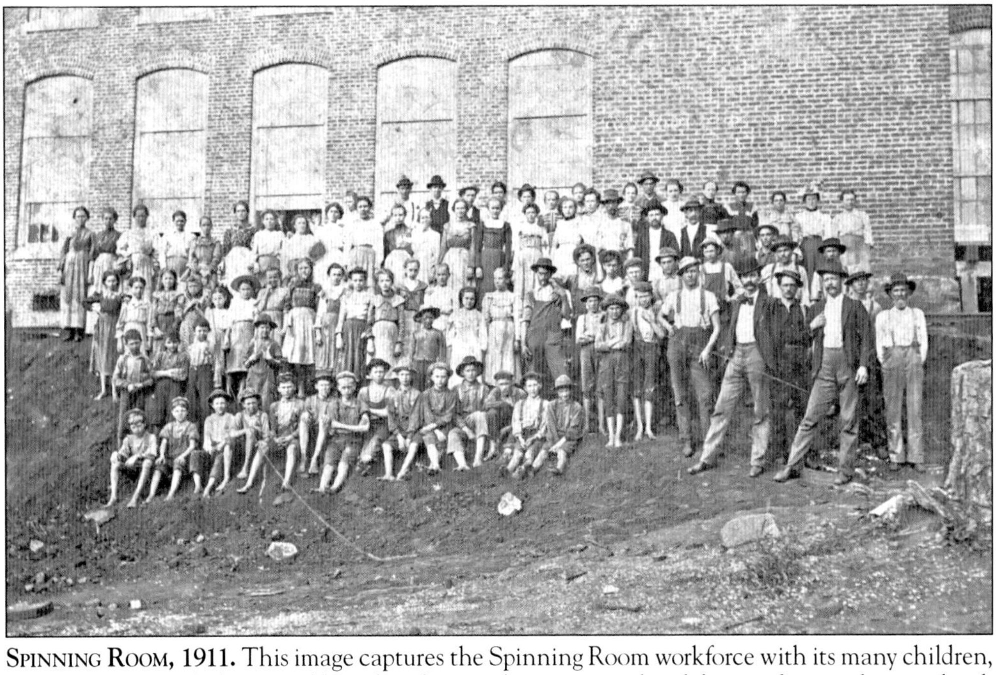

SPINNING ROOM, 1911. This image captures the Spinning Room workforce with its many children, over 80 percent of whom could read and write, having completed four or five grades at school. (Courtesy of Textile Heritage Center at Cooleemee.)

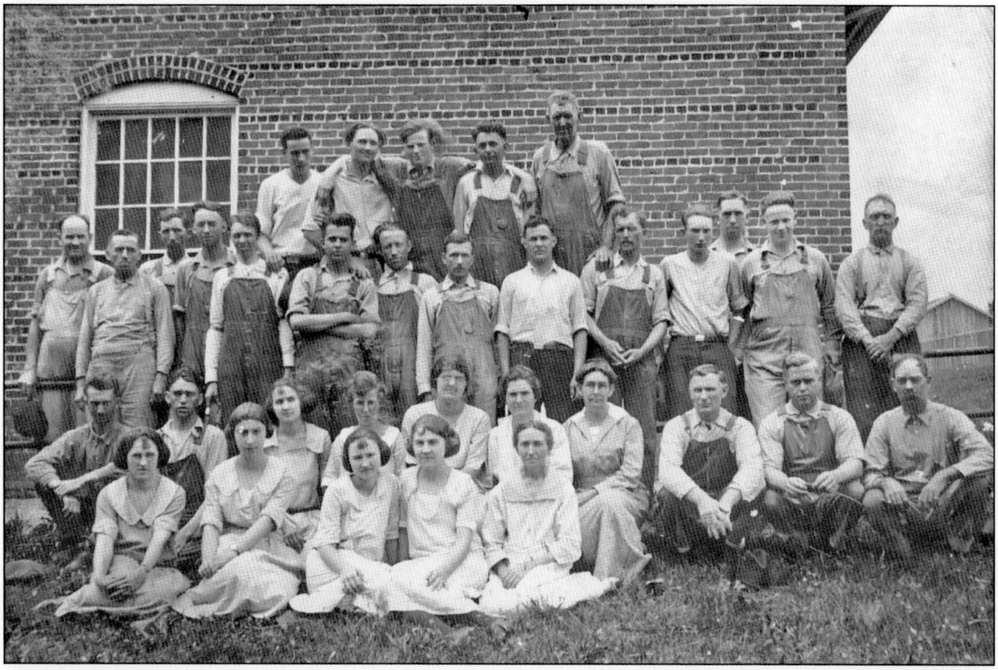

Napper Room, 1922. Workers in the Napper Room made flannels in 1922. (Courtesy of Textile Heritage Center at Cooleemee.)

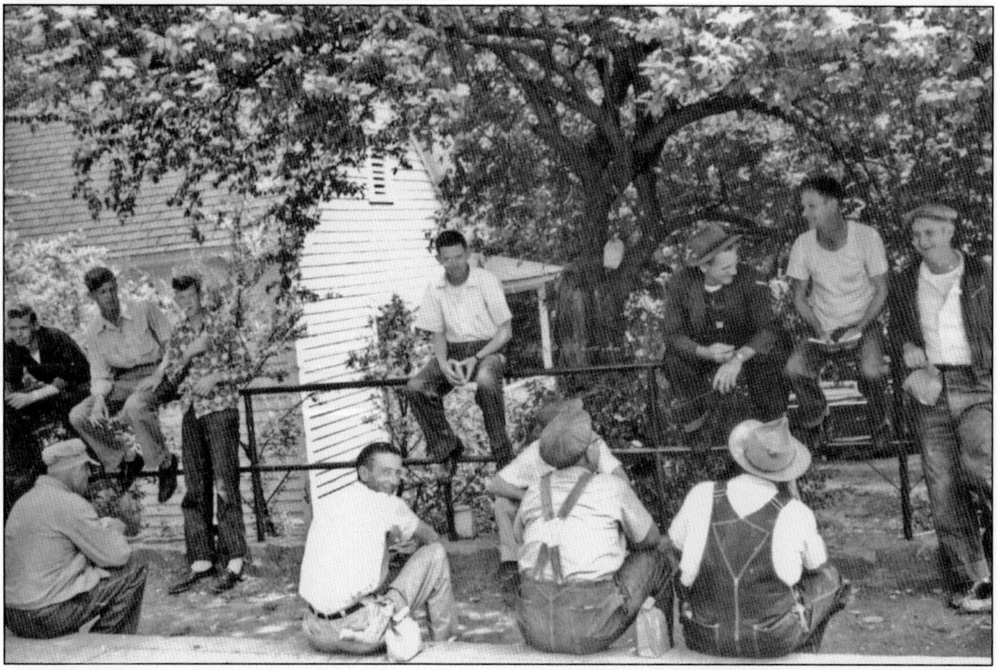

Old Iron Rails at Square. The mill ran one 12-hour shift from 6:00 a.m. until 6:00 p.m., with an hour for dinner, until the late 1920s. After operating with two 10-hour shifts for the next decade, the mill moved to three 8-hour shifts in the 1930s while hiring more workers from rural areas of Davie and Rowan Counties. Second-shift men often gathered on the old iron rails below the café on the square. (Courtesy of Textile Heritage Center at Cooleemee.)

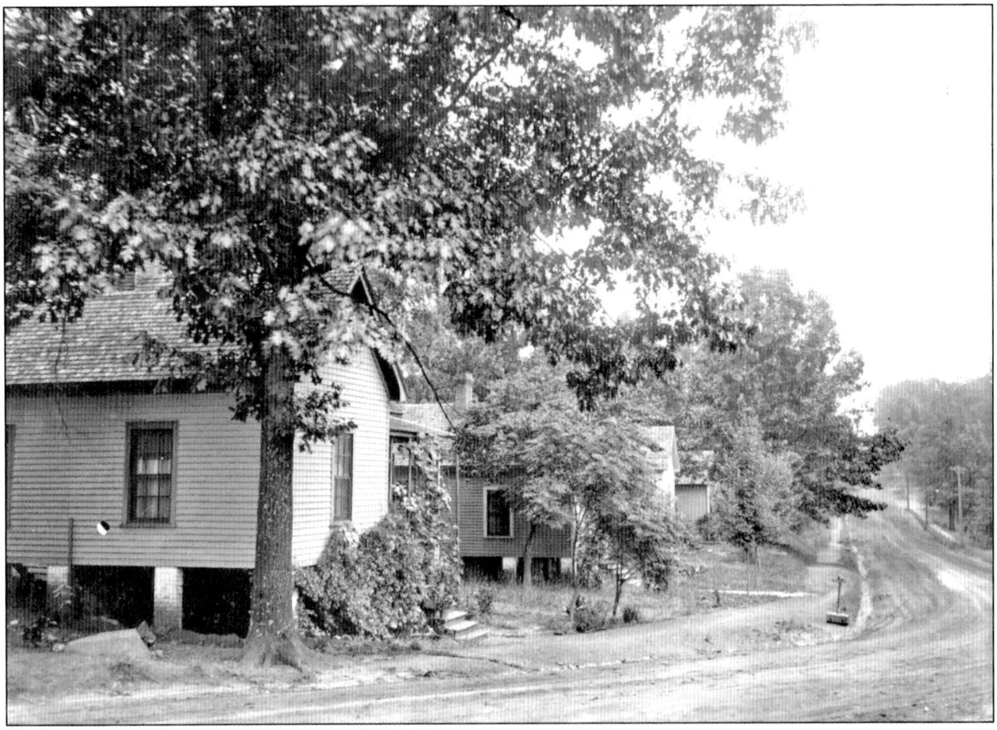

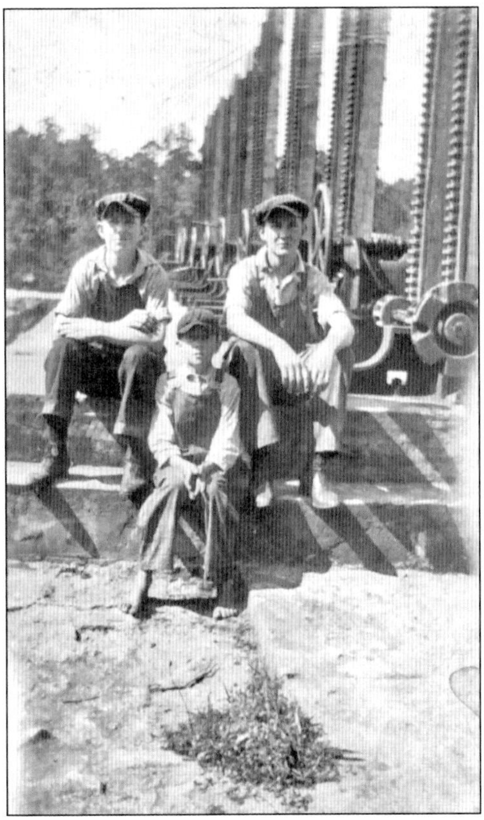

Street Scene with Water Pump. The mill built more than 360 houses, most with four rooms and a lot large enough for a garden and a smokehouse. Residents hauled water to each home from community pumps. From the 1920s until 1953, when the mill offered to sell the houses, rent remained at 25¢ per room per week. After World War II, paving replaced the dirt streets packed with coal cinders. (Courtesy of Textile Heritage Center at Cooleemee.)

Three Young Mill Hands. Boys enjoyed fishing and swimming at "The Bullhole," considered off-limits for girls. These three boys sit on the dam in front of its headgates to the millrace. (Courtesy of Textile Heritage Center at Cooleemee.)

Playing Marbles. Large extended families with grandparents and plenty of cousins cared for the abundant children. Simple toys included marbles purchased at the company store or "pee dabs" handmade from clay and baked in mother's wood cookstove. Girls played jacks and jumped rope. (Courtesy of Textile Heritage Center at Cooleemee.)

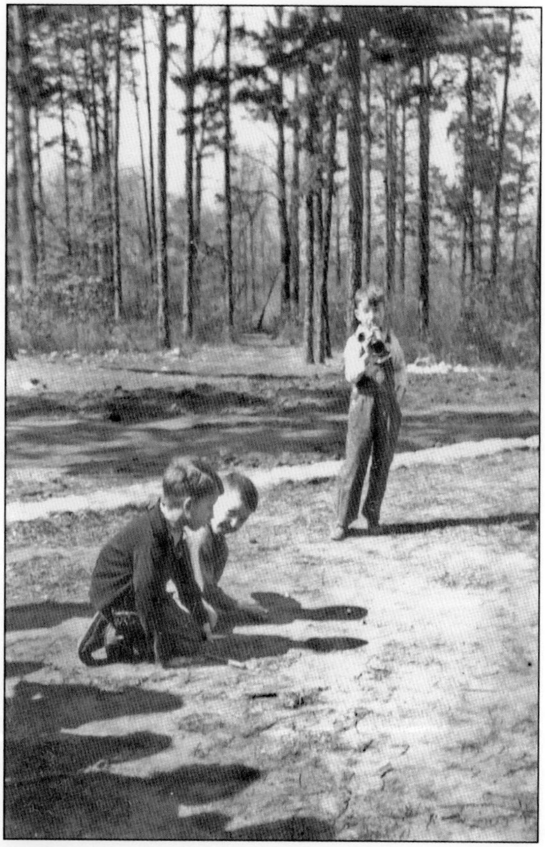

Center Street. Residents used brush brooms to sweep their dirt yards, like these lining the Center Street hill toward the cotton mill below. The mill company regularly painted the houses inside and out, and installed electric power in 1927 and indoor plumbing in 1932. (Courtesy of Textile Heritage Center at Cooleemee.)

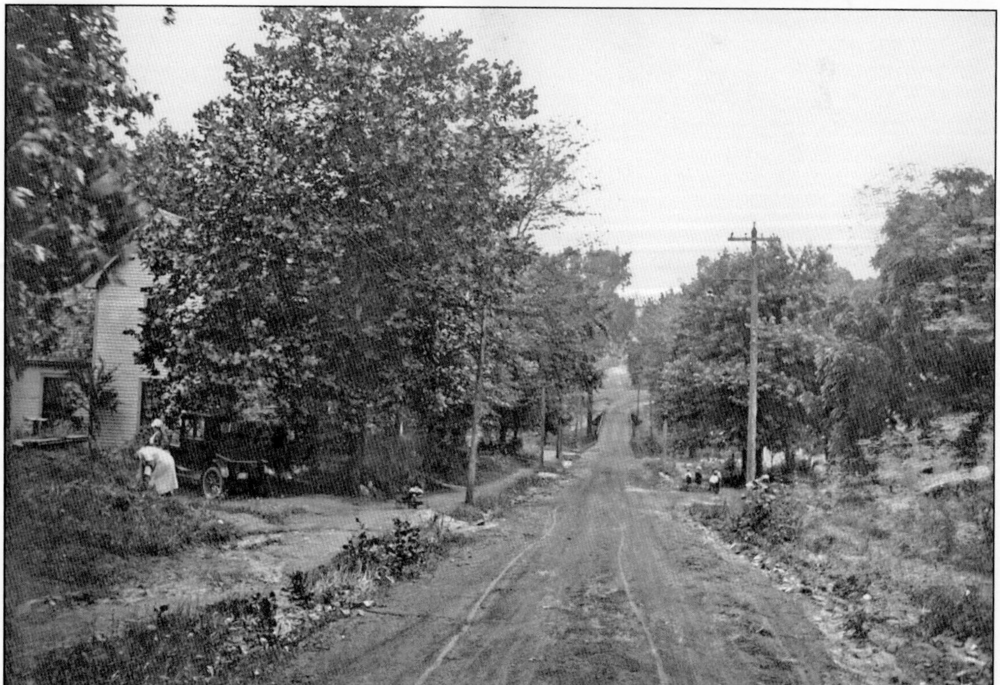

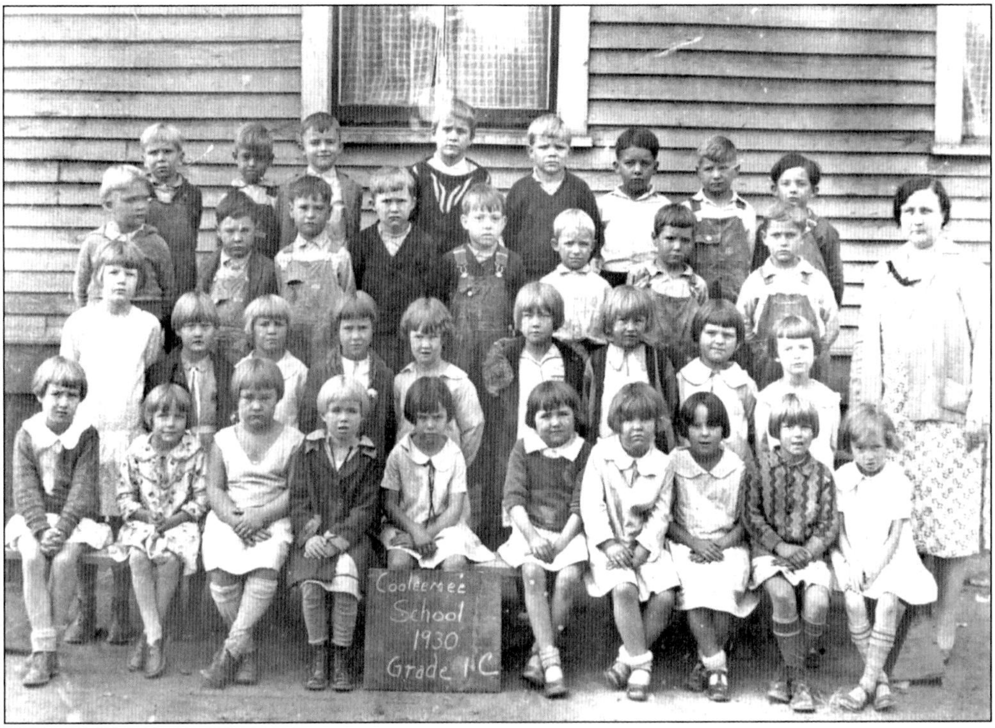

OLD WOOD SCHOOL. In 1903, Erwin Mills' new modern school for white children replaced the one-room "field schools" in which children progressed at their own speed. Davie County's first graded school faced Watts Street at the corner of Cross Street. Most teachers attended college beyond normal school. Above, Emma Grimes's first-grade class poses in 1930. (Both, courtesy of Textile Heritage Center at Cooleemee.)

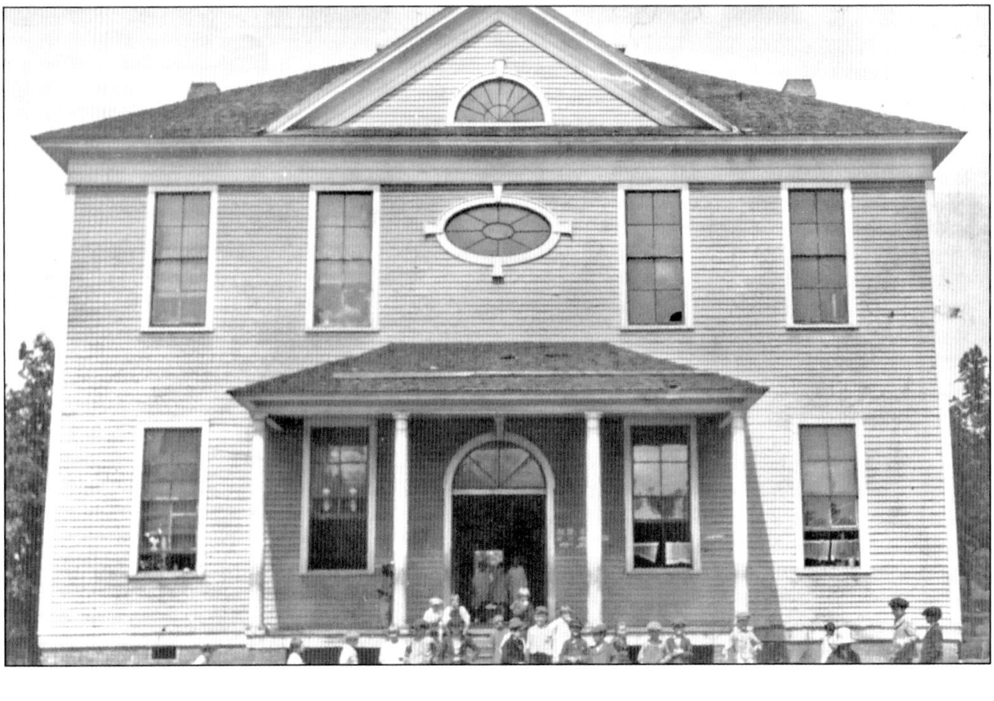

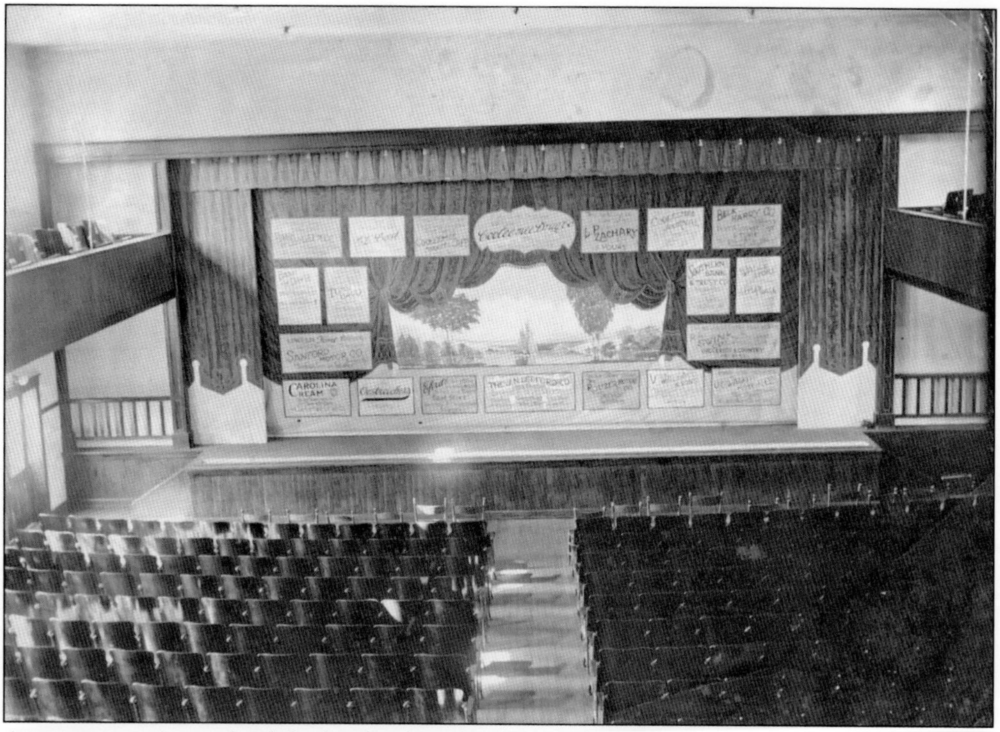

AUDITORIUM. A new brick high school in 1924 boasted an 800-seat auditorium and eventually housed all grades. Many mill family children graduated from this high school in the late 1930s. (Courtesy of Textile Heritage Center at Cooleemee.)

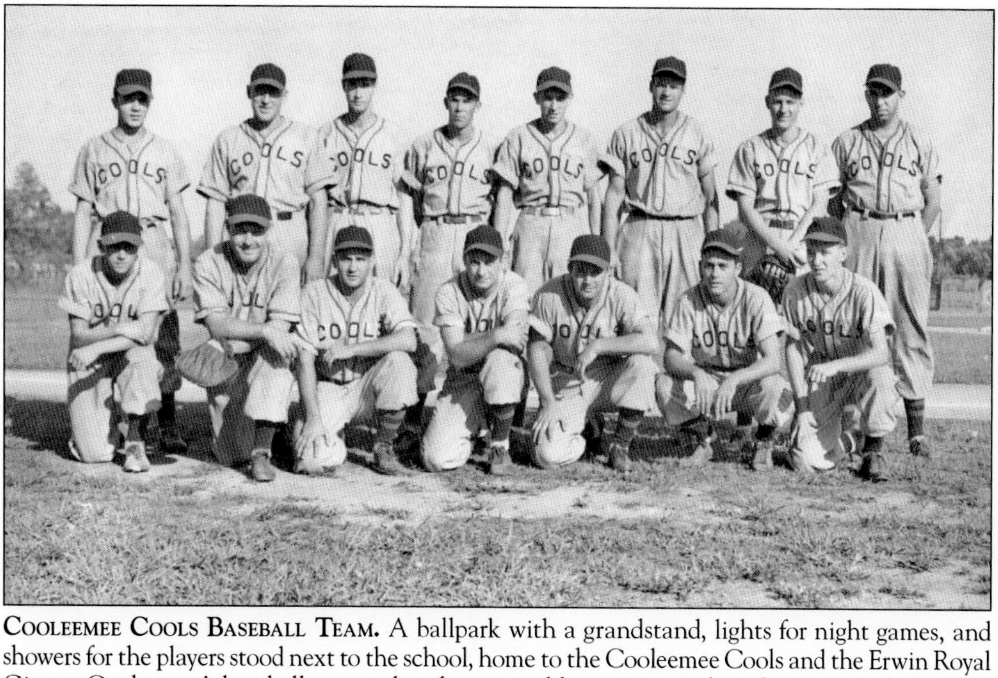

COOLEEMEE COOLS BASEBALL TEAM. A ballpark with a grandstand, lights for night games, and showers for the players stood next to the school, home to the Cooleemee Cools and the Erwin Royal Giants. Cooleemee's baseball teams played in several leagues, even for a few years as part of the farm system of the St. Louis Cardinals. (Courtesy of Textile Heritage Center at Cooleemee.)

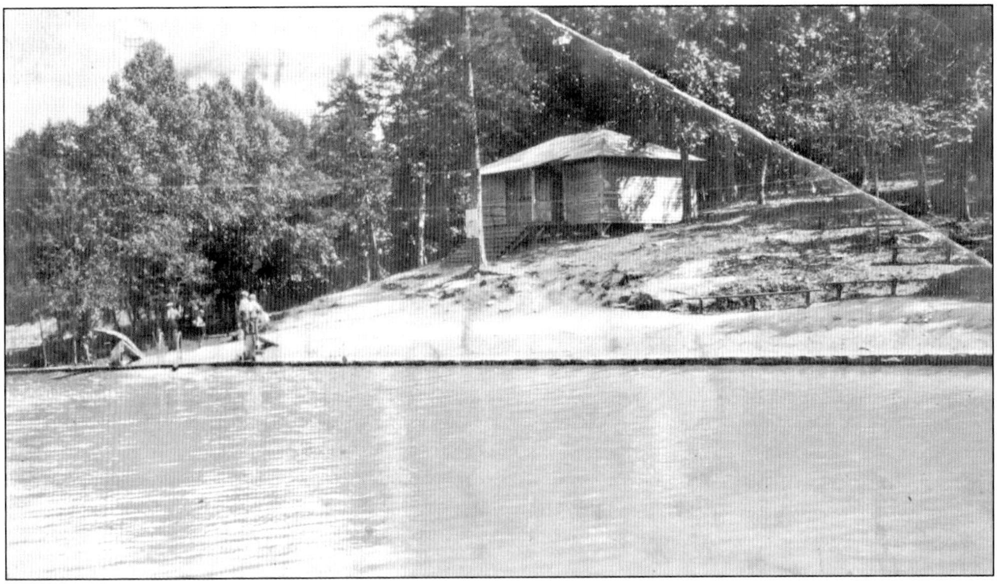

Stone Pool and Bathhouse. A freshwater stream filled one of the state's earliest public bathing pools, complete with lights for nighttime swim competitions. Its bathhouse rented towels and suits. Excursion trains brought passengers to Cooleemee for a day of shopping and swimming in the stone pool. (Courtesy of Textile Heritage Center at Cooleemee.)

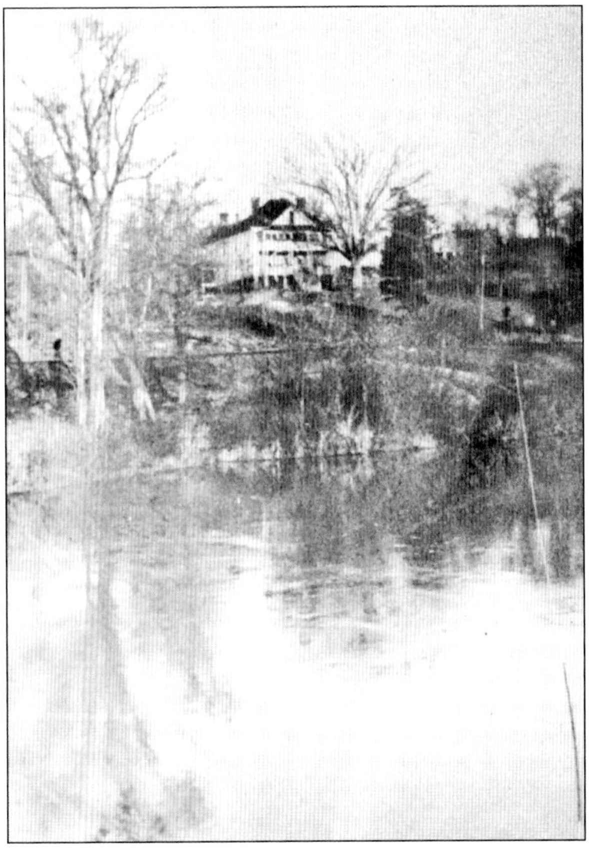

Riverside Hotel. Overlooking the river on the Davie side stood the Riverside Hotel at the end of Cross Street just off Main Street. With a grand parlor and dining room, the hotel housed many teachers and visiting executives and salesmen. (Courtesy of Textile Heritage Center at Cooleemee.)

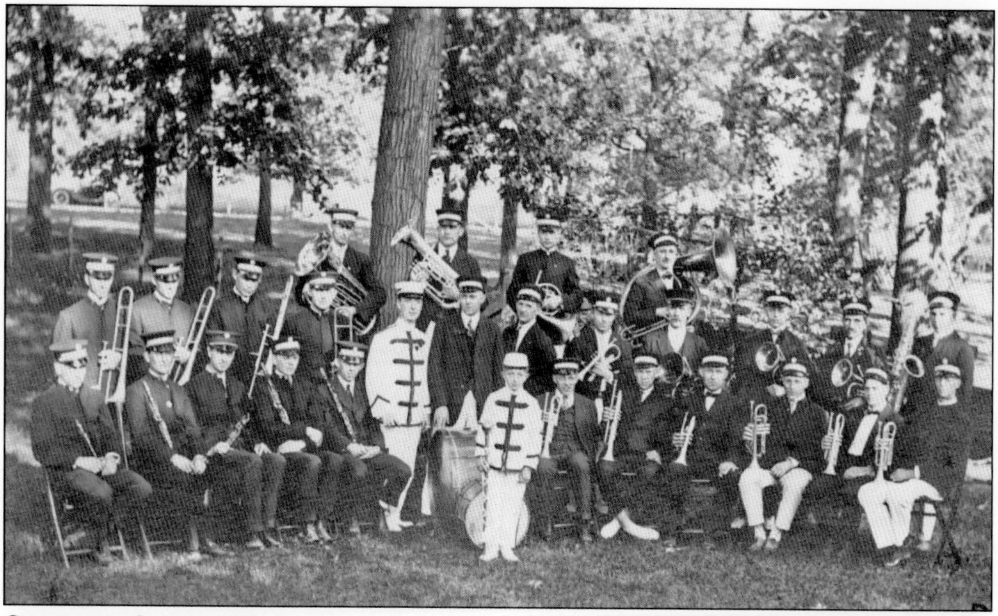

Cooleemee Concert Band. The mill organized the band with 20 members in 1917, providing uniforms and instruments. A. A. Hartman served as the first director, followed by Joe Nance, Ernest Fritz, Prof. ? Shaw, Roberts Mills, and Floyd A. Nail. The band performed for Christmas, Fourth of July, picnics, and other amusements in the mill village. Some members later played with other bands, such as Wake Forest College, Clark Brothers Circus, Ringling Brothers Circus, and John Philip Sousa.

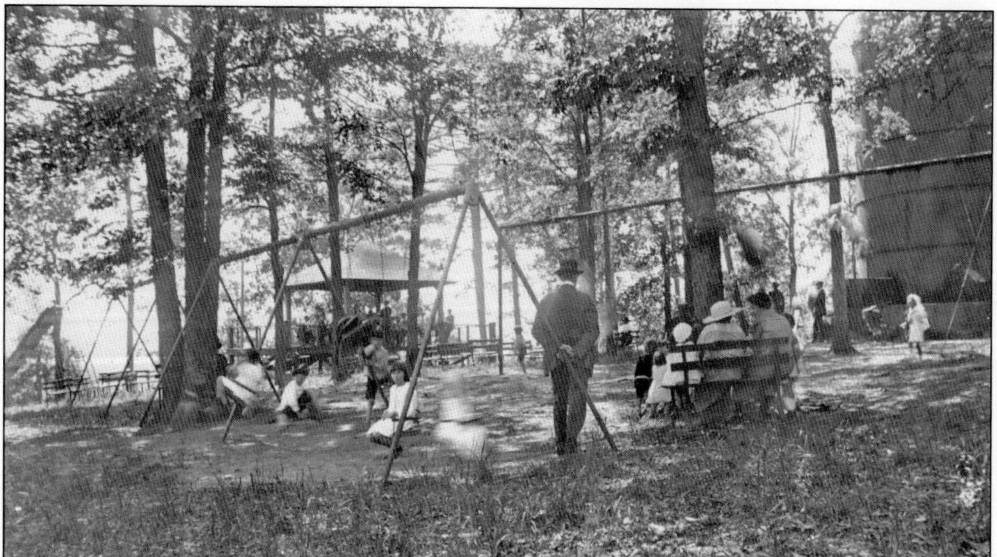

Park Hill Playground. The fully equipped Park Hill playground on Main Street featured seesaws, swings, tennis courts, and a bandstand where many gathered on Sunday evenings to hear the band and sing hymns. Cooleemee's community life beyond the mill included civic groups like the all-female Cotton Club and fraternal orders such as the Redmen and the Patriotic Sons of America, with the Textile Workers Union of America, organized locally in the late 1930s, perhaps the largest group in town. (Courtesy of Textile Heritage Center at Cooleemee.)

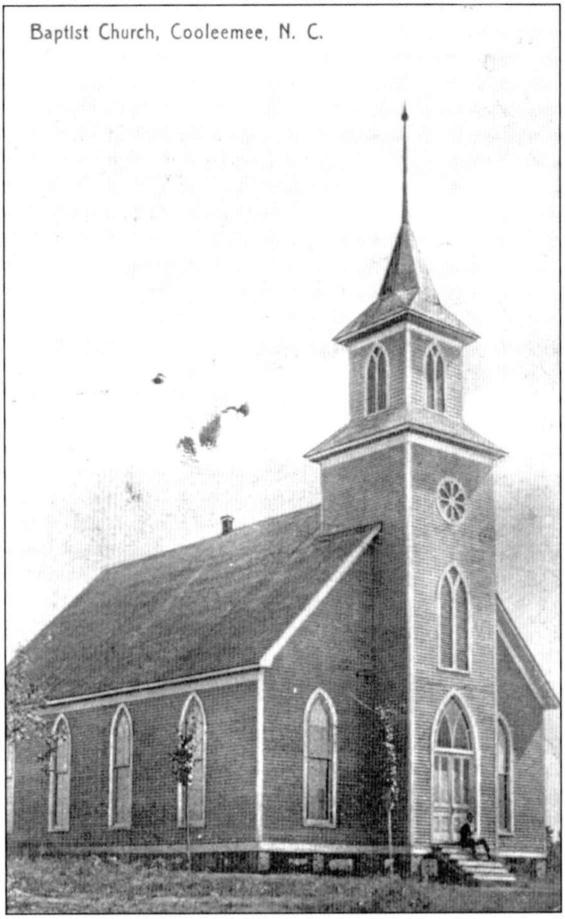

COOLEEMEE BAPTIST CHURCH. Erwin Mills donated land for six houses of worship, with four founded in 1901: Cooleemee Baptist Church (with the largest congregation), Good Shepherd Episcopal, Cooleemee Methodist, and Cooleemee Presbyterian. Friendship Baptist (1905) and Erwin Temple Colored Methodist Episcopal Church (1928) followed. With potbellied stoves for heat, these earliest wood churches each burned and was rebuilt in brick. Most families regularly attended Sunday services, which bolstered their ancestors' traditional values, based on the Ten Commandments and the Golden Rule. Christmas Eve meant packed churches, while summers saw vacation Bible schools and tent revivals. (Both, courtesy of Textile Heritage Center at Cooleemee.)

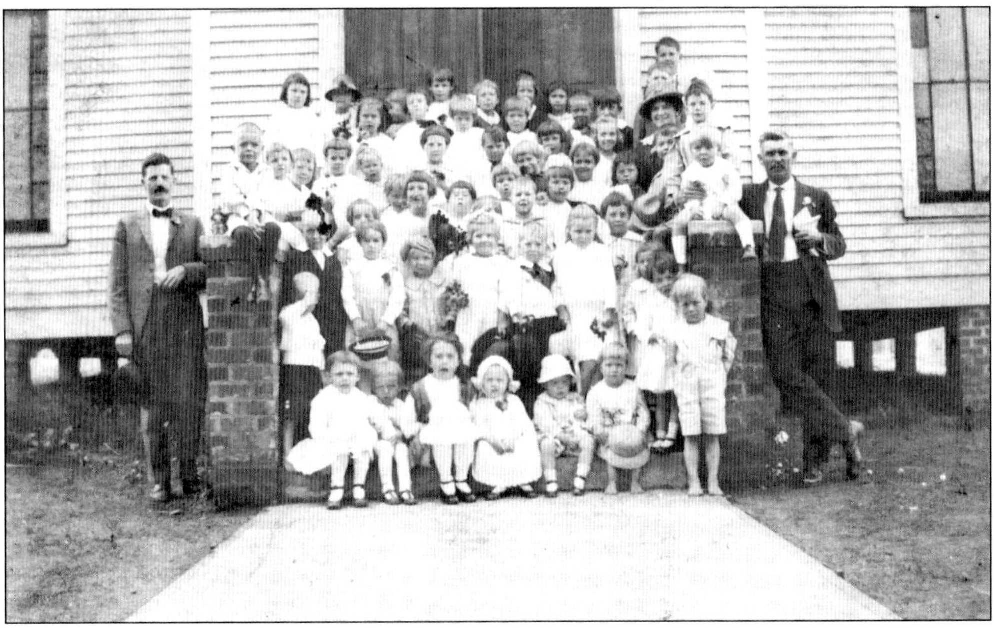

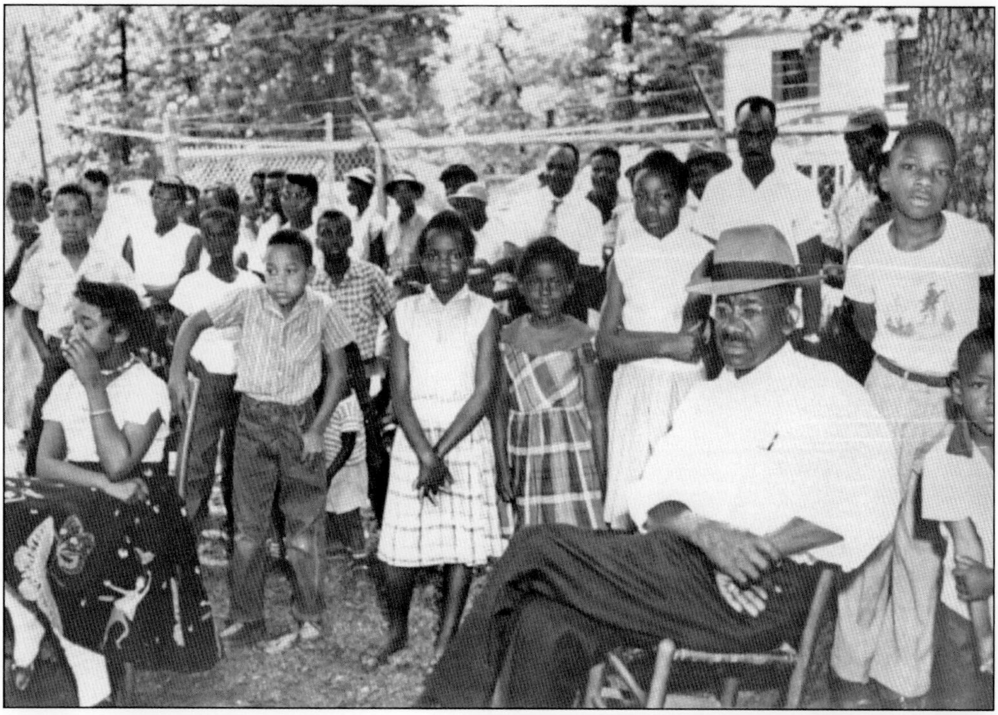

AFRICAN AMERICAN COMMUNITY. The town's small African American community had roots in nearby plantations before the Civil War. Black families in town originally lived on "Dam Hill," but in the mid-1930s, they moved to new mill houses near Friendship Baptist Church and North Cooleemee School. Black men hired by the mill opened bales of cotton or boxed and loaded finished cloth. As part of the mill's outside crew, some removed garbage and cleaned outdoor toilets. Black women usually served as laundresses if they worked outside the home. (Both, courtesy of Textile Heritage Center at Cooleemee.)

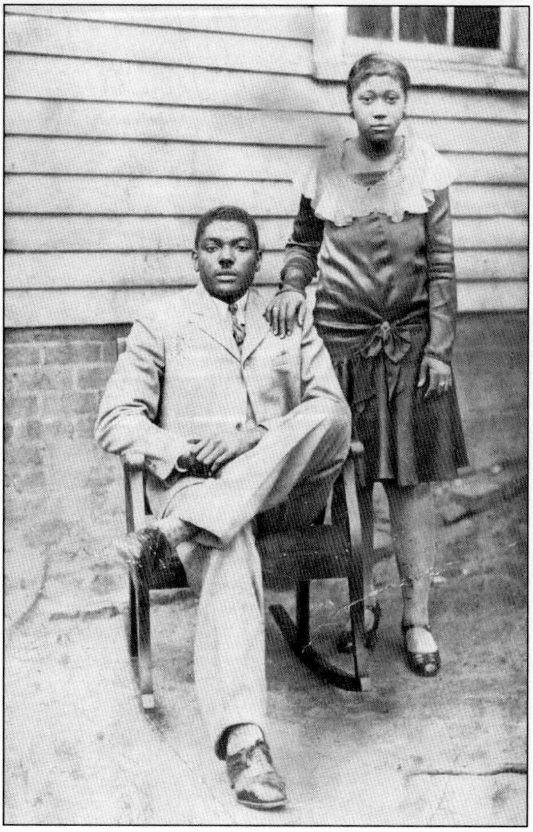

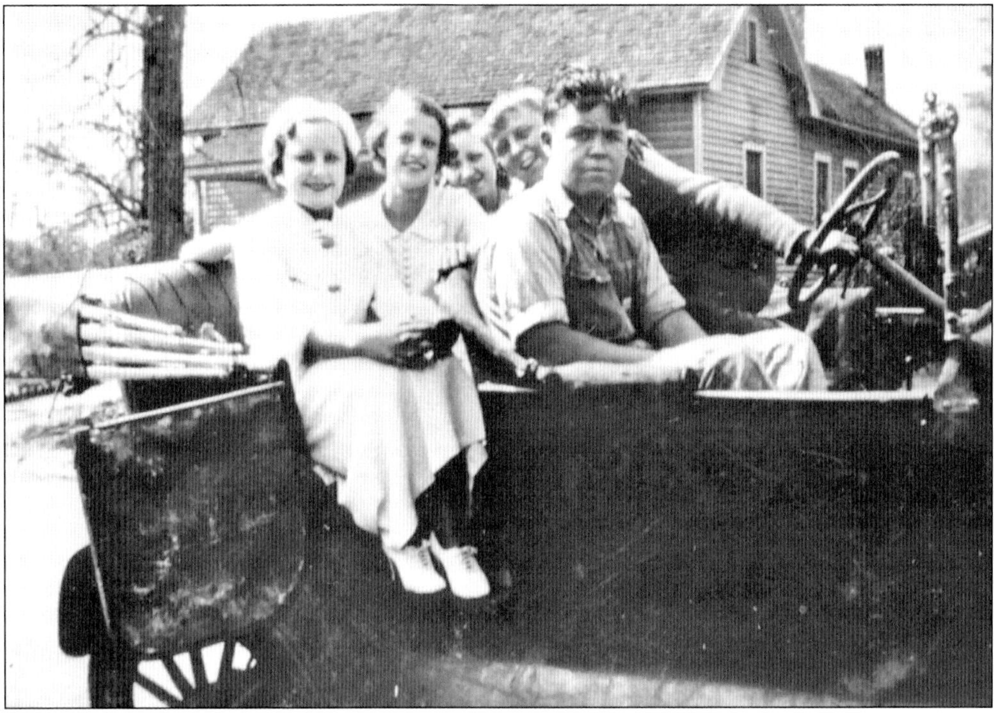

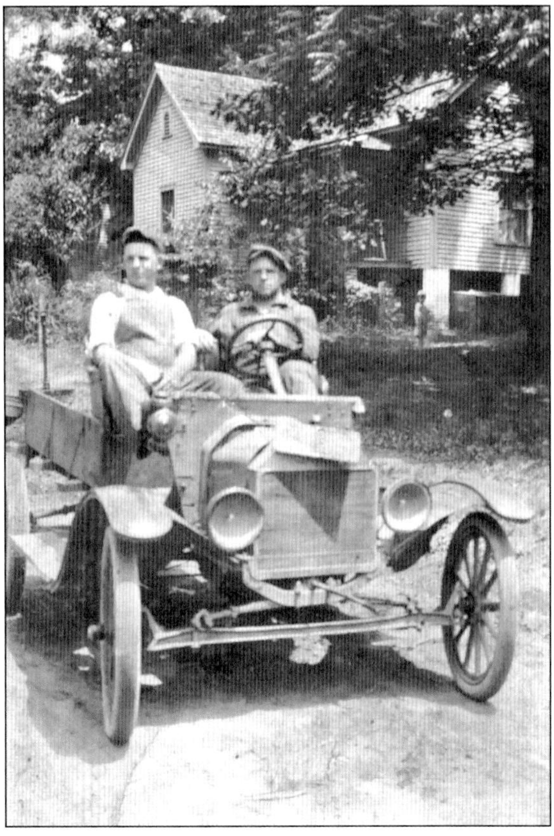

Automobiles. The overseer of the Weave Room owned the first automobile in Cooleemee, followed closely by the mill manager. Tradition maintains that local men dismantled and rebuilt the engine of the first Ford Model T in Cooleemee so they could become self-reliant mechanics. Cars remained a novelty until after World War II. (Both, courtesy of Textile Heritage Center at Cooleemee.)

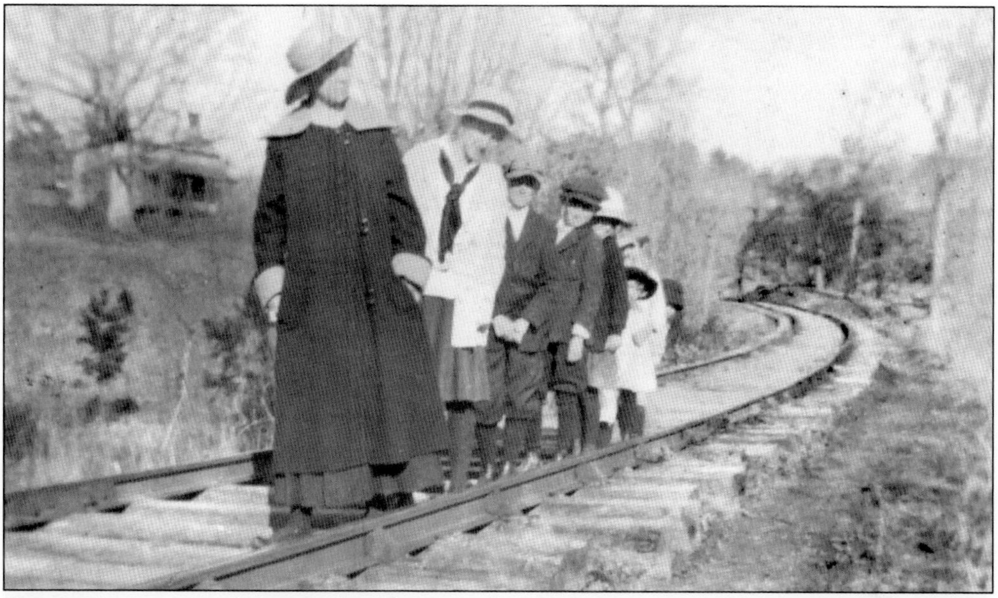

SUNDAY STROLL. Sundays started in church and was followed by dinner, which usually consisted of a chicken or two from the family stock, either fried or stewed with dumplings. Leisurely Sunday afternoons entailed visiting other homes or strolling up to the junction along the railroad spur line. (Courtesy of Textile Heritage Center at Cooleemee.)

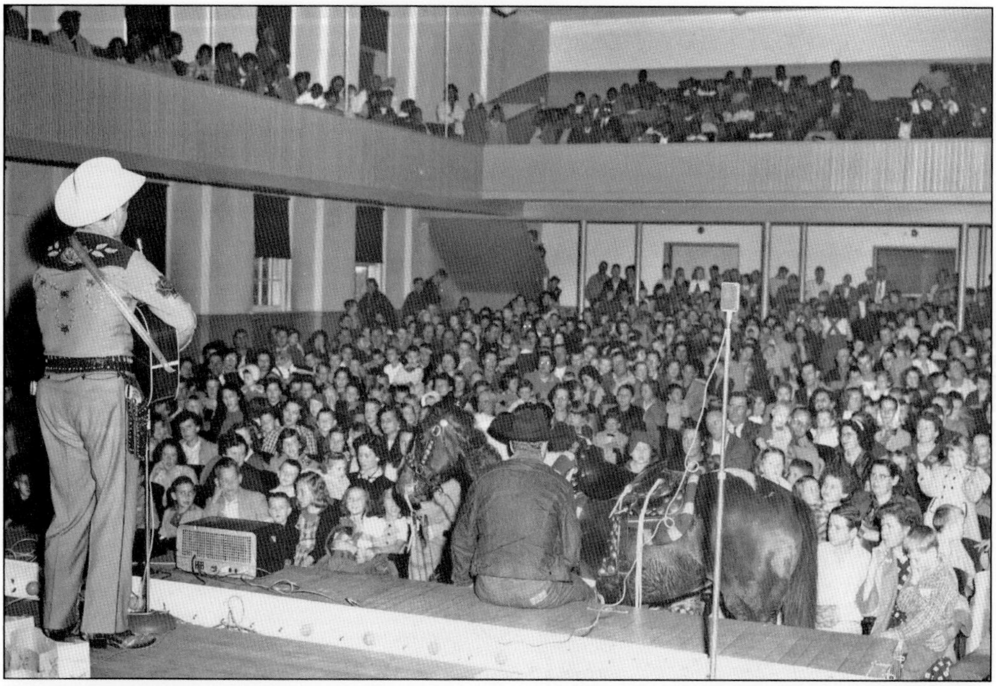

FRED KIRBY. North Carolina's singing cowboy, Fred Kirby, appears with his horse, Calico, at the auditorium for the annual union Christmas party. Since the large stage accommodated even full-court basketball games, the auditorium provided an ideal venue for many large community events, such as fiddlers' conventions, plays, pageants, graduation exercises, and musicals. (Courtesy of Textile Heritage Center at Cooleemee.)

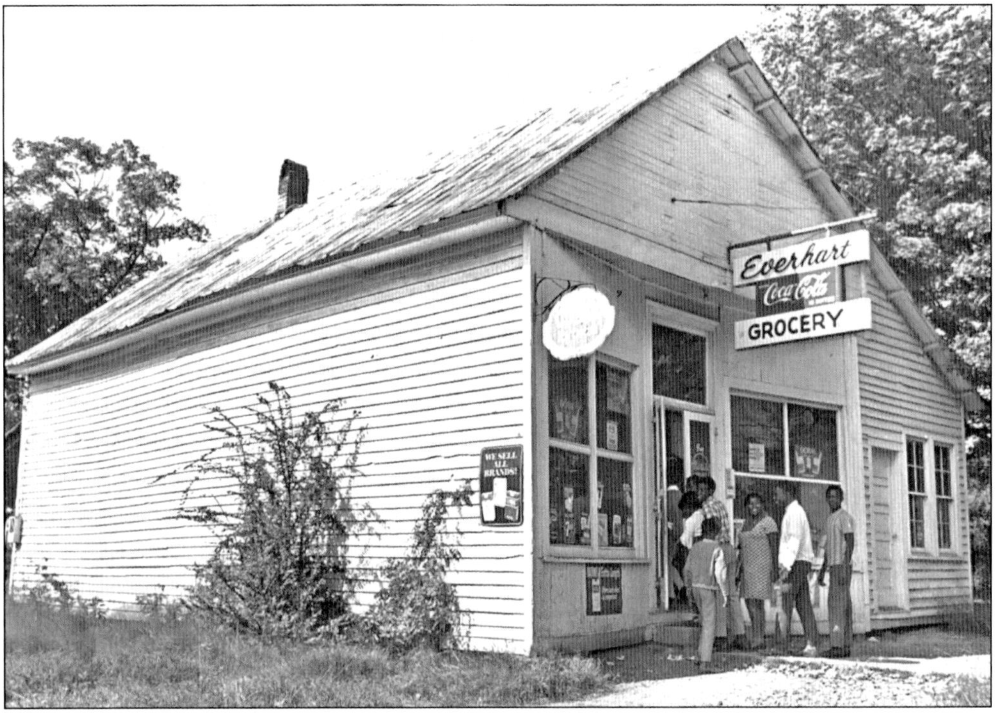

NORTH COOLEEMEE. On the way to Greasy Corner, North Cooleemee ran independently of mill company control, with its own stores, taverns, cafés, and homes. The Everhart store (pictured above) took orders and made home deliveries. Q. M. Goodman's service station (shown below) offered gas, hot dogs, and a pool table. (Both, courtesy of Textile Heritage Center at Cooleemee.)

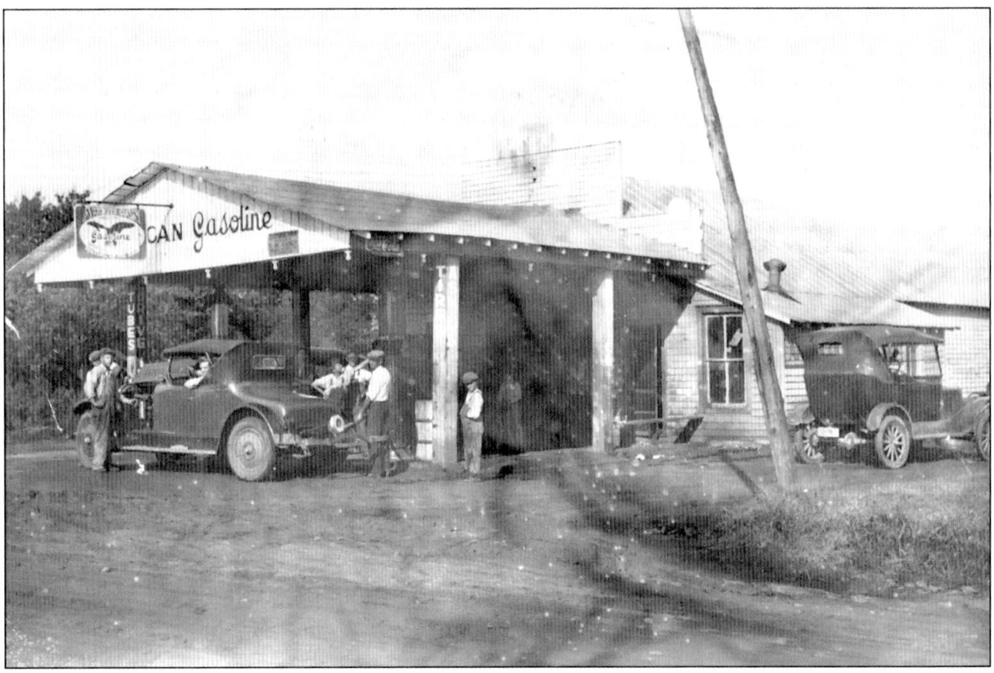

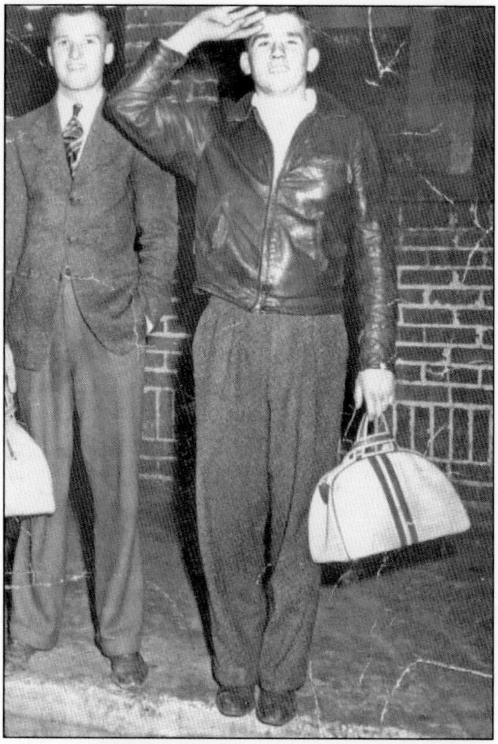

World War II. Hundreds of Cooleemee men and some women served in World War II, following the long tradition of military service of their ancestors back to the American Revolution. On the home front, mill employees attended "Buy War Bonds" rallies like this one (shown below). Town residents experienced blackouts and rationing for consumer goods. Following the war, many changes came to Cooleemee. (Both, courtesy of Textile Heritage Center at Cooleemee.)

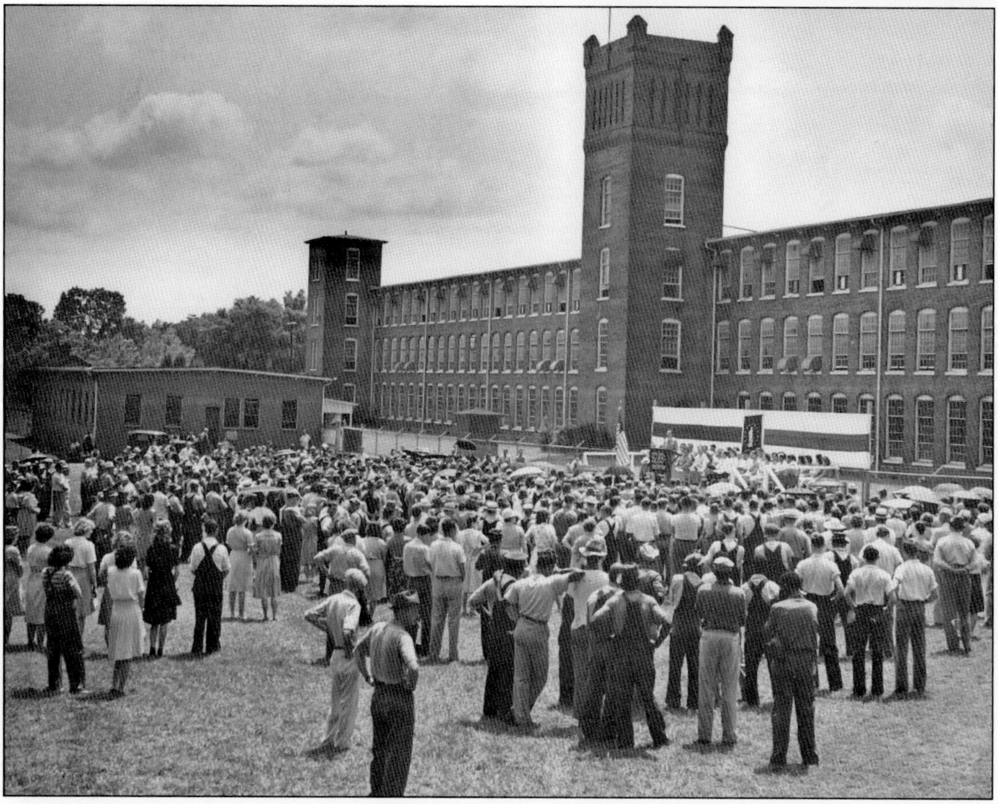

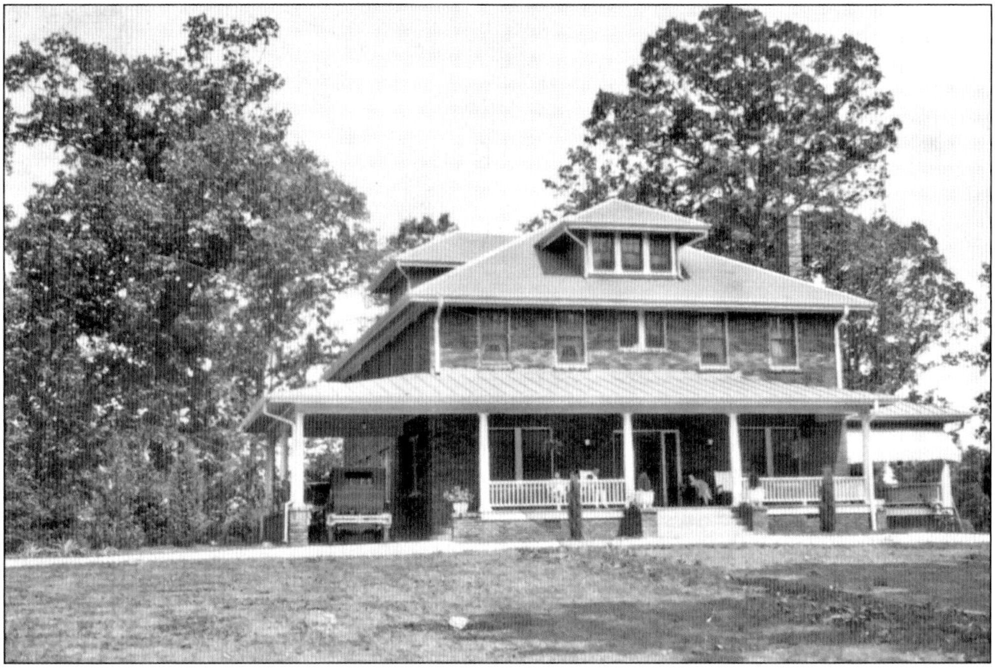

Zachary House. James W. and Lillian Zachary and their 12 children lived in this large house on Church Street. In 1948, Erwin Mills transformed the old general manager's house into a recreation center with pool tables, table tennis, and a variety of board games for the town's first generation of teenagers. A library upstairs hosted "Story Hour," enriching preschoolers. (Courtesy of Textile Heritage Center at Cooleemee.)

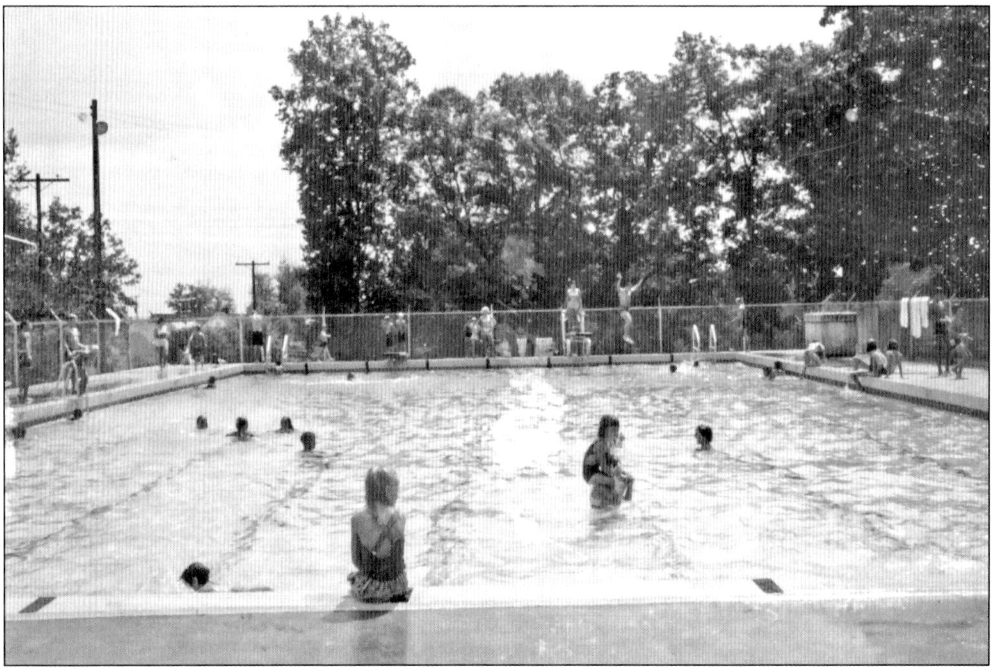

Good Times at the Pool. The next year, an Olympic-sized swimming pool opened. Entry tickets cost 10¢. (Courtesy of Textile Heritage Center at Cooleemee.)

Four

COUNTY SCENES AND PLACES

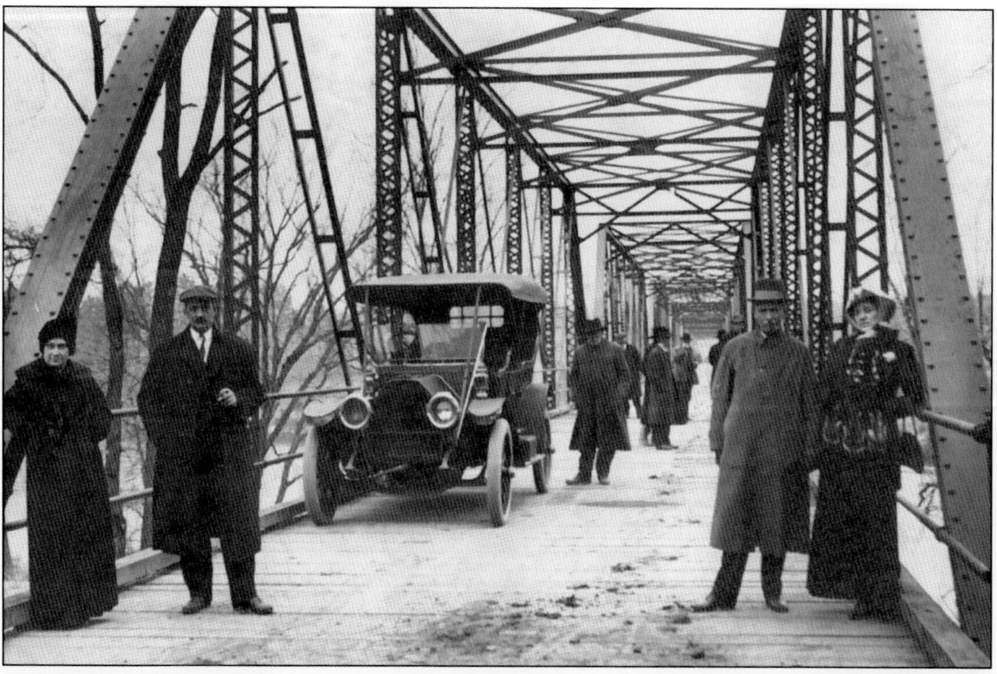

HALL'S FERRY BRIDGE. Begun in 1913, the steel bridge connected Forsyth and Davie Counties across the Yadkin River at the location currently occupied by the Katherine Crosby Bridge. The Vincennes Bridge Company of Indiana built the bridge for $31,000. Construction was supervised by engineer J. N. Ambler. Hall's Ferry operated at the crossing from 1848, making its last trip on Easter Monday 1914.

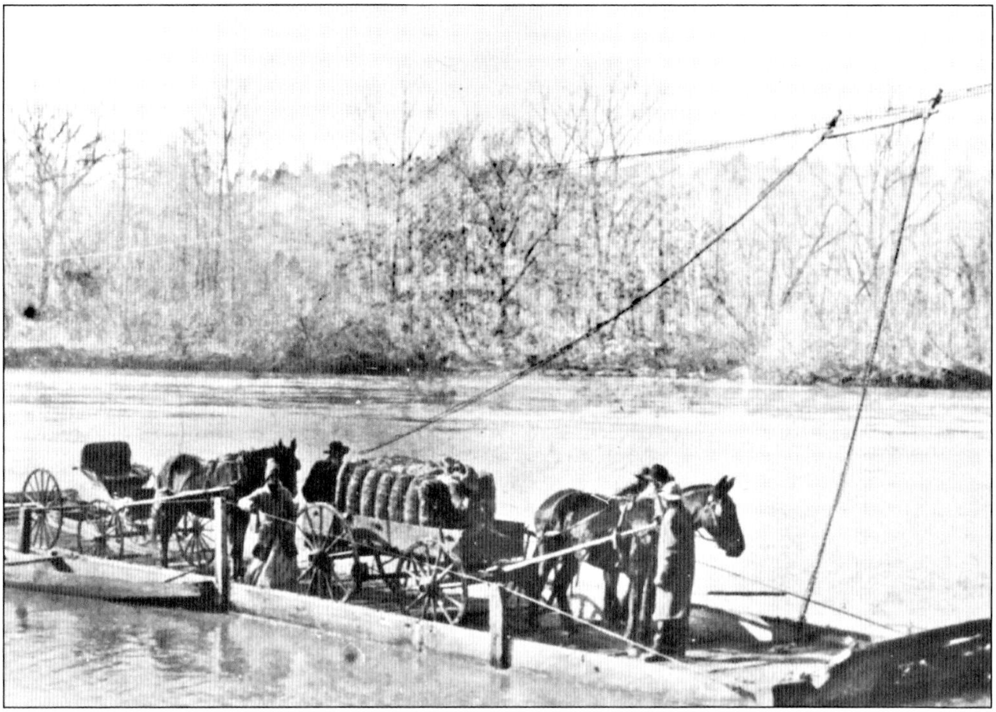

Early Ferry across the Yadkin River. Ferries represented a common and necessary means of travel in North Carolina. This ferry crossed the river between Lexington and Mocksville.

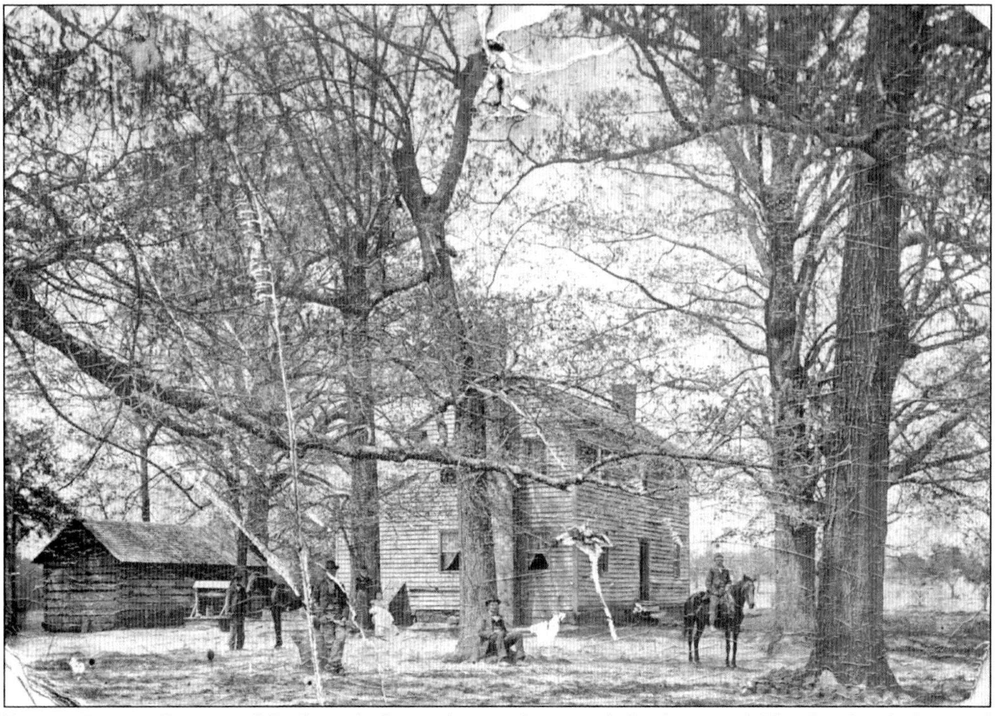

Rural Davie County. Unidentified people stand around the home of Charlie Cook, located near present-day Highway 601. Cook's home no longer exists.

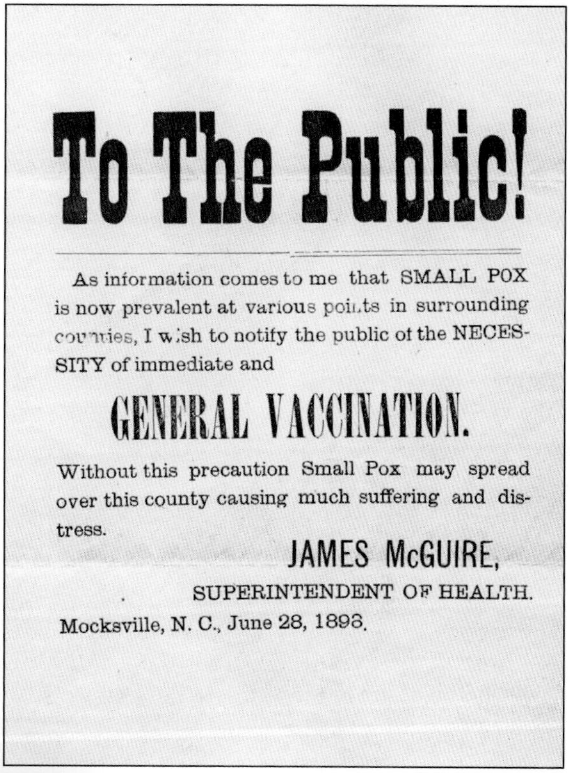

To The Public!

As information comes to me that SMALL POX is now prevalent at various points in surrounding counties, I wish to notify the public of the NECESSITY of immediate and

GENERAL VACCINATION.

Without this precaution Small Pox may spread over this county causing much suffering and distress.

JAMES McGUIRE,
SUPERINTENDENT OF HEALTH.

Mocksville, N. C., June 28, 1893.

Pest House. Pest houses isolated patients with communicable diseases from the community, as Dr. A. W. Wiseman's in Jerusalem did during a smallpox epidemic. The image below shows one of the pest houses in Davie County.

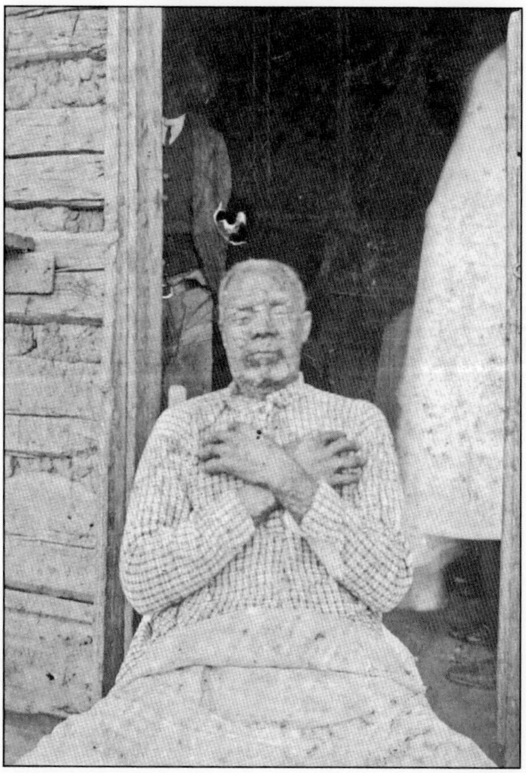

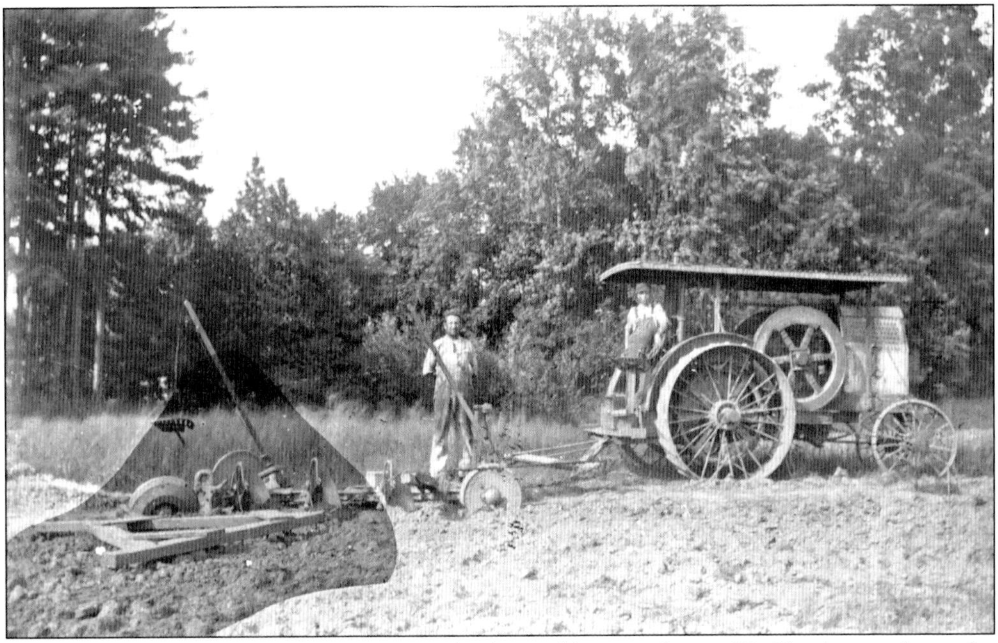

Farming at Boxwood Lodge. John C. Charles and his son, James W. Charles, work on the grounds at Boxwood Lodge. The 1,500-acre grounds of Boxwood included the lodge, a guest cabin, a greenhouse, various outbuildings, a fruit orchard, and several gardens (formal and informal flower, rose, and vegetable). The National Park Service added the lodge to the National Register of Historic Places in 1995.

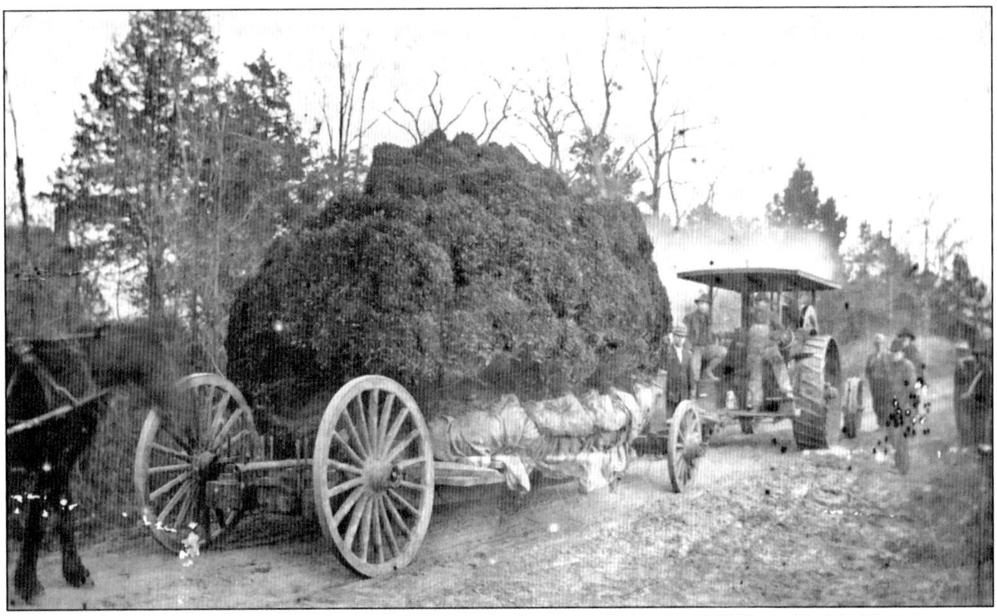

Boxwood Farm. John and James Charles move a boxwood plant to William Rabb Craig's estate in 1912. After the death of her husband, Margaret Cunningham Craig (later Woodson) made North Carolina her permanent home, tearing down the old home and hunting lodge, the Yadkin River Lodge, and constructing the Boxwood Lodge, named for the English boxwoods hauled in by wagon for the original lodge. Delano and Aldridge of New York designed the new lodge.

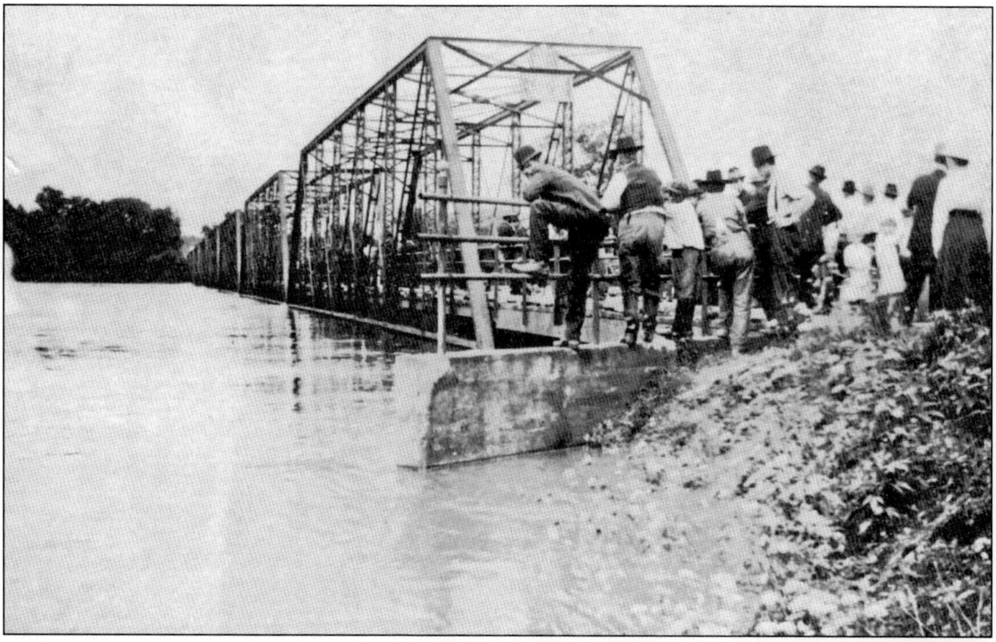

GREAT FLOOD, JULY 1916. Two back-to-back Caribbean hurricanes drenched North Carolina with record rainfalls, taking 80 lives and damaging $22 million worth of property when daily wages in 1916 averaged only $1. The swollen Yadkin River washed 2 feet over the new Hall's Ferry bridge, normally 30 feet above the water line. As the rising waters attracted many onlookers, Sheriff George W. Flynt of Forsyth County roped off the bridge at the Forsyth end to prevent traffic from crossing—a few minutes before one of the sections gave way. Z. N. Anderson took these pictures.

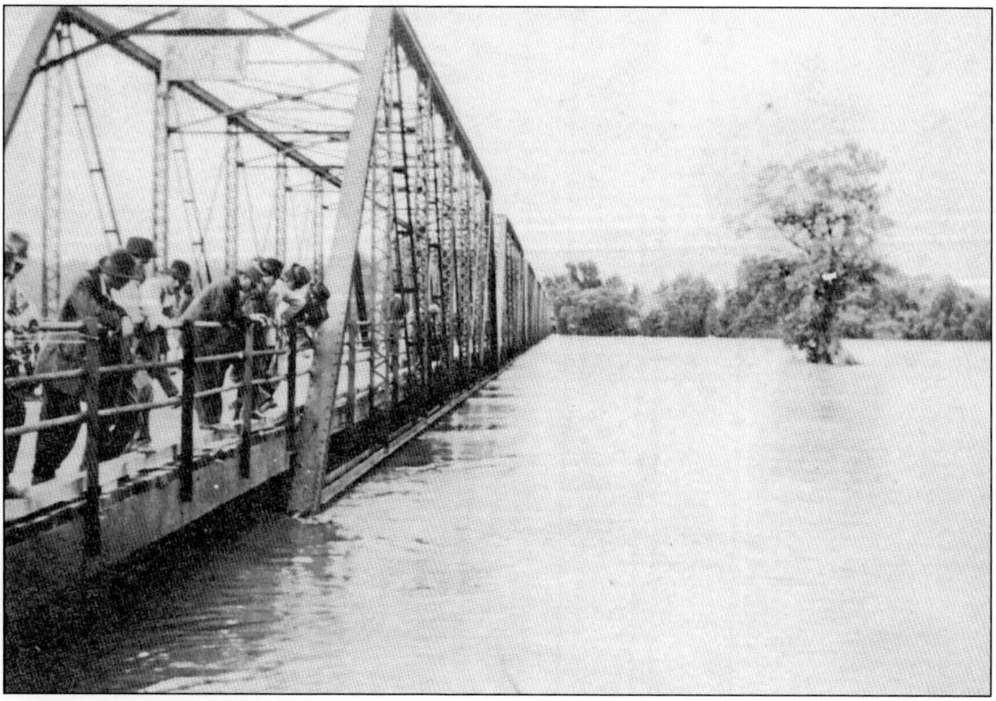

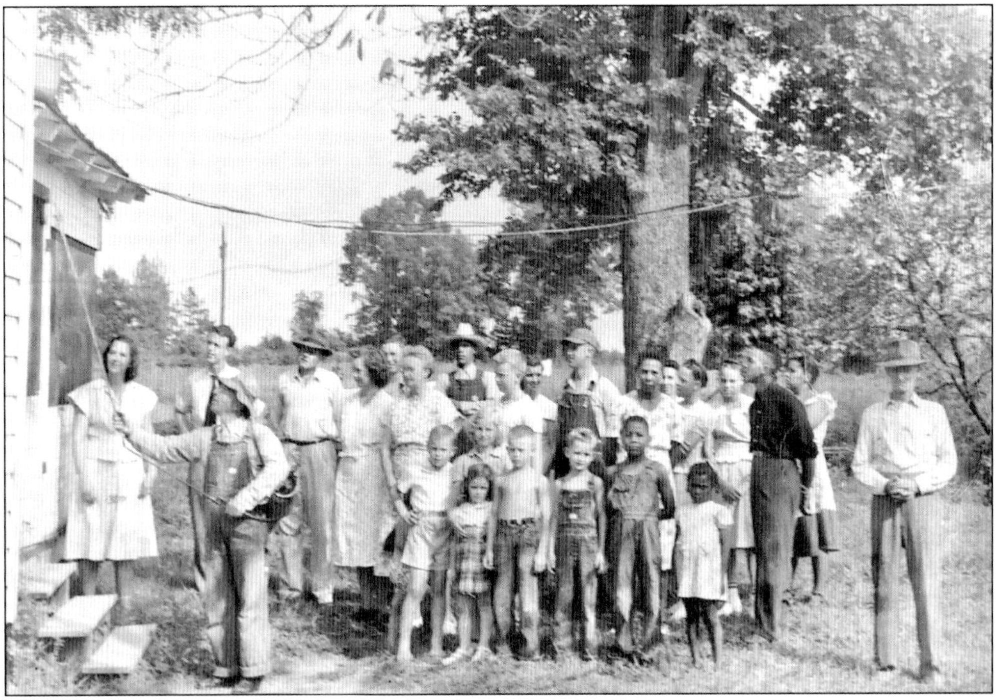

Spraying Demonstration. Carl Shell, the sanitarian of the Davie-Yadkin Health District, demonstrates the application of a new pesticide, DDT, to a community group at the Center Community Building. (Courtesy of Neil Anderson.)

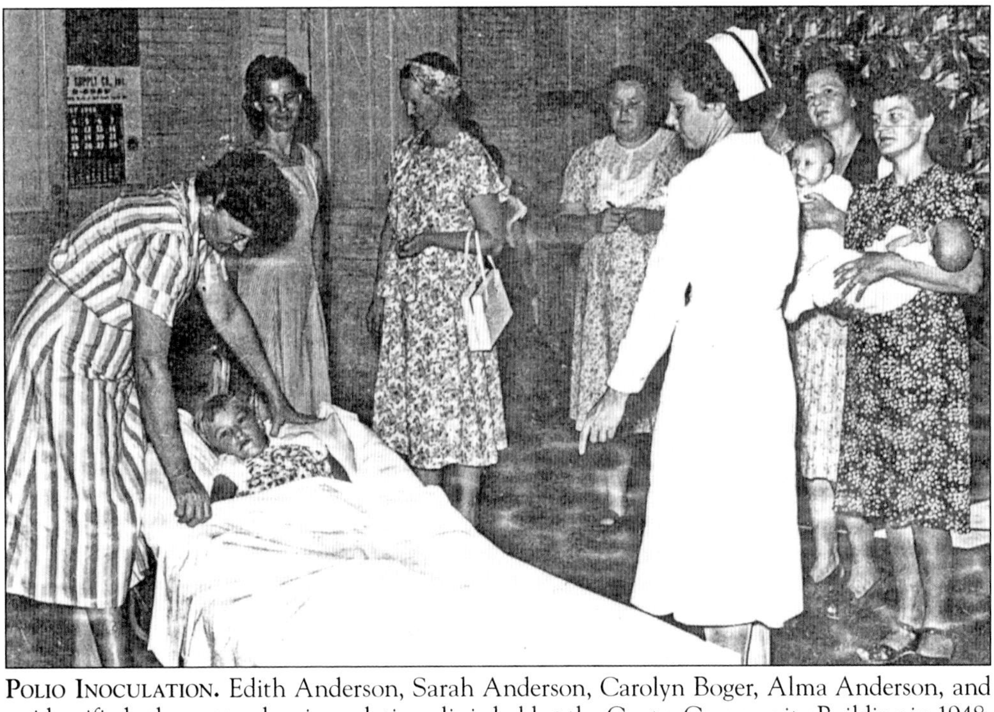

Polio Inoculation. Edith Anderson, Sarah Anderson, Carolyn Boger, Alma Anderson, and unidentified others attend an inoculation clinic held at the Center Community Building in 1948. (Courtesy of Neil Anderson.)

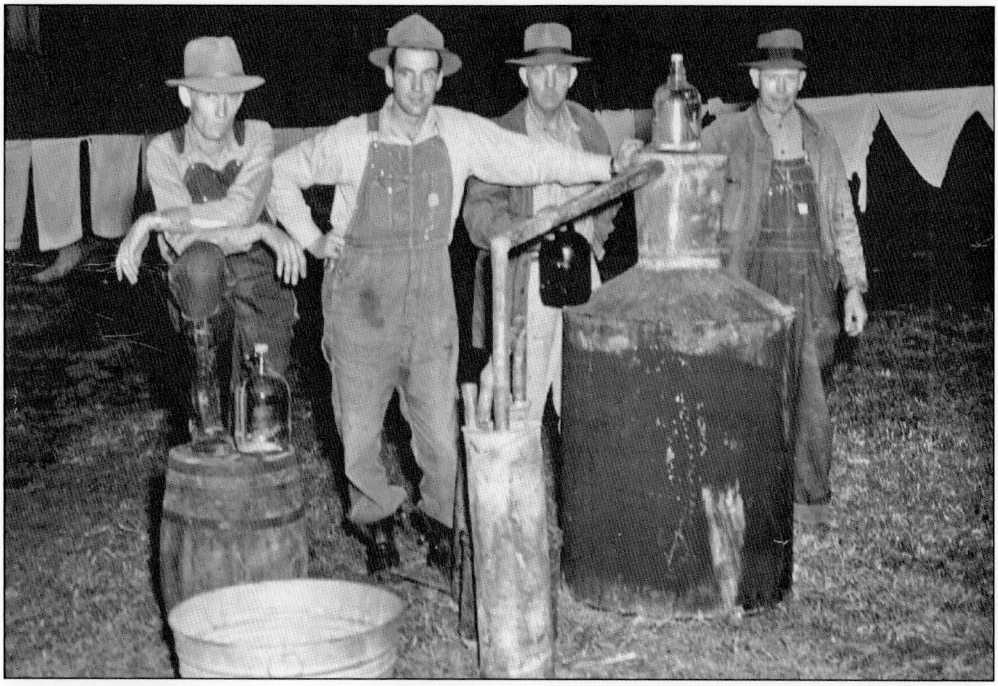

Jerusalem Township Still. Deputies destroy a still found near Cherry Hill. From left to right are Jason Sheek, Ben Ellis, F. A. Mitchell, and A. M. Laird. R. S. Meroney wrote in the March 31, 1952, *Davie Record*, "One could buy whiskey at any one of these stills for a dollar per gallon. There were often 12 or 15 barrels of whiskey stored in the depot for shipment, and one night someone bored a hole in the floor with an auger into two barrels and caught the stuff in tubs as it ran out."

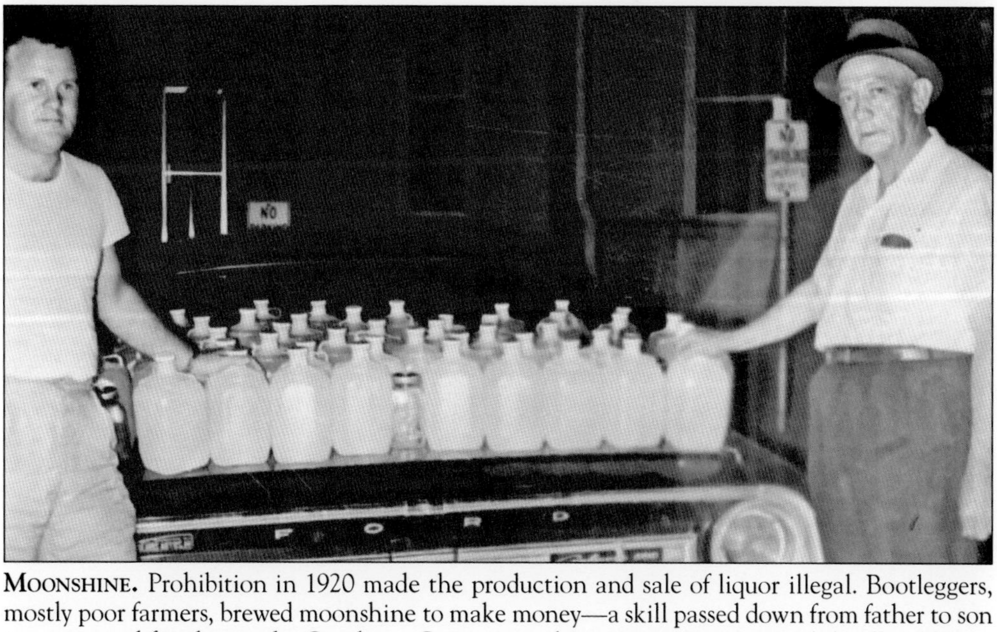

Moonshine. Prohibition in 1920 made the production and sale of liquor illegal. Bootleggers, mostly poor farmers, brewed moonshine to make money—a skill passed down from father to son in some rural families in the Carolinas. Some moonshine runners transported the illegal liquor in supercharged cars. Both federal and state officials aggressively pursued the moonshiners. The photograph shows Deputy Sheriff Leonard "Jug" Howard (right) with apprehended moonshine.

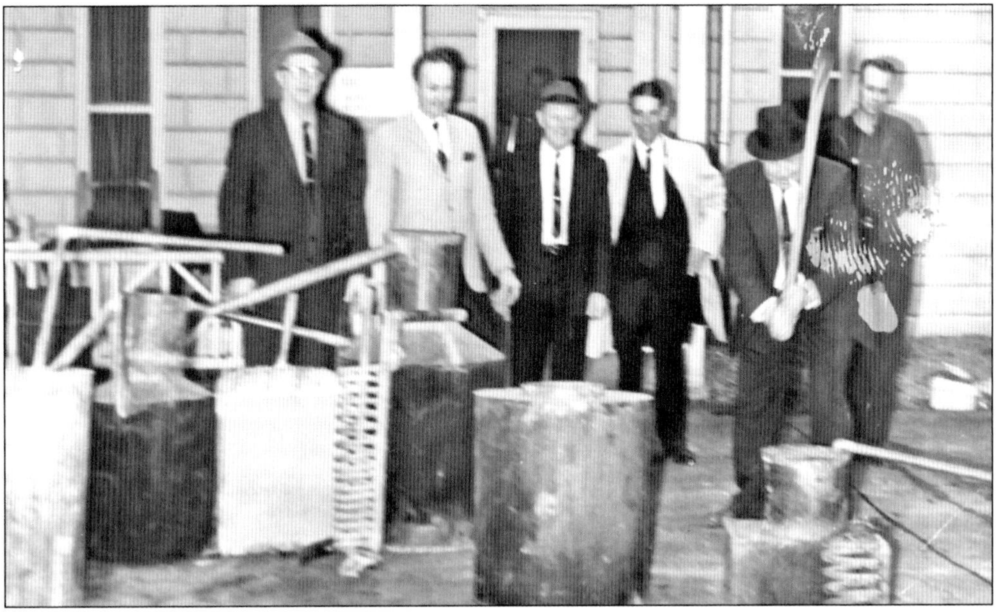

Moonshine Still. George W. Smith, Albert Howard, C. W. "Buddy" Alexander, and three unidentified men destroy confiscated stills in front of an old jail. In the "Local and Personal News" column of the May 29, 1912, edition of the *Davie Record*, an excerpt appeared from the *Cooleemee Journal*: "A good citizen living near the big Yadkin River during the heavy rains recently saw floating down the river almost a complete still house consisting of one copper still and worm, four or five big mesh tubs, a wheelbarrow, and one barrel of whiskey. A very liberal reward will be paid for the return of the last mentioned item to the *Journal* office."

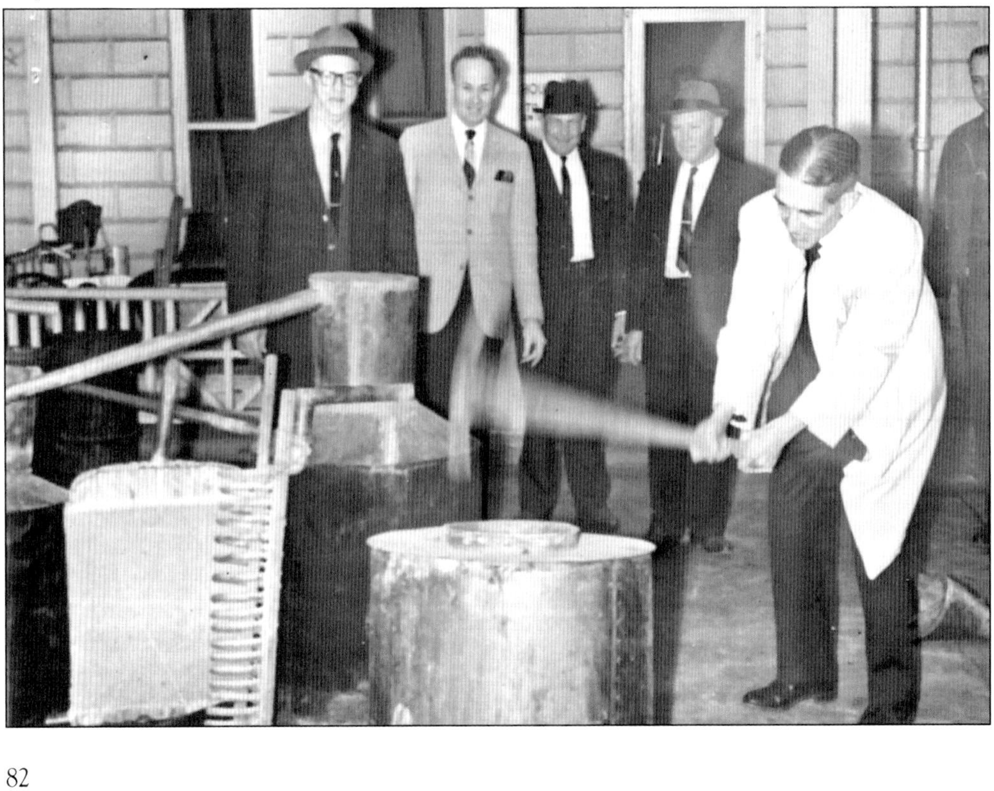

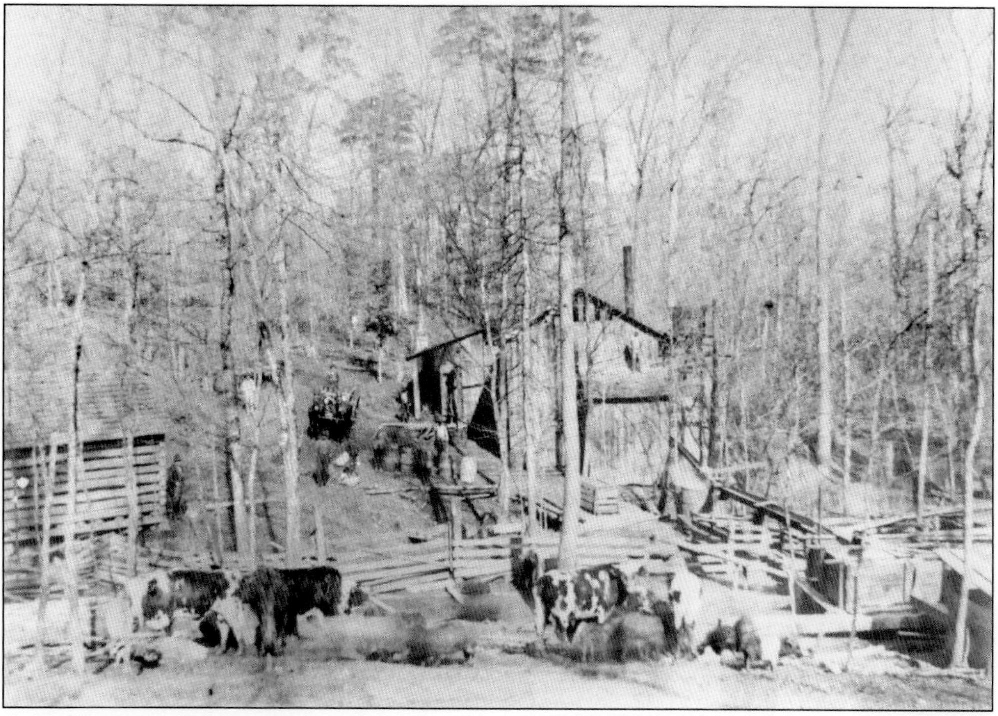

A. E. Hartman Distillery, c. 1900. This distillery helped make the Advance community the whiskey-making capital of North Carolina in the 1890s. A local historian, Minnie Zerrell Talbert Bryson, reported, "A person could stand on the steps of the Methodist Church and count the smoke from nine distilleries."

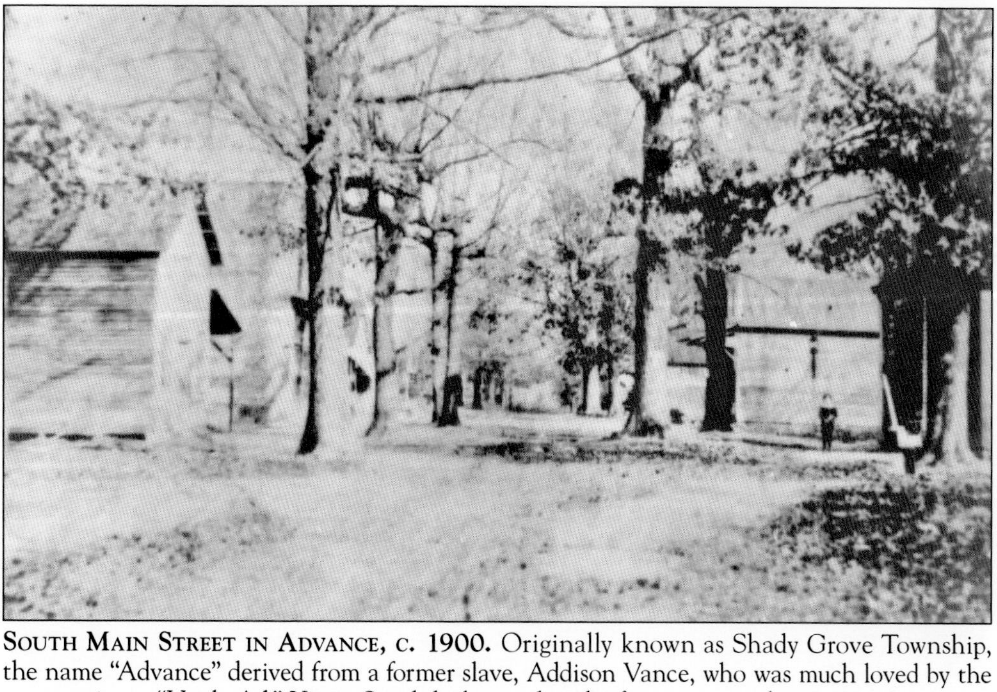

South Main Street in Advance, c. 1900. Originally known as Shady Grove Township, the name "Advance" derived from a former slave, Addison Vance, who was much loved by the community as "Uncle Ad." Henry Smithdeal served as the first mayor and postmaster.

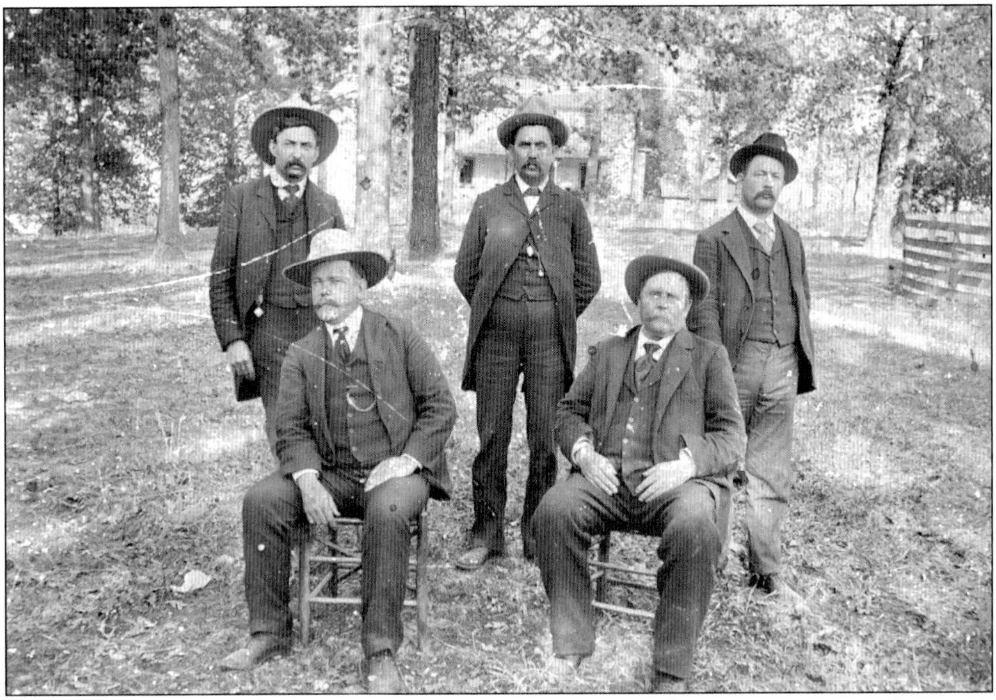

A Good Day for a Visit. Ed Morris, owner of the *Davie Record*, visits with Alex Bailey, Brack Bailey, ? Sherman, and an unidentified man, perhaps at the old Bailey home near the railroad tracks in Advance.

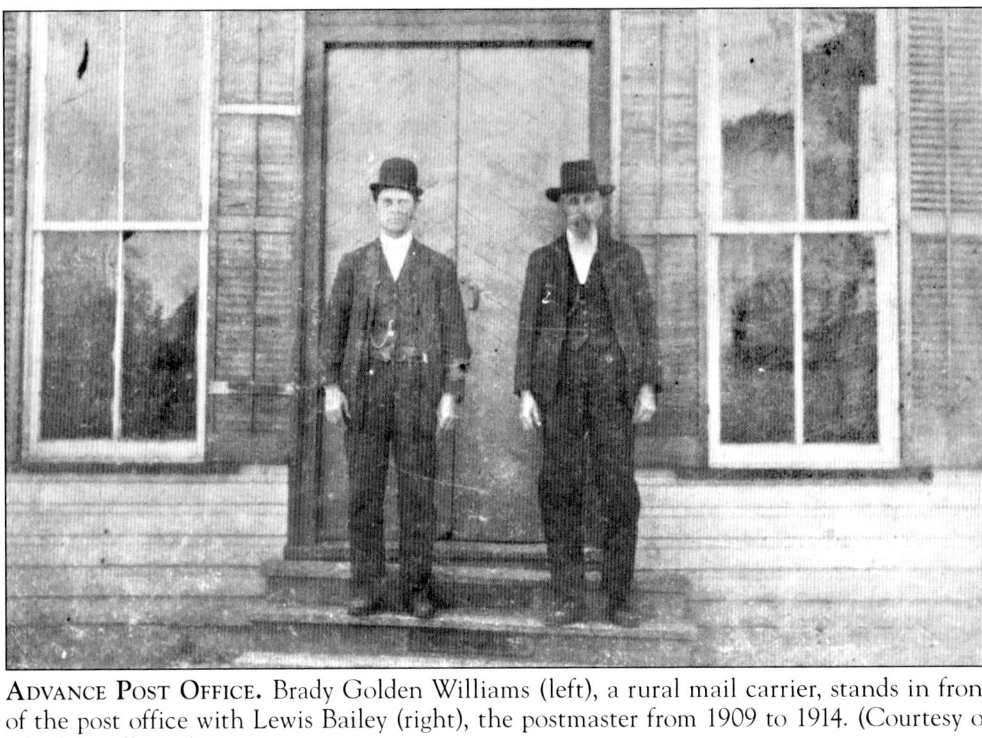

Advance Post Office. Brady Golden Williams (left), a rural mail carrier, stands in front of the post office with Lewis Bailey (right), the postmaster from 1909 to 1914. (Courtesy of Charles Williams.)

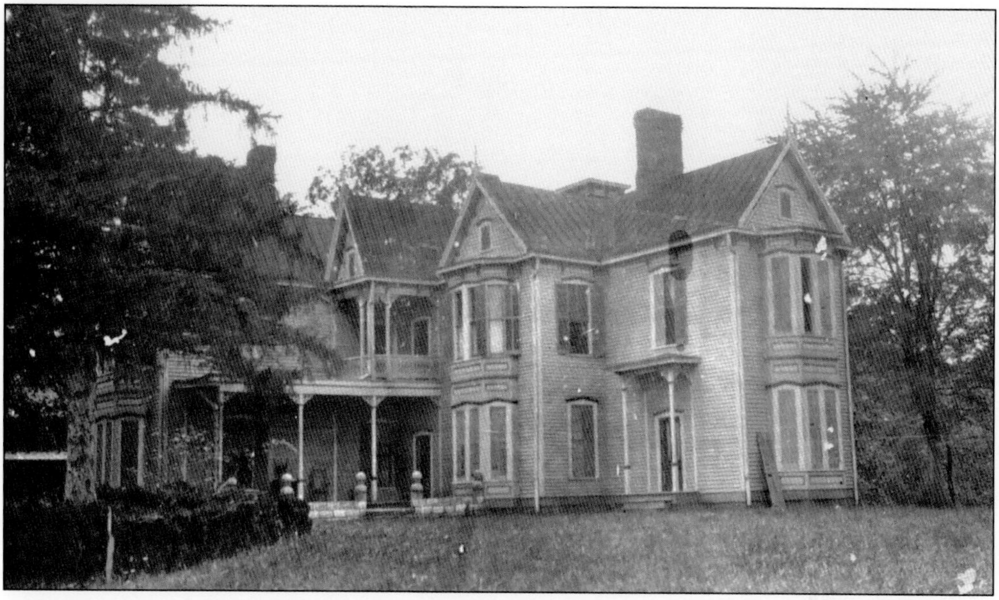

Marchmont. H. L. Austin designed and built this house for William Booe March and his daughter, Mary Frances March Williams, in 1885–1886. March served as sheriff of Davie County (1842–1850) and in the North Carolina House of Representatives (1854–1858) and Senate (1864). The second floor featured doors that folded back on themselves to create a large open space for dances and parties. March's house, which was eventually torn down, stood in ruins for years.

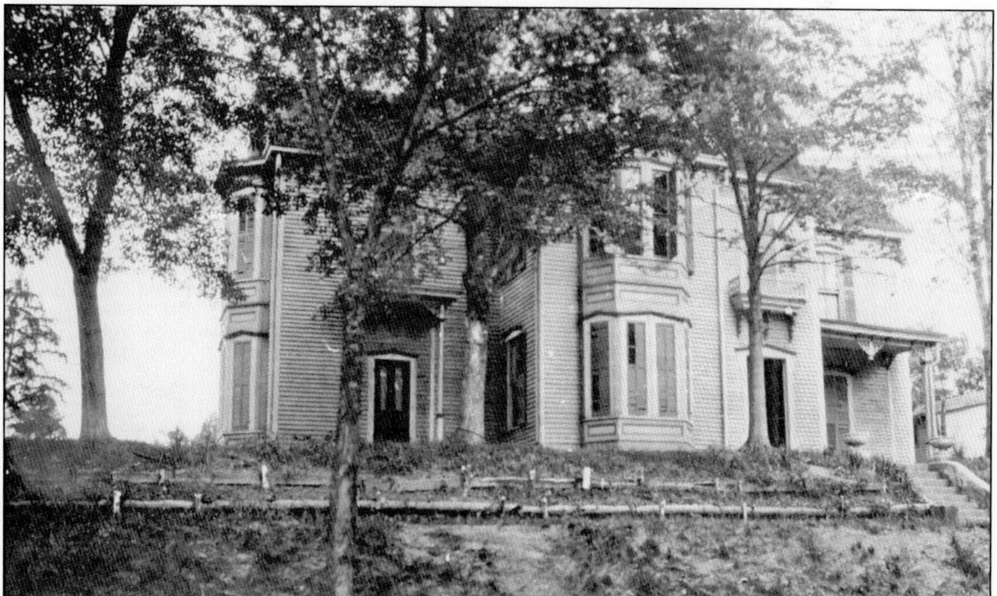

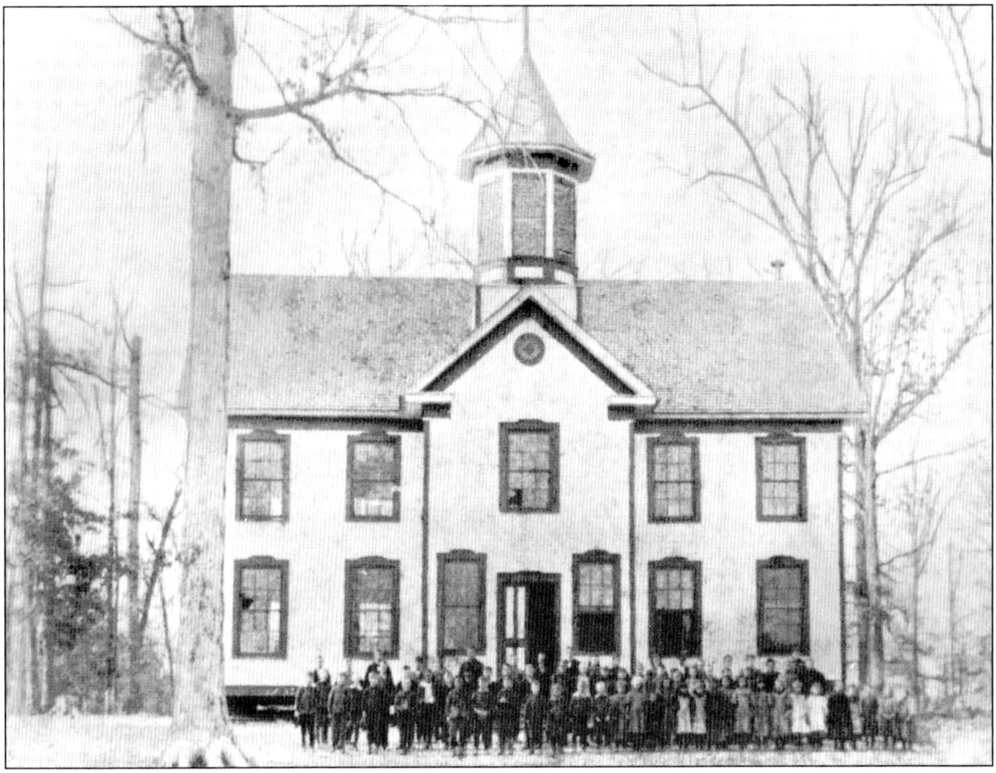

Advance Academy, c. 1900. Families in the community who could afford the tuition sent their children to the academy instead of the local one-room schoolhouse from 1893 to 1924. With primary school downstairs and high school on the second floor, the academic curriculum included spelling, reading, writing, arithmetic, geography, grammar, history, philosophy, algebra, geometry, chemistry, physiology, Latin, Greek, bookkeeping, telegraphy, and music. The old school now serves as a community building.

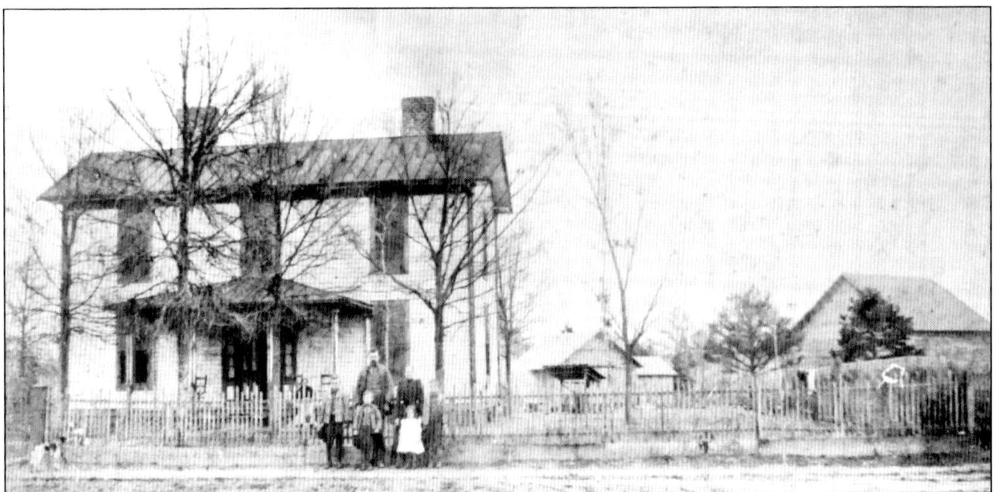

Atley Elser Hartman House. Alfred Douthit built the house in the Shady Grove Township for his daughter Martha Ellen Douthit Hartman, the wife of A. E. Hartman, in 1890. The house stood on Hartman's 1,000-acre farm.

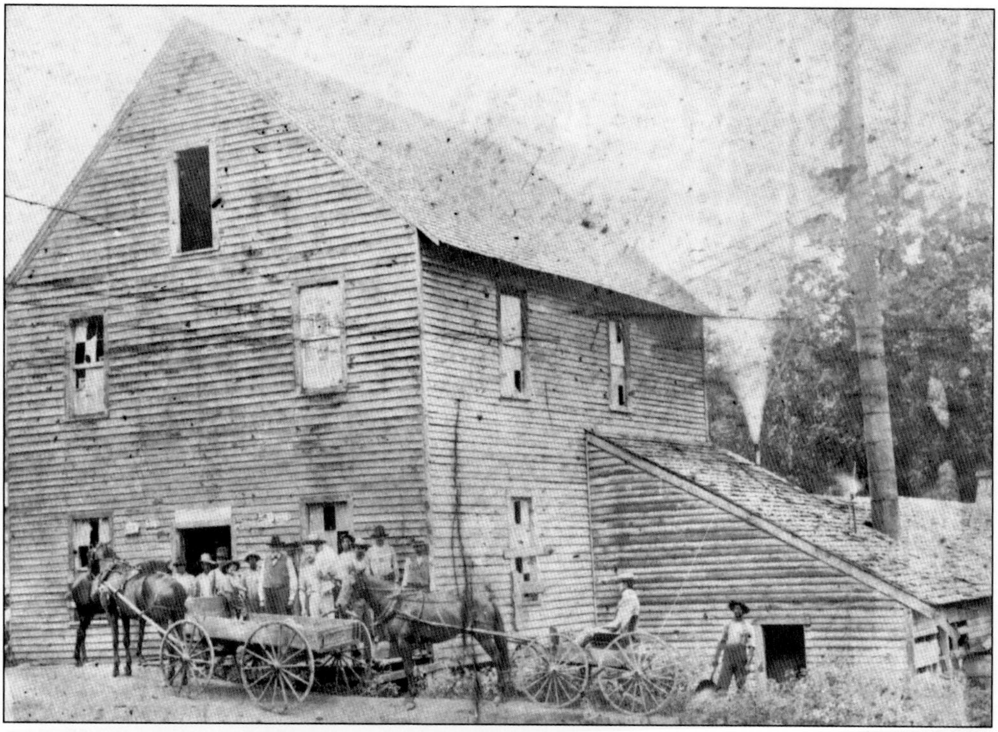

CANA ROLLER MILL. J. W. Etchison and Thomas Eaton built the original Etchison Mill in 1885. Ownership passed to a Mr. Brewer and then J. C. Booe in 1908. Steam from a wood-burning stove powered the grindstone. The Cana Roller Mill burned in 1928 or 1929.

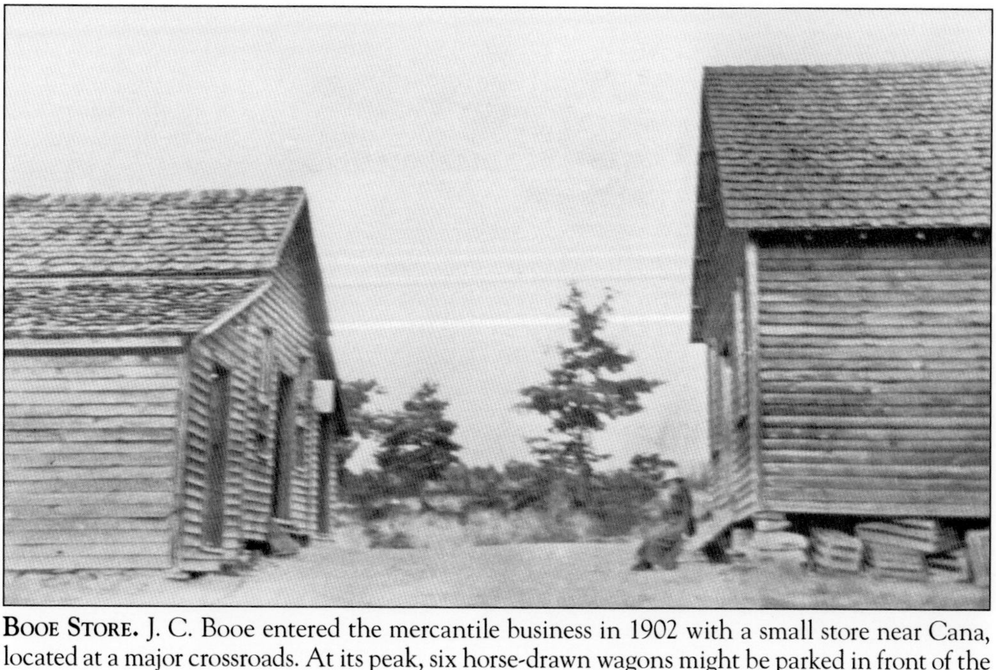

BOOE STORE. J. C. Booe entered the mercantile business in 1902 with a small store near Cana, located at a major crossroads. At its peak, six horse-drawn wagons might be parked in front of the store at the same time. Booe's eldest daughter, Naomi, enjoyed working in the store. She graduated as valedictorian from Oxford College in Oxford, North Carolina, in 1912.

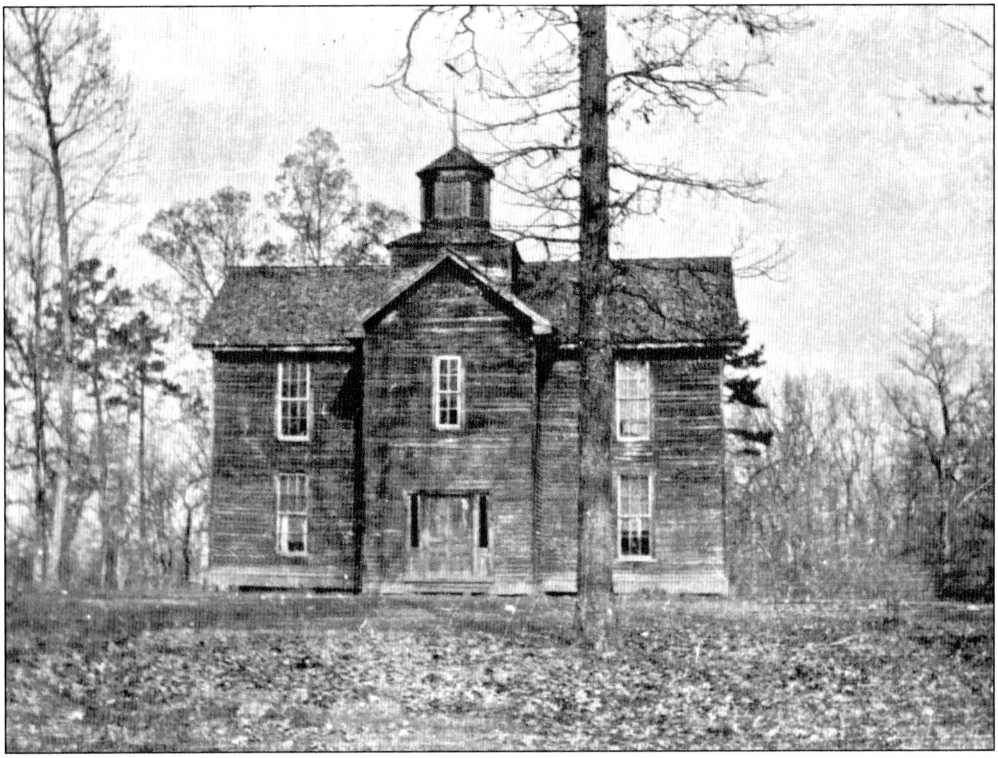

Cana Academy. Annie Charles of the Thomasville Female College opened the Cana Academy with 32 pupils on December 31, 1883.

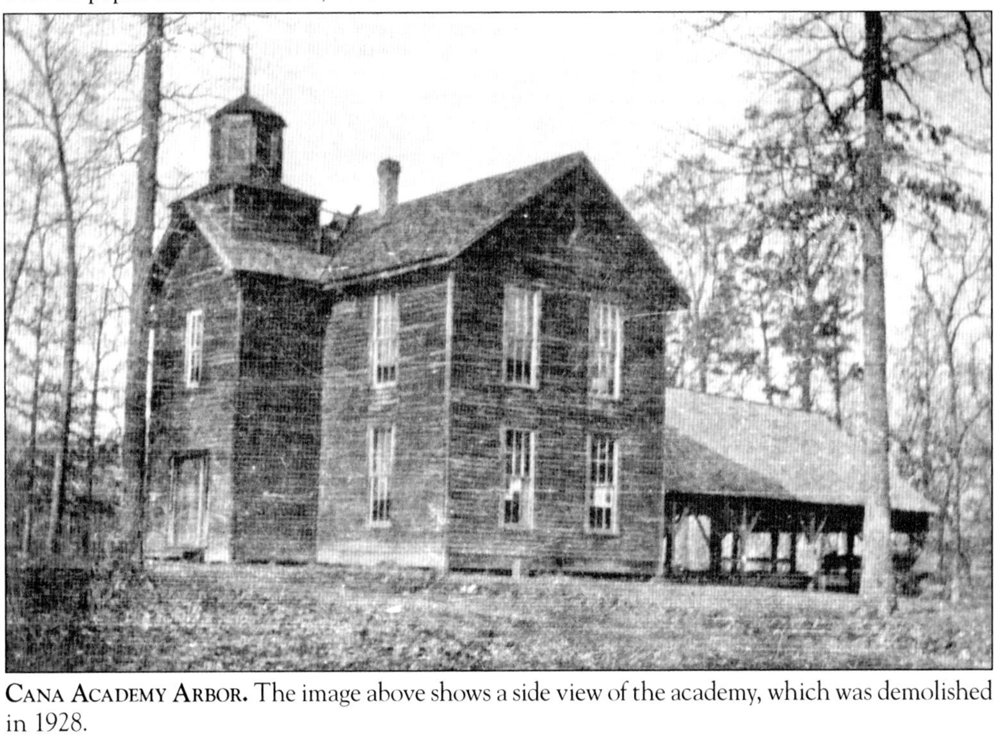

Cana Academy Arbor. The image above shows a side view of the academy, which was demolished in 1928.

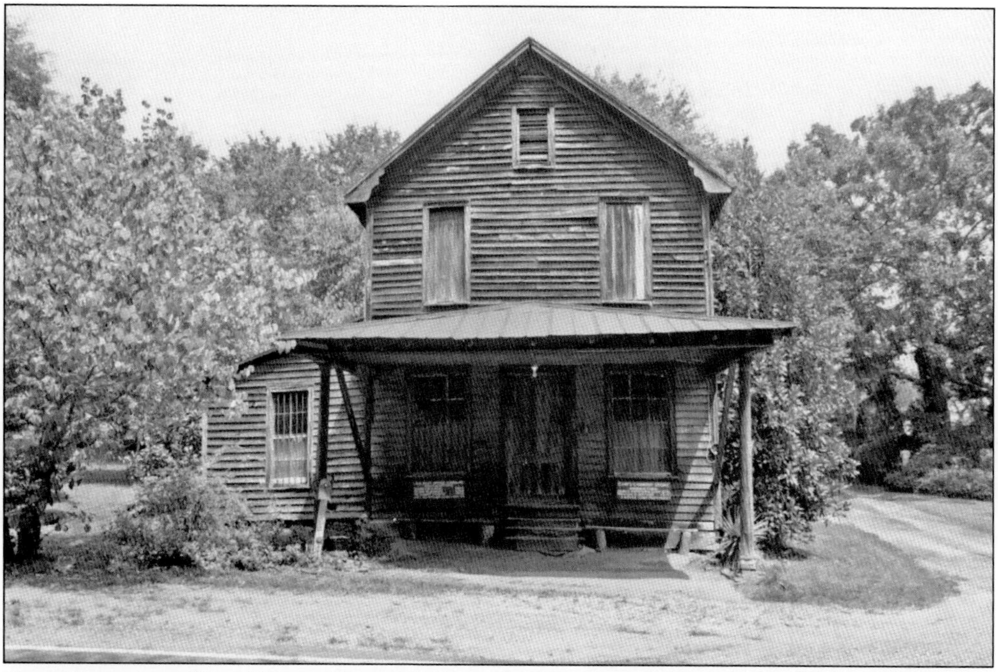

CANA STORE AND POST OFFICE. James H. Cain, the first postmaster, managed the post office first in his home (1875) and then in his store (1890). The National Park Service listed the building on the National Register of Historic Places in 2001.

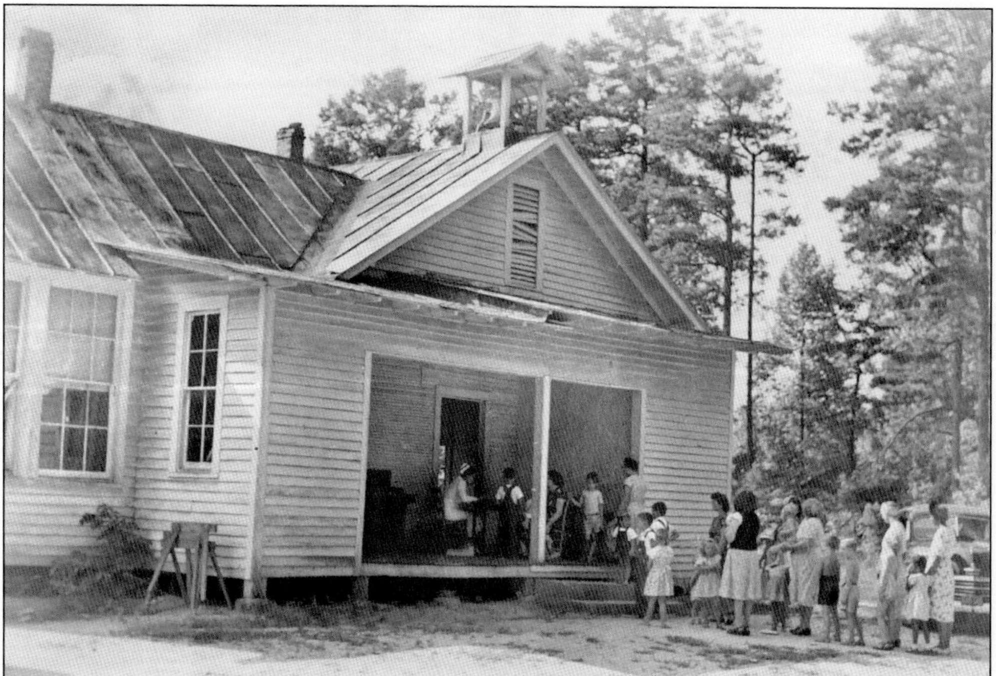

COMMUNITY IMMUNIZATIONS. Mothers and children line up outside of one community school to participate in county-wide immunizations to prevent the spread of disease.

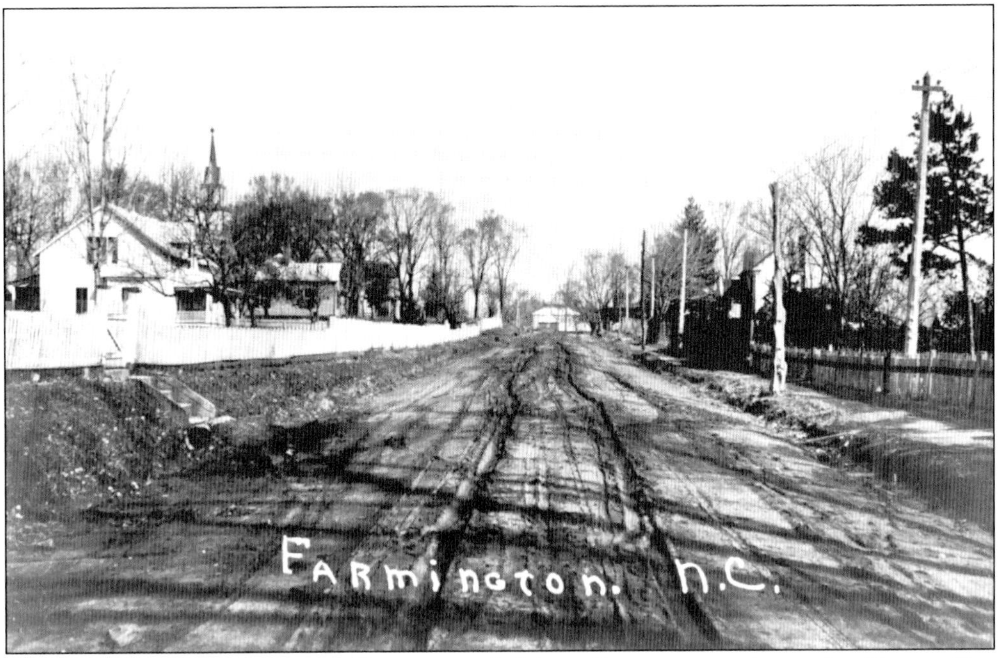

MAIN STREET, FARMINGTON. Farmington's Main Street runs along the Huntsville-Mocksville Road.

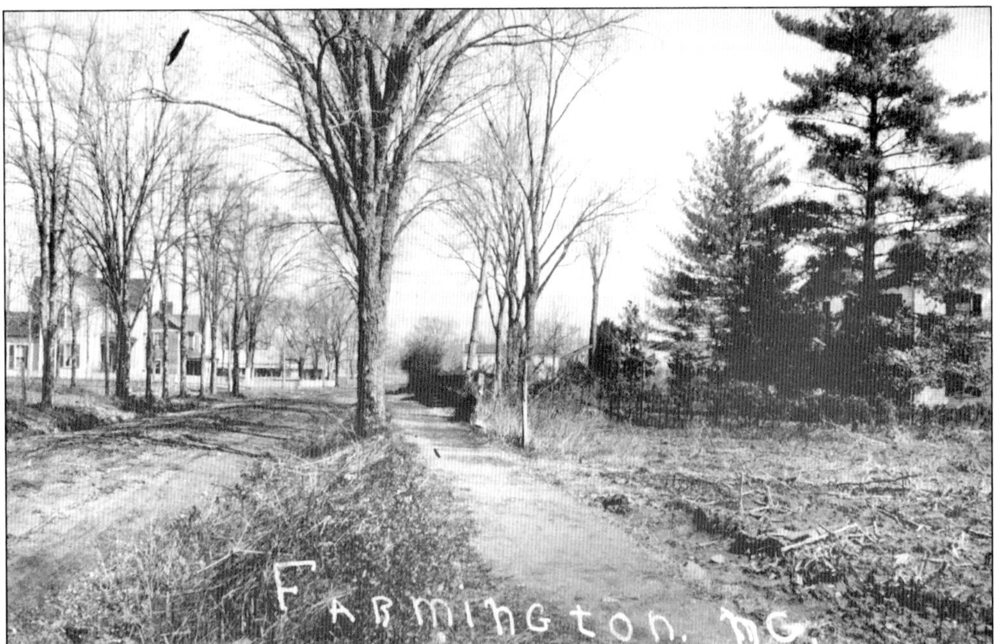

FARMINGTON. Farmington developed from the original Bryan Settlement in 1755. Around 1800, immigrants from Currituck County, North Carolina, settled in the area, renaming the town Little Currituck until around 1837, when the community got a post office and its current name of Farmington.

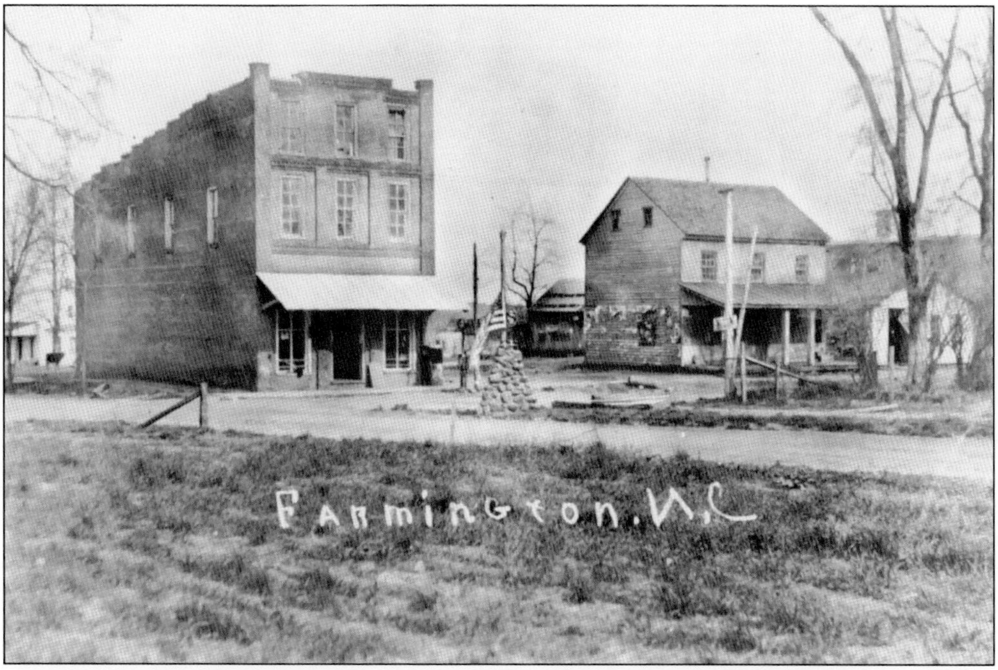

Farmington Crossroads. George Wesley Johnson built these two brick (left) and wooden frame (right) stores. Johnson also owned a blacksmith shop, a woodworking shop, a coffin shop, a brickyard, a tannery yard, a tin shop, and a furniture manufacturing shop.

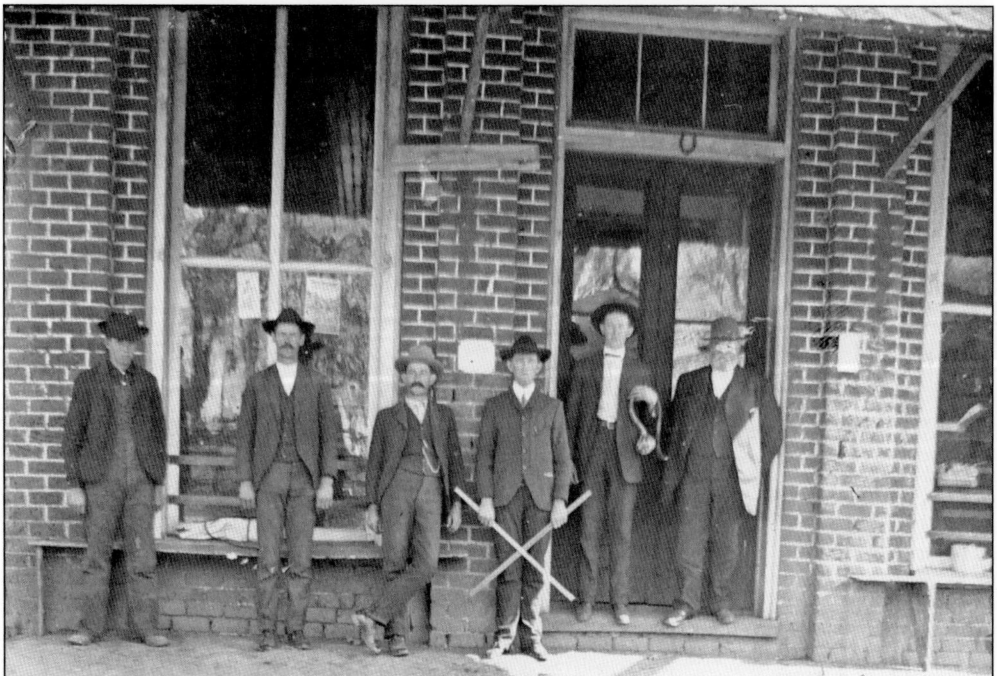

Johnson Store. George Wesley Johnson's first store in Farmington also held the post office in 1837. The photograph shows Dr. William G. Johnson (far right) with unidentified men in front of the store.

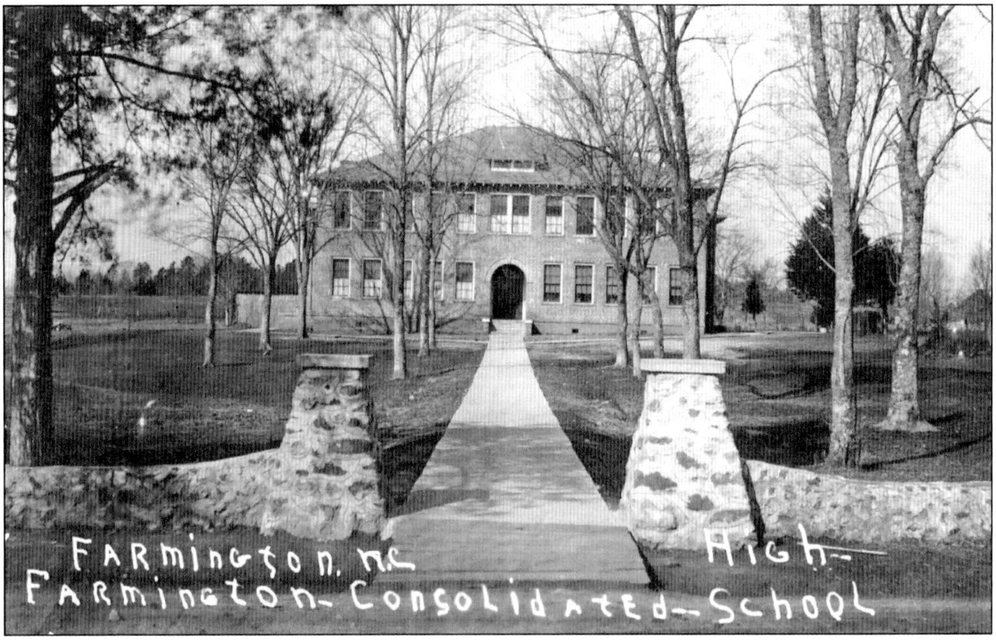

FARMINGTON CONSOLIDATED HIGH SCHOOL. The county's first brick-veneer school opened on October 3, 1911, operating until 1944–1945.

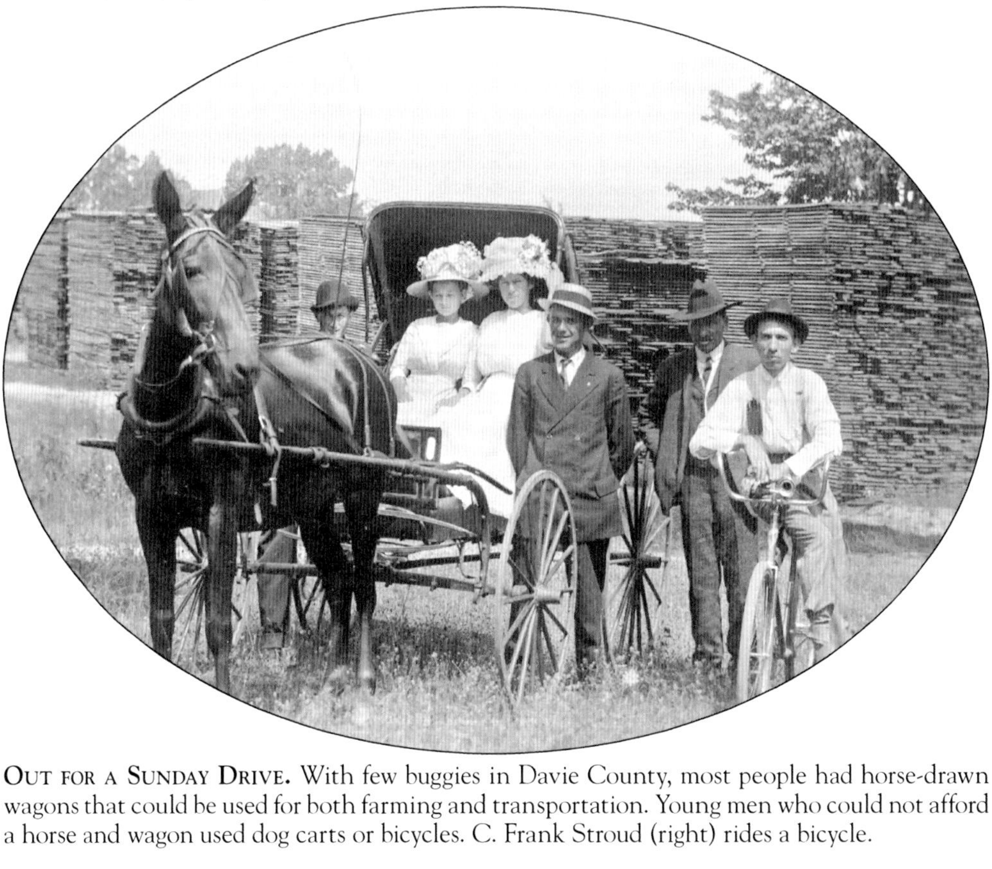

OUT FOR A SUNDAY DRIVE. With few buggies in Davie County, most people had horse-drawn wagons that could be used for both farming and transportation. Young men who could not afford a horse and wagon used dog carts or bicycles. C. Frank Stroud (right) rides a bicycle.

Five

Cooleemee Plantation

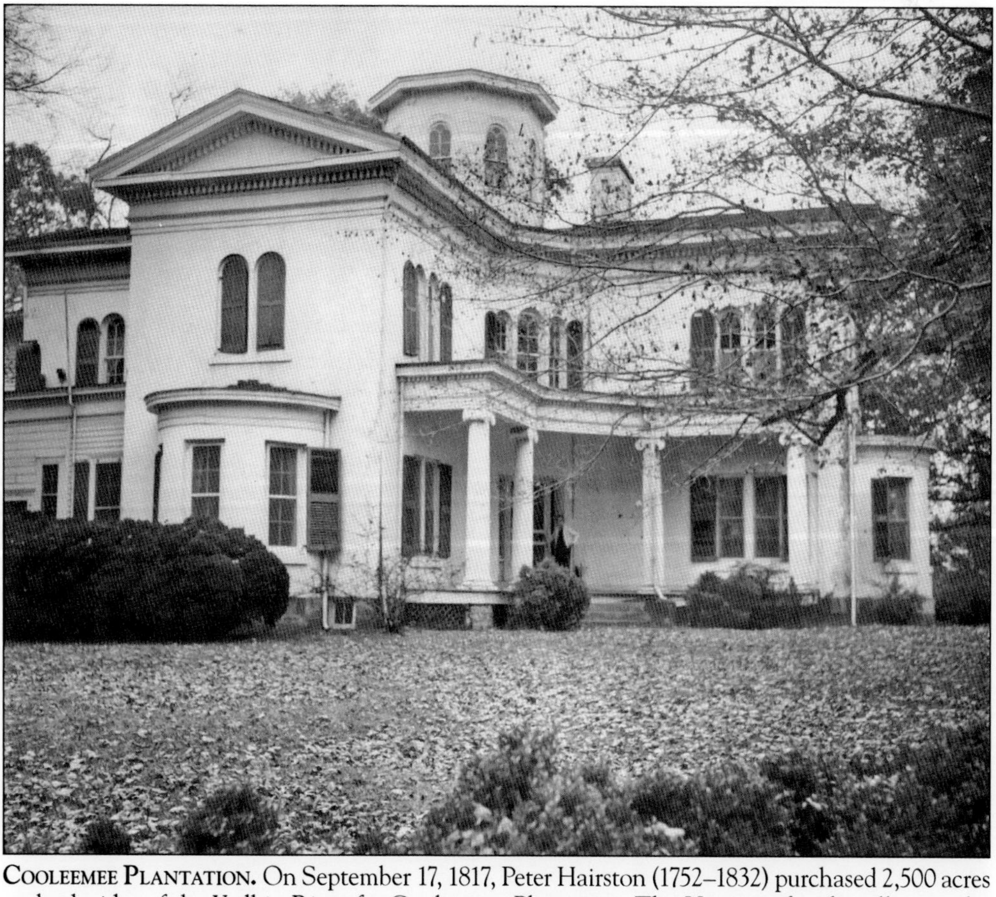

Cooleemee Plantation. On September 17, 1817, Peter Hairston (1752–1832) purchased 2,500 acres on both sides of the Yadkin River for Cooleemee Plantation. The Hairston family still owns the house, which was constructed from 1853 to 1855. (Courtesy of Peter W. Hairston.)

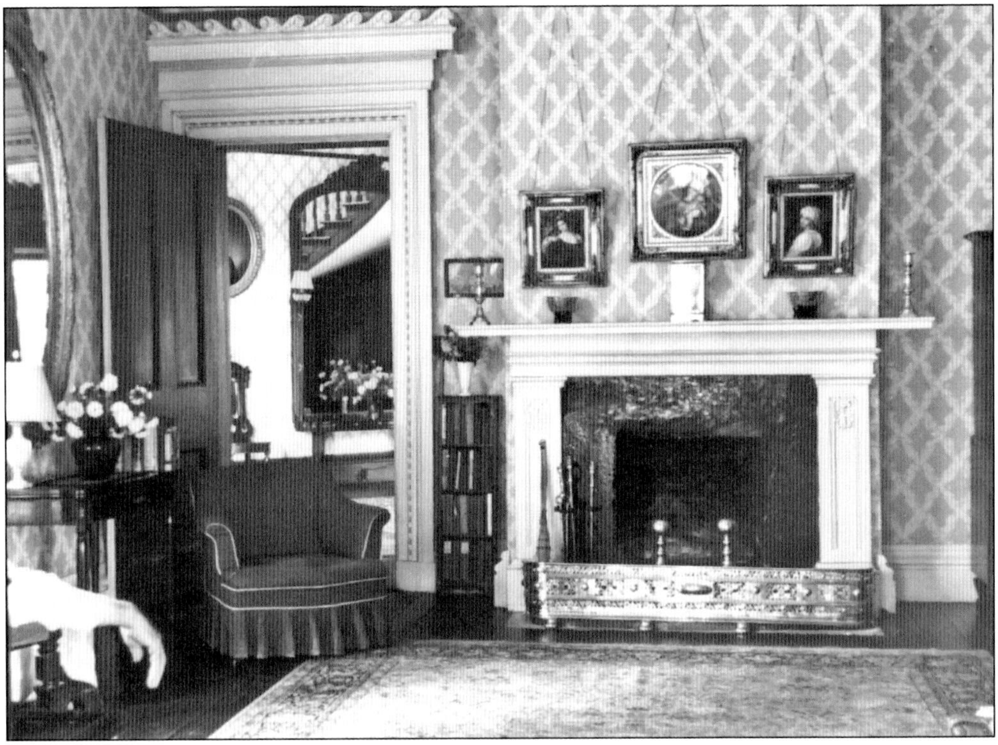

Cooleemee Plantation Interior. The photographs capture the entrance hall and living room in the 1930s. (Both, courtesy of Peter W. Hairston.)

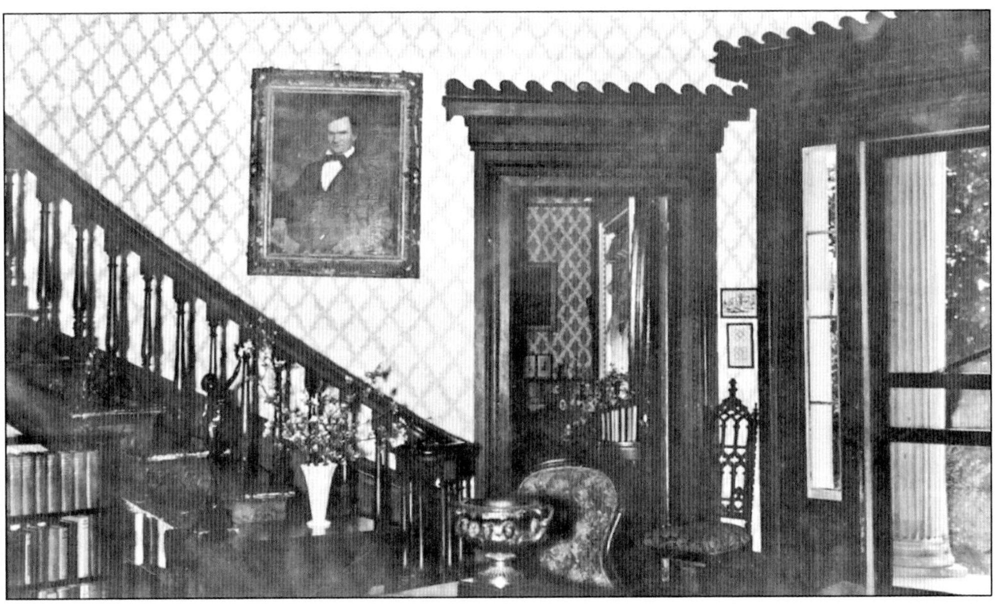

PETER WILSON HAIRSTON (1819–1886). Hairston inherited Cooleemee Plantation from his great-grandfather and built the present house. (Courtesy of Peter W. Hairston.)

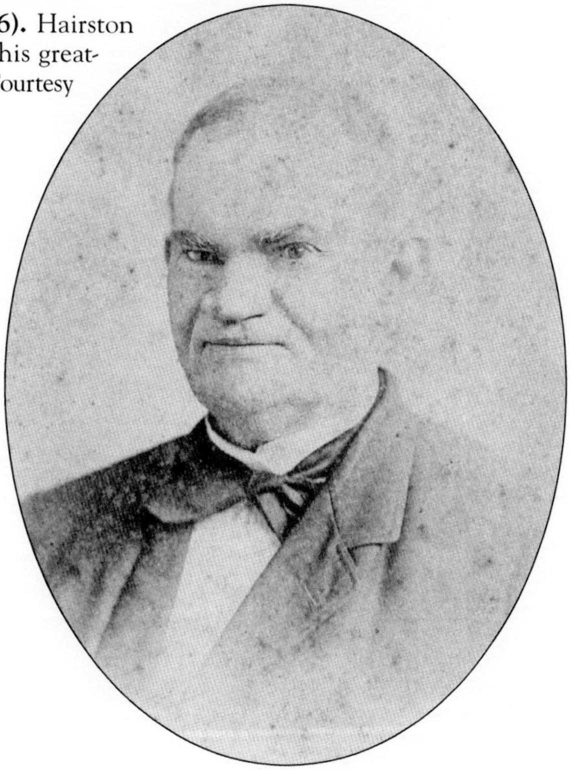

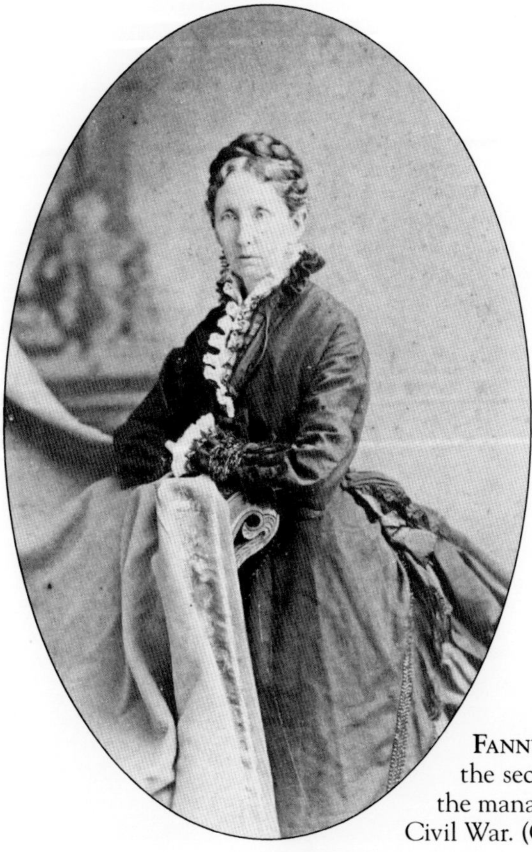

FANNY CALDWELL HAIRSTON (1834–1907). Fanny, the second wife of Peter Wilson Hairston, oversaw the management of Cooleemee Plantation during the Civil War. (Courtesy of Peter W. Hairston.)

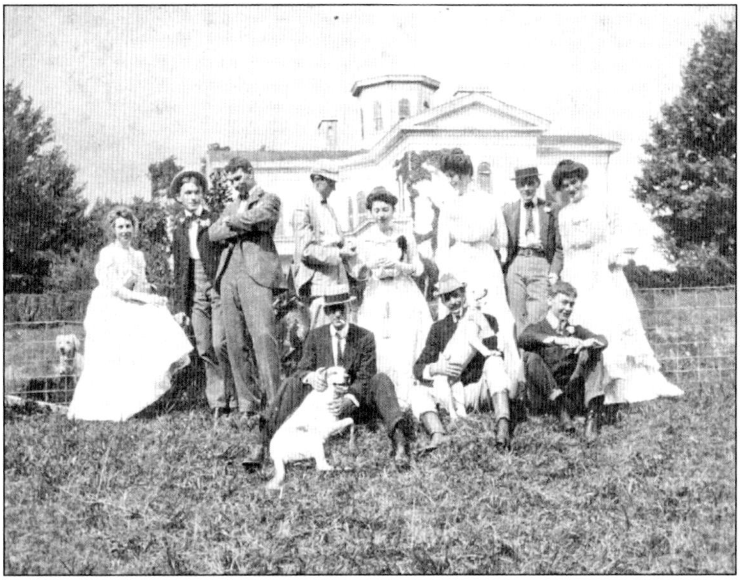

House Party, 1901. Houseguests from Winston and Salisbury enjoyed parties and hunting. (Both, courtesy of Peter W. Hairston.)

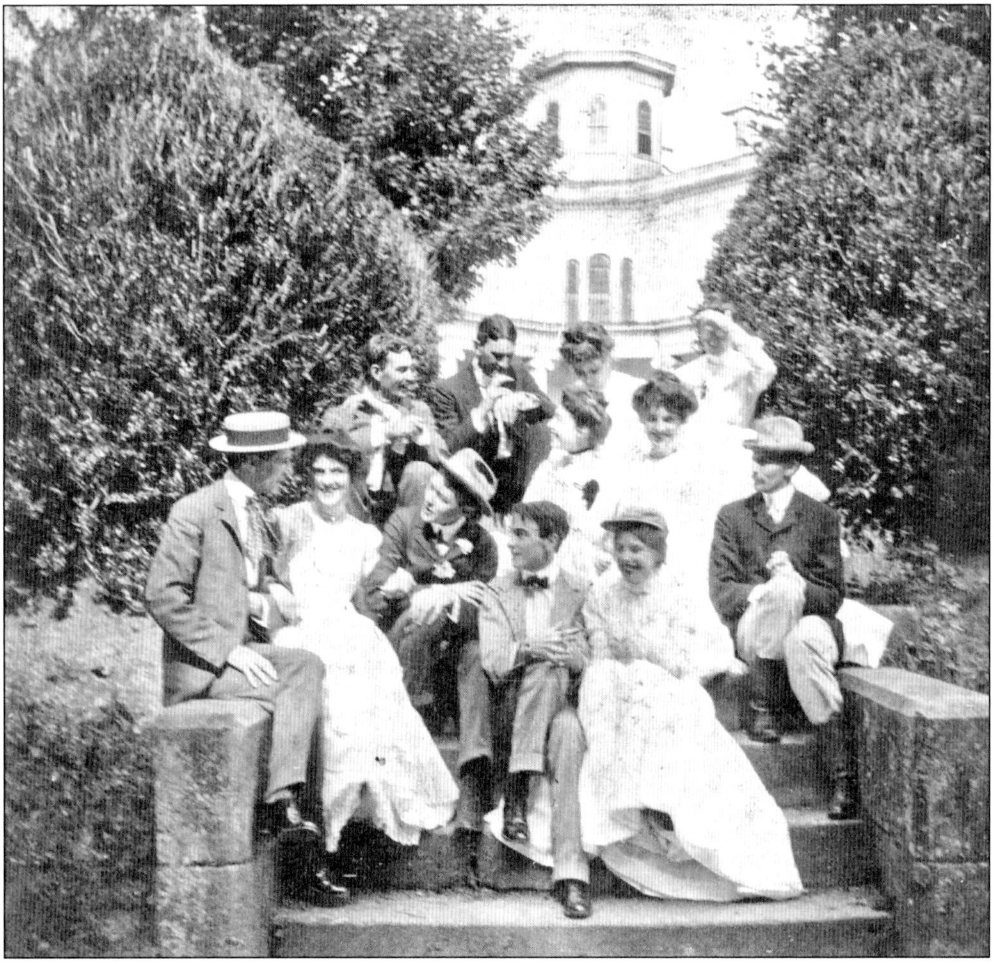

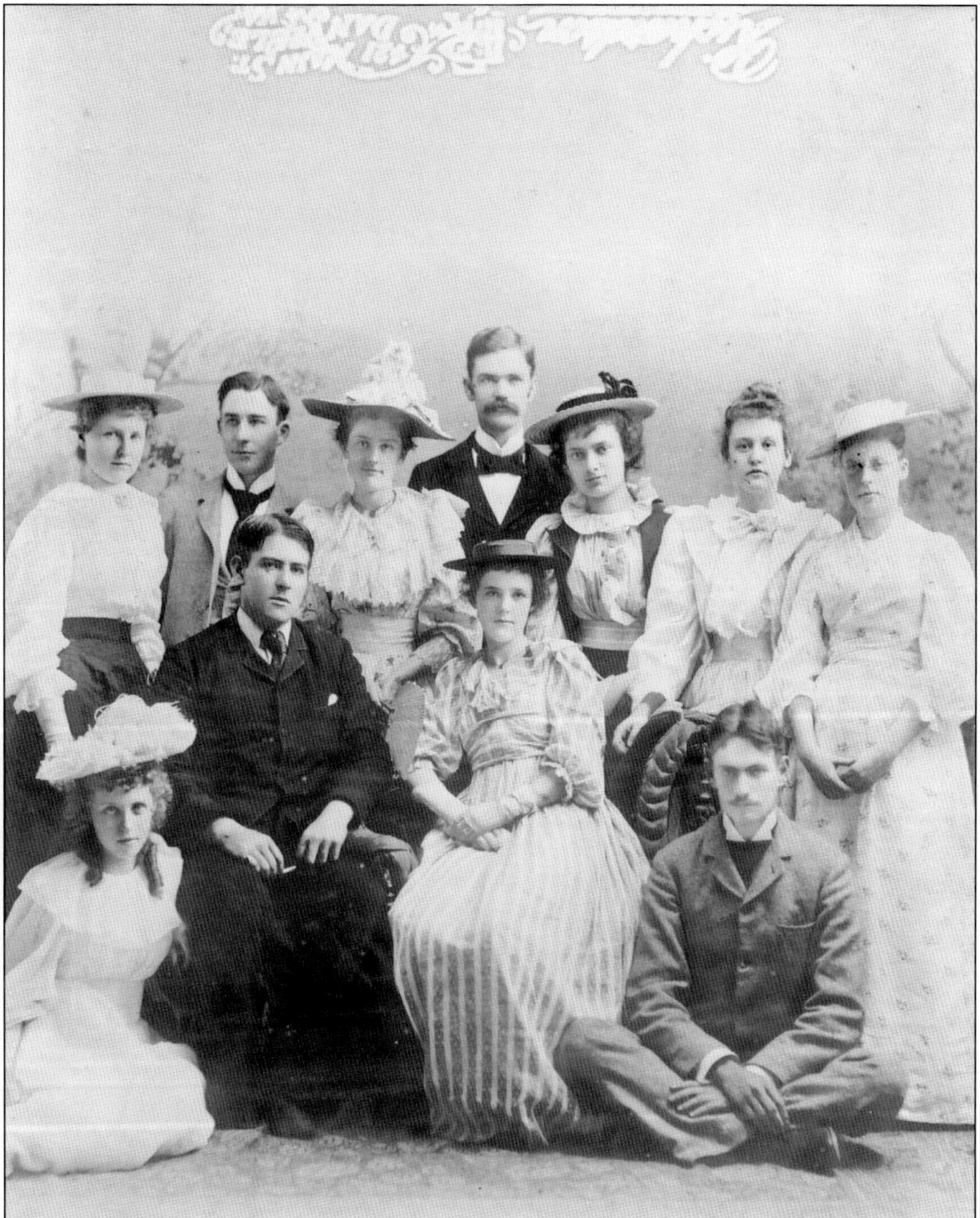

House Party, c. 1896. The Hairstons entertained guests, including, from left to right, (first row) Bessie Henderson, Walter Murphy, Ruth Kluttz, and Peter W. Hairston; (second row) Daisy Scales, Jim Gaither, Alice Caldwell, White McKenzie, Nannie Craig, Fanny Caldwell, and Jeanne Kluttz. (Courtesy of Peter W. Hairston.)

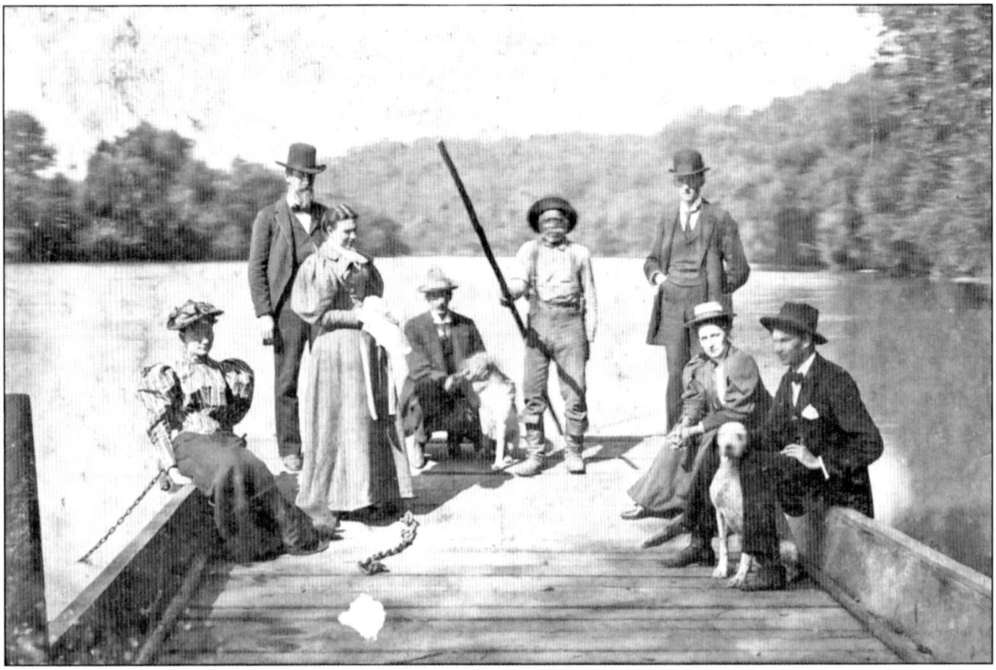

Cooleemee Plantation Ferry, c. 1900. The Hairston family's private ferry across the Yadkin River operated until 1931. The photograph shows, from left to right, Ruth and Agnes Hairston, ? Redmond (standing), Frank Hairston (seated), Righteous Hairston (ferryman), ? Redmond II, an unidentified woman, and Peter Hairston (seated). (Courtesy of Peter W. Hairston.)

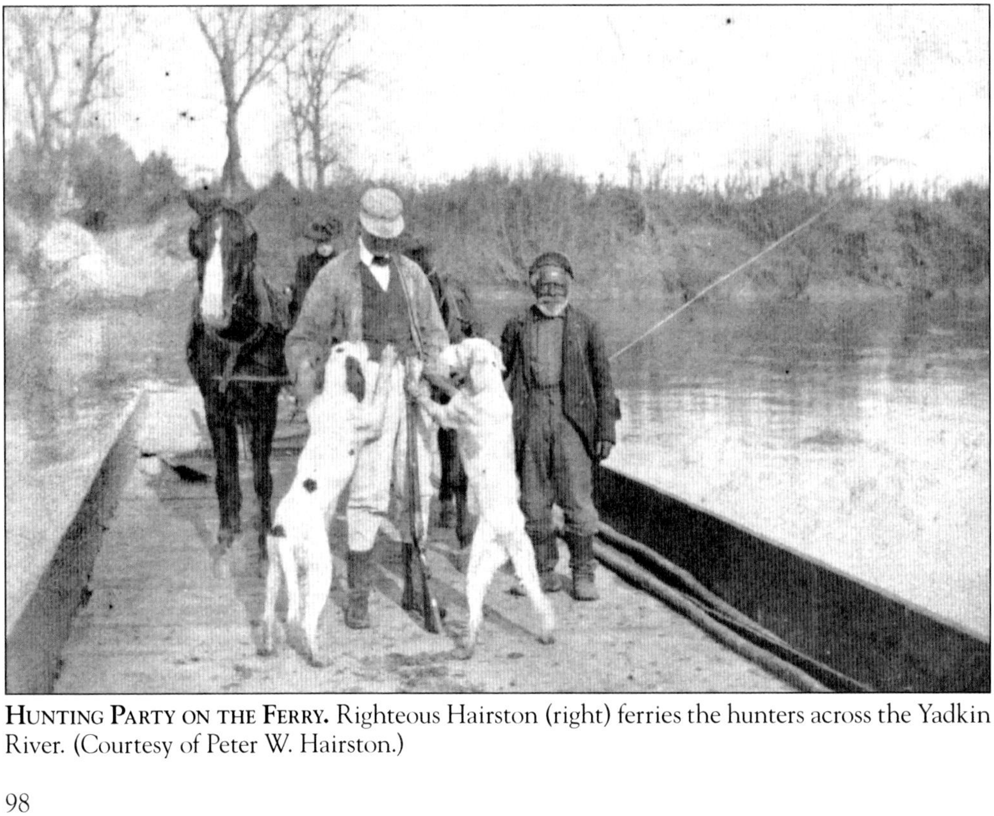

Hunting Party on the Ferry. Righteous Hairston (right) ferries the hunters across the Yadkin River. (Courtesy of Peter W. Hairston.)

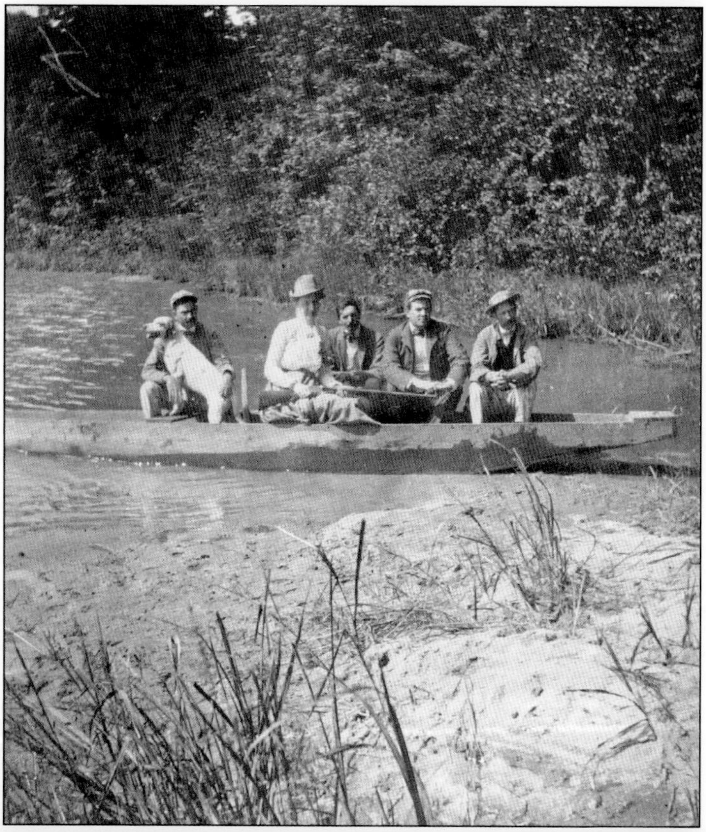

HUNTING PARTY ON THE YADKIN, C. 1900. A hunting party glides down the river in a bateau. (Courtesy of Peter W. Hairston.)

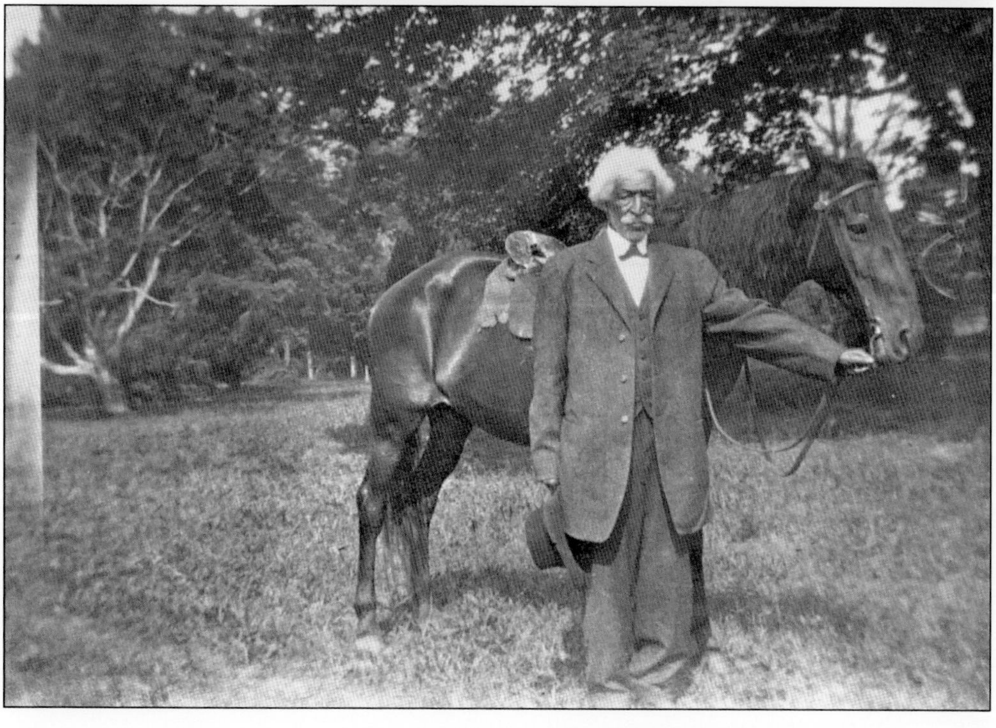

JOHN GOOLSBY. Goolsby, the coachman at Cooleemee Plantation, hid the Hairstons' household silver from Yankee soldiers during the Civil War. (Courtesy of Peter W. Hairston.)

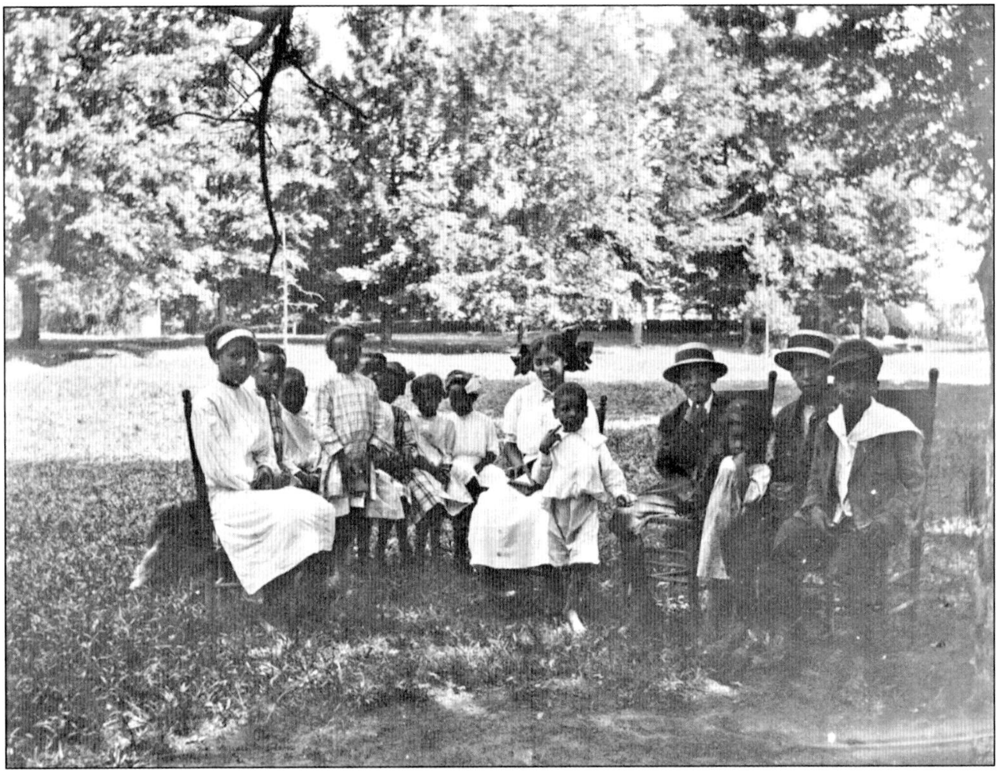

Family of Hairston Goolsby. Hairston, son of John Goolsby, managed the daily operations of the plantation and farm. (Courtesy of Peter W. Hairston.)

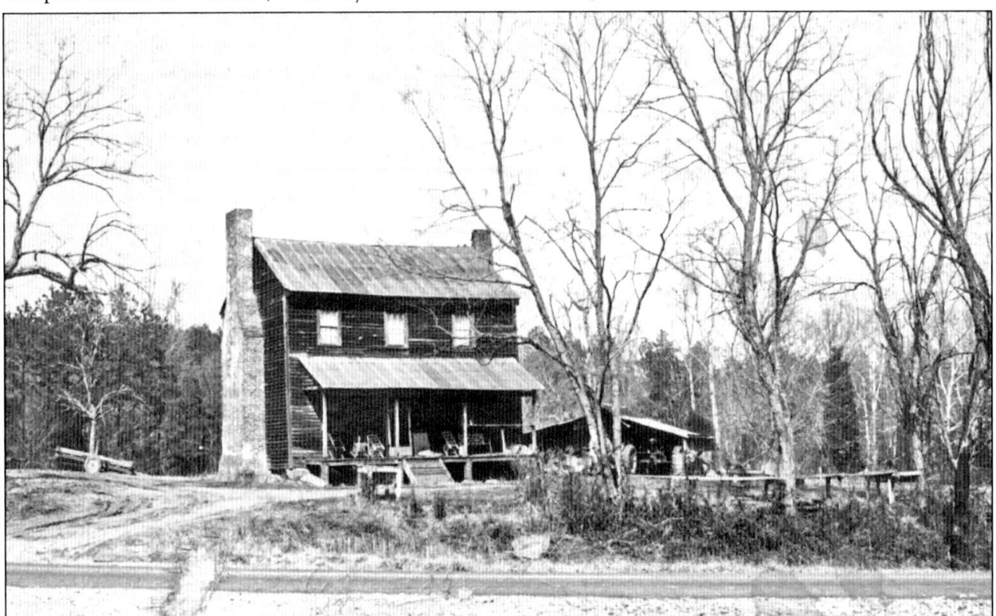

Frederick Cope House, 1989. Frederick Cope probably built this house after 1826. In 1850, Cope sold the house and three tracts of land totaling 293.5 acres to Peter Hairston, whose overseer, Grief G. Mason, lived in the house. (Courtesy of Peter W. Hairston.)

Six

EDUCATION

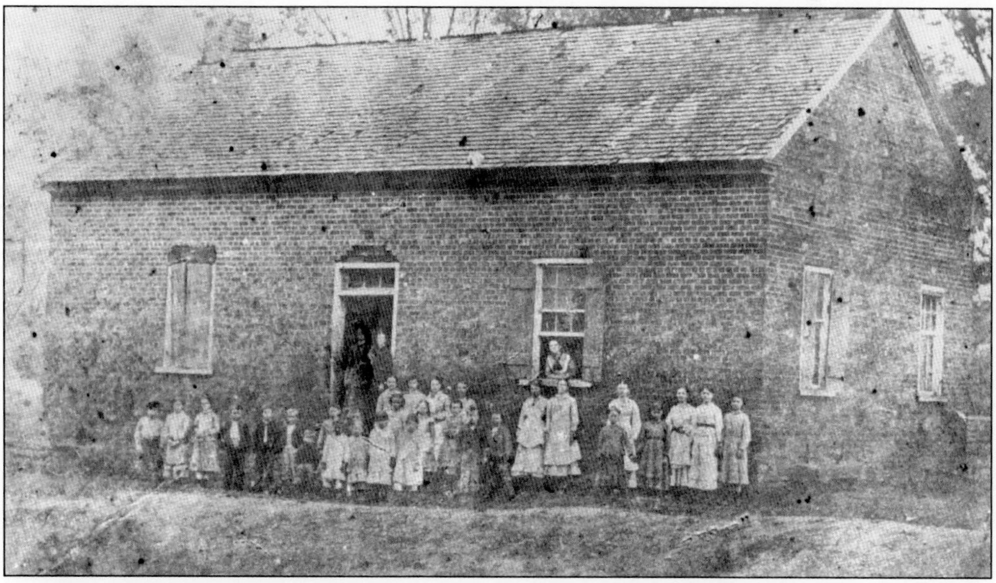

OLD BRICK ACADEMY. The academy, located near the site of the Mocksville Depot, served as a schoolhouse for about 40 years.

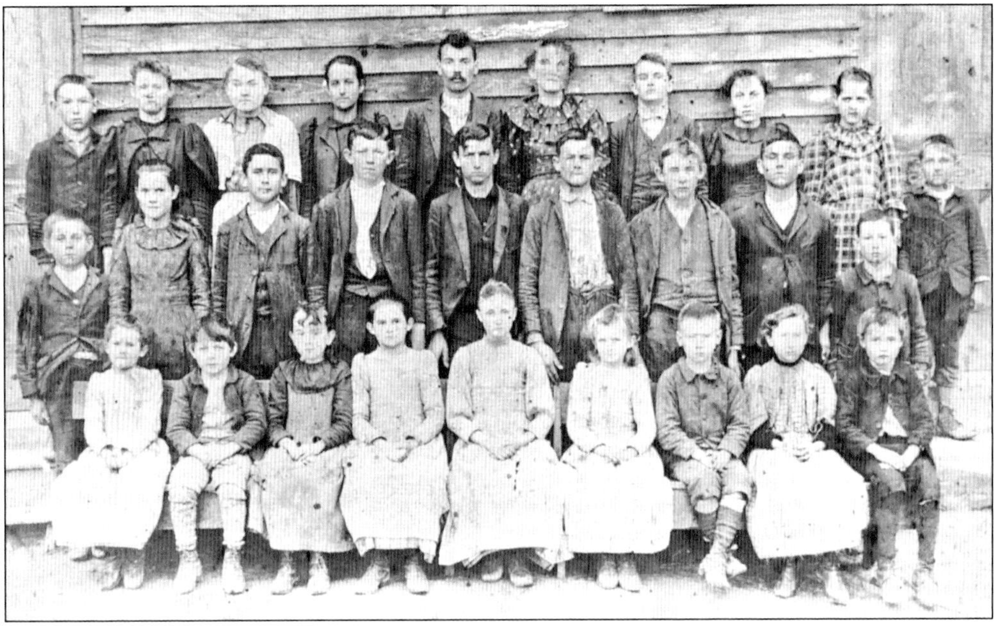

Oak Grove School, Mocksville, 1892. This photograph shows students, from left to right, (first row) Essie McClamroch, Abb Sain, Mary Call, Rose McClamroch, Luster Whitaker, Daisy McClamroch, Jim Smith, Essie Sain, and Chall Sain; (second row) Sanford Nail, Dora McClamroch, Jim McClamroch, Jim Ellis, Albert McClamroch, Cole McClamroch, Will Ijames, Amberst Turrentine, and Johnny McDaniel; (third row) Bud Sain, Mamie Ellis, Kate Douthit, Dorcas Jane McClamroch, Jesse Foster, Minnie Douthit, Walt McClamroch, Emmie Sain, Mary Eanes, and Willie Long.

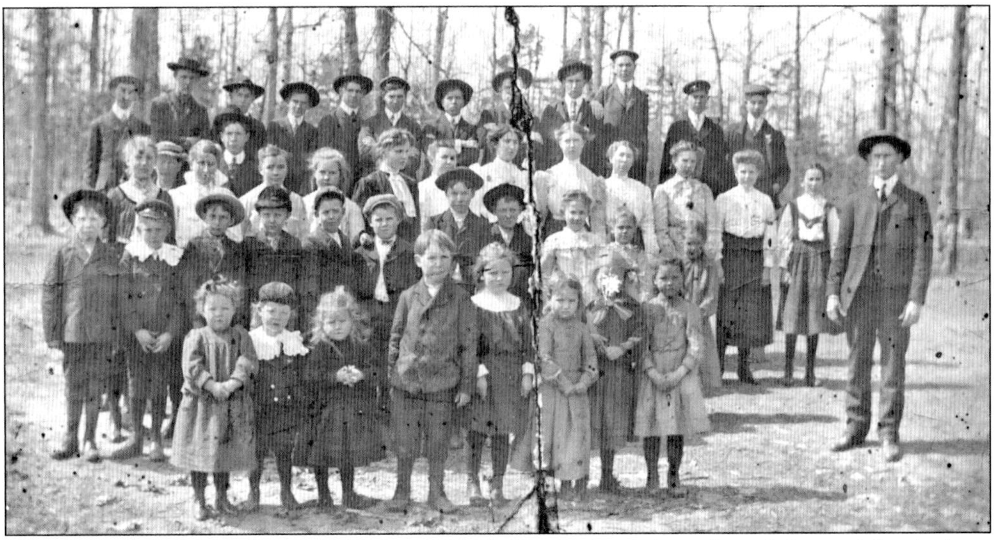

Liberty School, c. 1898. Teacher Sam R. Latham stands on the right at Liberty School, about one mile northeast of Liberty Church, with students, including Henry Daniel (fourth row, second from left), Grant G. Daniel (fourth row, fourth from left), and James Arthur Daniel (fourth row, fifth from left). Students sat on two long benches in the classroom and hung their lunch pails on nails driven into the walls. The Liberty School consolidated with another school in 1921, with both the house and lot sold in 1925.

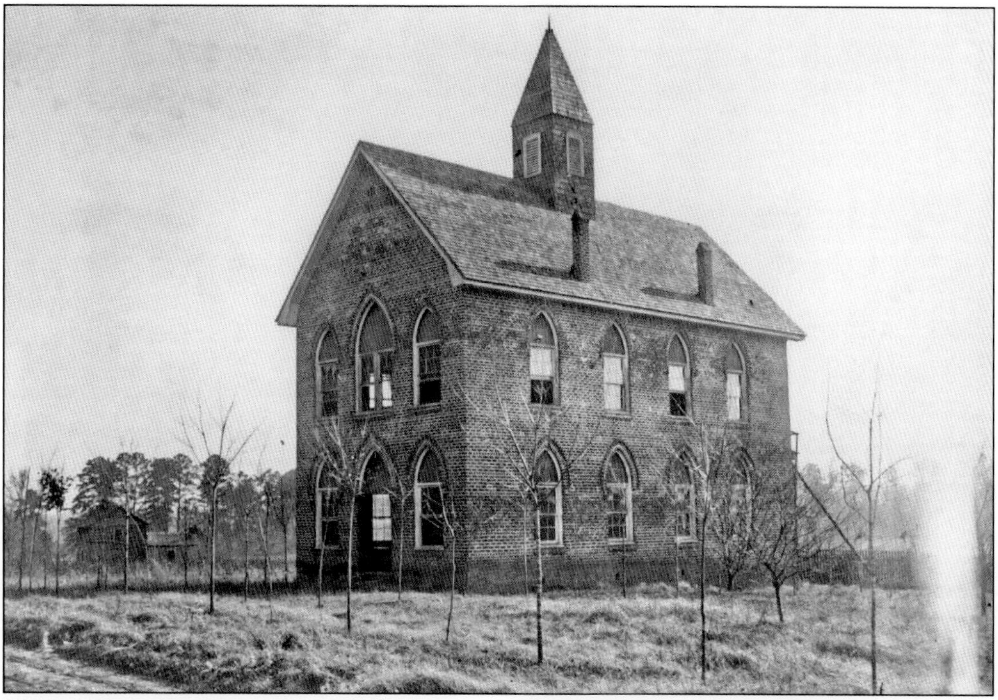

HODGES BUSINESS COLLEGE. To teach business to young boys, John D. Hodges in 1894 established the college in a brick building on Cherry Hill Road, with 2,500 square feet, a pyramidal roof, and square bell tower. Just $36 paid for three months' tuition, room, and board. The business school closed in the early 1900s, and the building was turned into a boardinghouse. Now a private residence, the building represents Davie County on the National Register of Historic Places (2000).

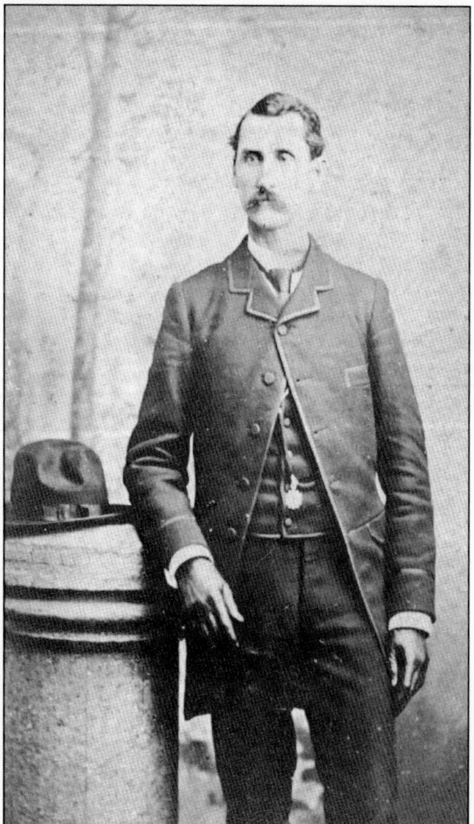

PROF. JOHN DANIEL HODGES (1845–1936). Hodges served in the 5th North Carolina Cavalry, Company H, during the Civil War. After the war, he took degrees from Trinity College (now Duke University, 1869–1873) and Yale University (an A.B. degree in 1874). He established the first high school in Union County, North Carolina (1875); taught Greek and modern languages at Trinity College (1879–1882); and founded Augusta Academy (1886) and then Hodges Business College (1894). Hodges also served as superintendent of the Davie County Schools for 10 years. (Courtesy of Larry Cope.)

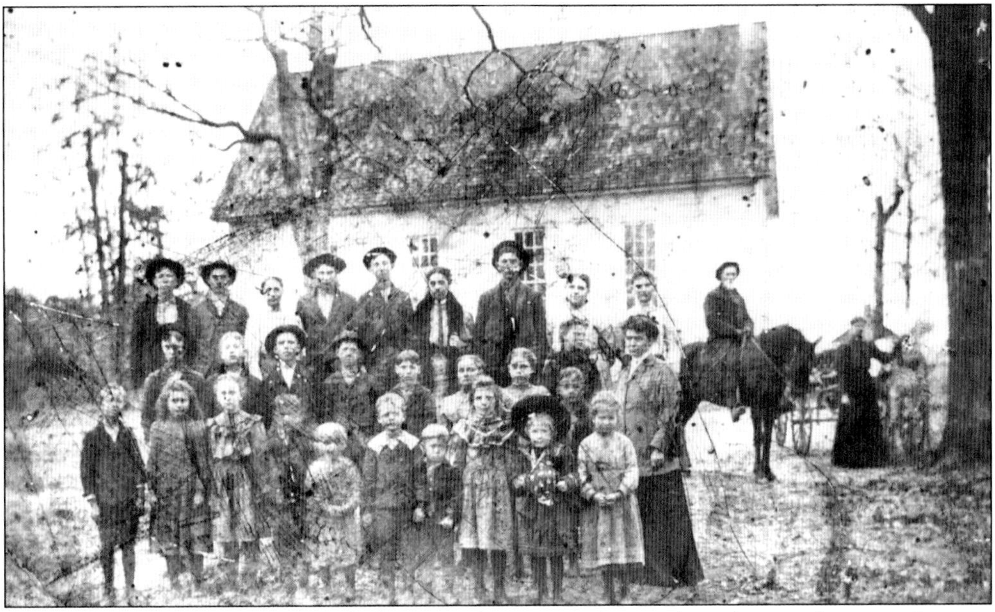

Bethel School. This photograph shows teacher Tempe Smoot (standing in the second row at right) and her students at Bethel, a private school run by the Bethel Methodist Church.

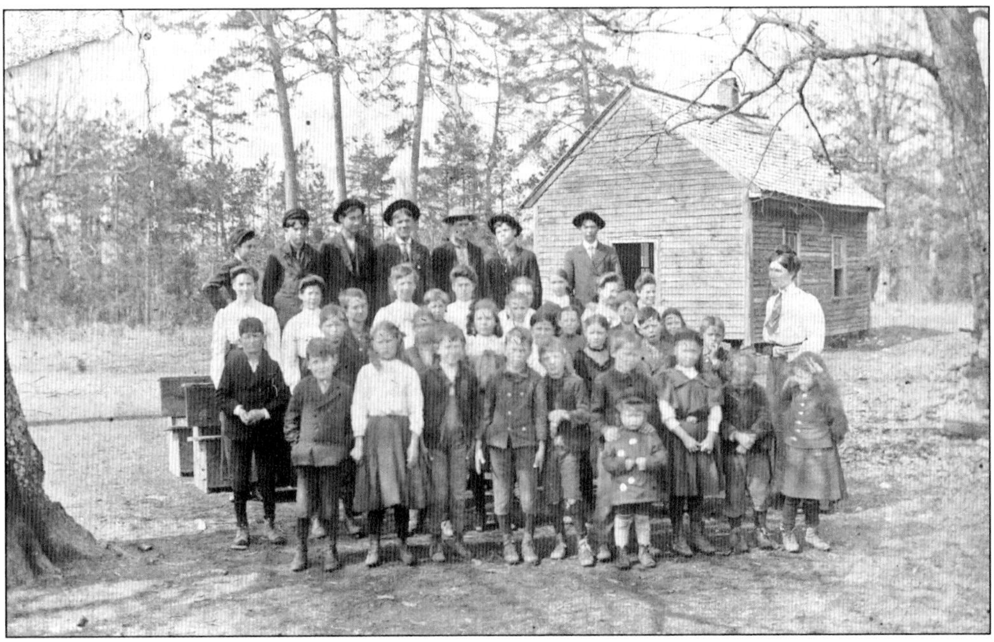

Turrentine School. John Turrentine sold 2 3/8ths acres of land on Dutchman's Creek on March 25, 1842, for a one-room schoolhouse. The Turrentine Baptist Church also held services in the schoolhouse. Teacher Mattie Collette (standing in the second row at right) appears in the photograph with students.

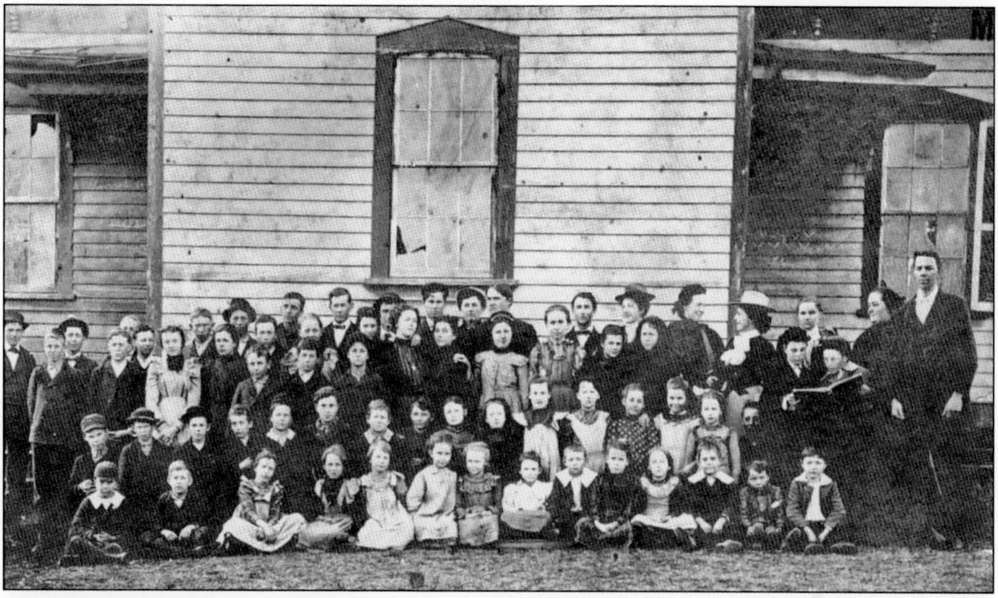

Farmington Academy, c. 1900. Leon Cash served as the academy principal in 1891. The board of trustees included Dr. J. W. Wiseman, F. M. Johnson, J. M. Johnson, S. C. Rich, and Dr. W. G. Johnson. The academy charged $1 per month tuition for first steps, $1.25 to $2 for intermediate, $2 to $3 for advanced and classical, and $2 for music. Board cost $8 per month, while an admission fee of 25¢ covered repairs, wood, crayons, and other incidental expenses. The academy advertised its building as "nearly new, well arranged for school work, and cost[ing] around $1,500."

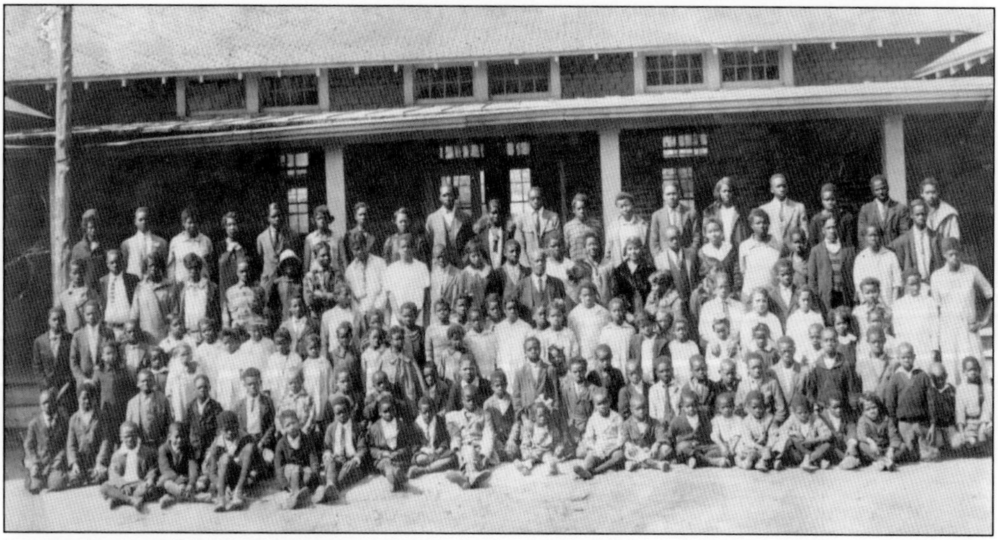

Davie County Training School. In the early 1900s, Dais and Hodge Gaither wrote to the Rosenwald Foundation for a grant to build a new school for black students in Davie County. The Julius Rosenwald Fund, seeking to improve opportunities and living conditions of African Americans and people of Jewish heritage in America, contributed to the construction of more than 5,000 rural schools for black children. The foundation financed the new local school building, using its standard construction plan (Floor Plan No. 1). In 1925, the Rosenwald Elementary School opened with grades 1 through 8, adding grades 9 through 12 in the 1940s. In the school year 1946–1947, the name was changed to the Davie County Training School.

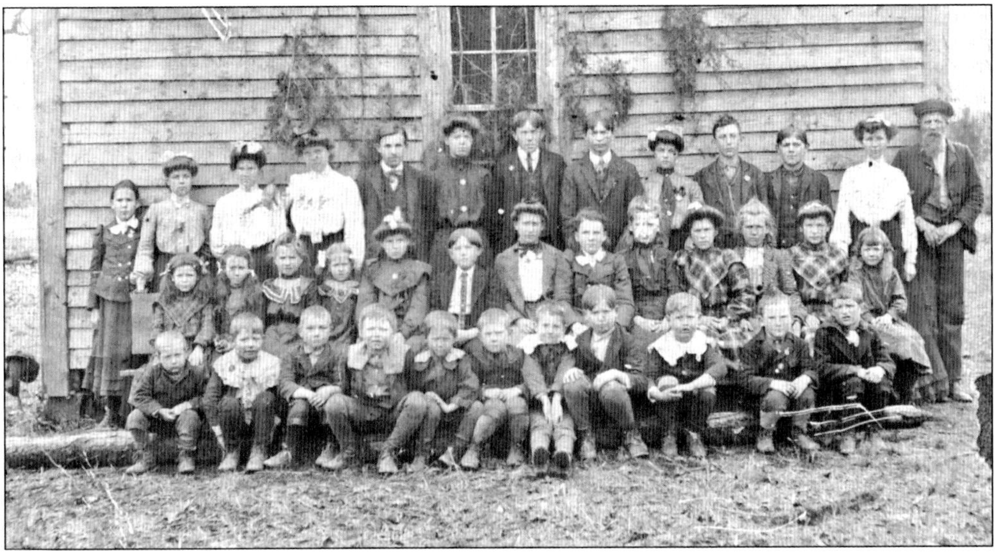

Class of Turrentine School, 1905. The photograph shows, from left to right, (first row) Willie Cope, Ernest James, John Thorton, Charles James, Frank James, Seba Cope, Gurner Foster, Edgar McCulloh, Preston McCulloh, Spencer Foster, and James Foster; (second row) Annie Foster, Annie Cope, Addie McCulloh, Annie McCulloh, unidentified, Bud Wagoner, Lille McCulloh, Ninner Foster, Beryl McCulloh, Bertha Foster, Mamie McCulloh, Alice Foster, and Brassie James; (third row) Beulah Foster, Dosha Foster, Vickie Foster, Pearl Wagner, Joe Everhart, Rose McCulloh, Eugene Wagner, Will Foster, Sallie Foster, Mack Foster, Ed Lagle, Maggie Foster (teacher), and her father, Denny Foster.

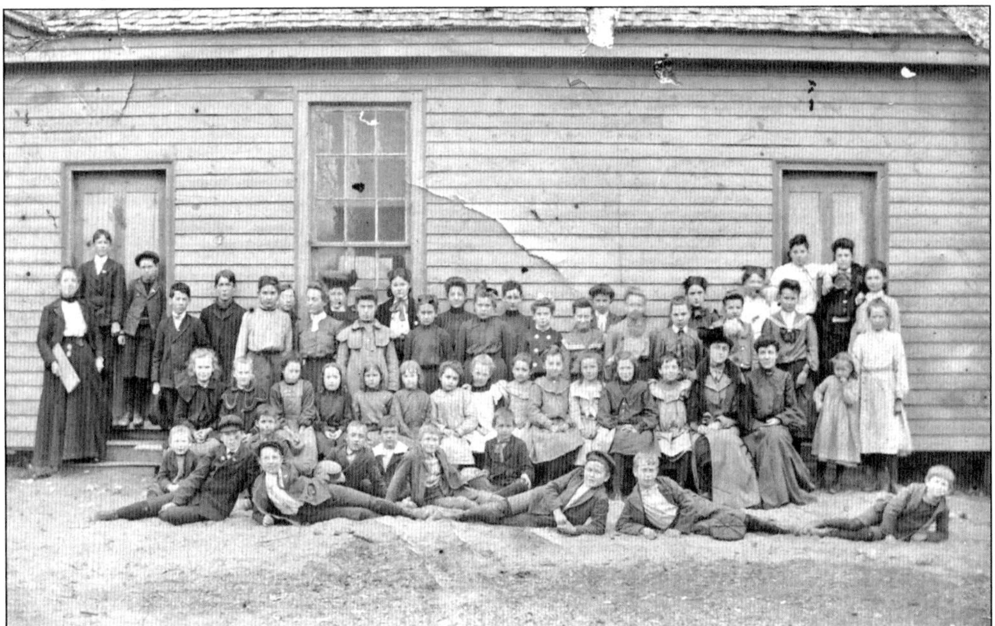

Sunnyside Seminary, 1905. In 1892, Mattie Eaton and Laura Clement opened the Sunnyside Seminary, named after Washington Irving's home, Sunnyside on the Hudson. A grove of sugar maples surrounded the two-room schoolhouse of the private, nondenominational seminary, which was demolished in 1947.

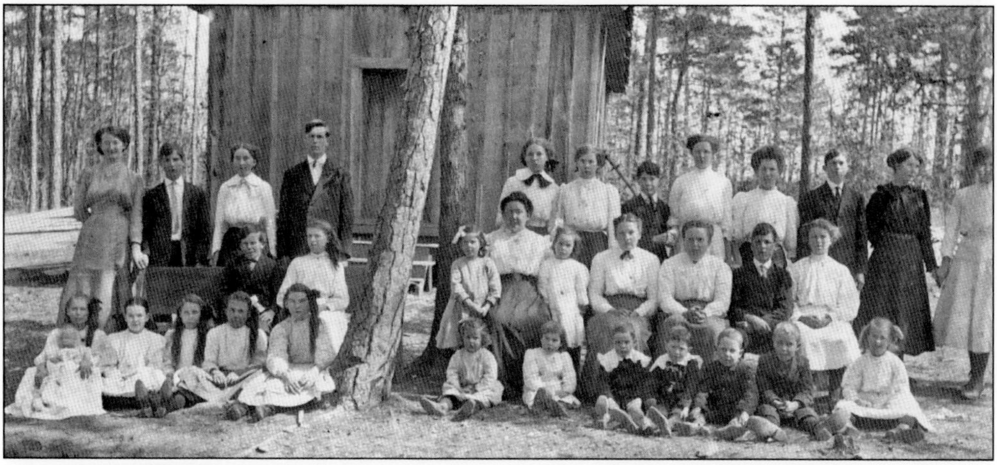

Mary Eliza Hudson. Mary Elizabeth Hudson (seated in the second row, fourth from the left) taught school in Cooleemee for more than 40 years. Her family settled in Davie County shortly after the American Revolution. Hudson attended the Cooleemee Episcopal Church. She died in April 1934. (Courtesy of Larry Cope.)

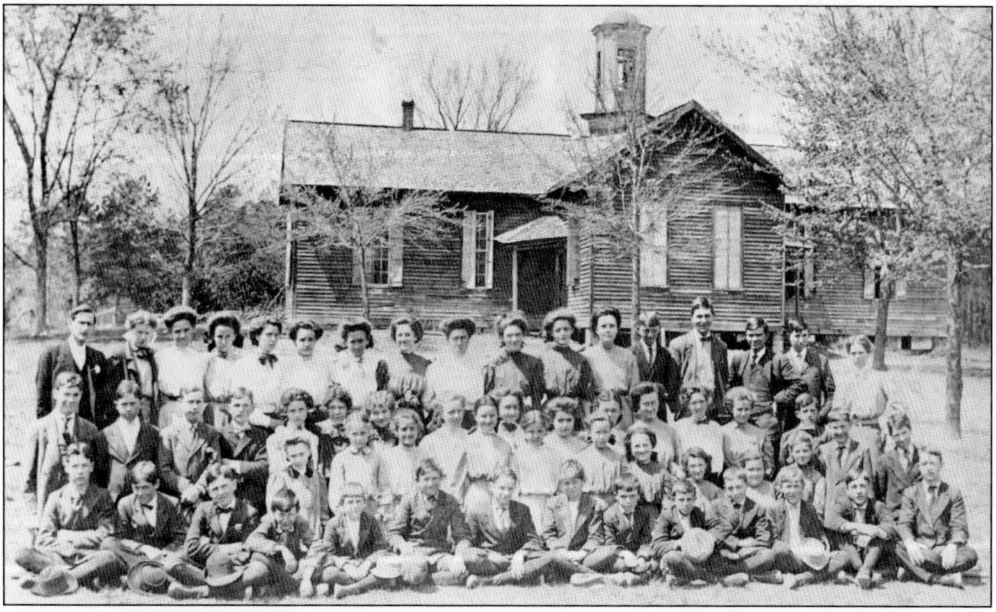

Mocksville Graded School, 1908. Students and faculty at the school included, from left to right, (first row) Kimbrough Sheek, Clegg Clement, Everette Horn, Maxie Brown, Norman Clement, Jack Allison, Hampton LeGrande, Lester P. Martin, Phillip Stewart, Mayo Foster, Claude Horn, Lonnie Griffin, Ranier Breneger, and Milton Call; (second row) Flora Davis, Elsie Horn, Ruth Miller, Mary Stockton, Margaret Meroney, Martha Call, Gelene Ijames, Ruth Parker, Frances Morris, Ralph King, and Jake Stewart; (third row) Fred King, Abram Nail, Thomas F. Meroney, Leroy Cashwell, Edna Stewart, Dorothy Gaither, Sara Clement, unidentified, Velma Martin, Rose Meroney, Ella Meroney, Louise Williams, Bonnie Brown, Martha Clement, Kopelea Hunt, and Frank Williams; (fourth row) Roy D. Jenkins (principal), Jessie Holthouser, Betty Linville, Bernice Wilson, Laura Clement, Clayton Brown, Mary Meroney, Frankie Wilson, Rose Owens, Jane Gaither, Caro Miller, Lena Brown, Walter Campbell, Aaron Bowles, Grant Daniel, Gaither Campbell, and Mary Fitzgerald (teacher). The old Sunnyside building stands in the background.

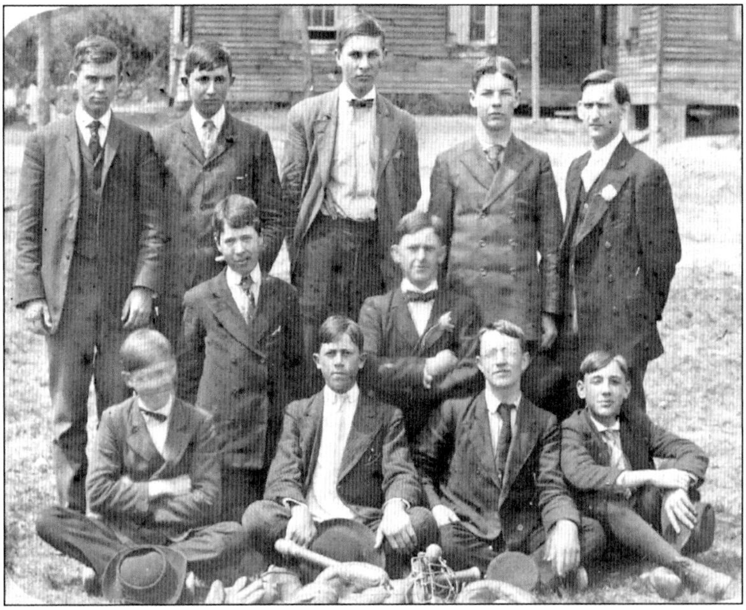

Baseball Team, 1910. Team members included, from left to right, (first row) Lester Martin, Abram Nail, Milton Call, and Ranier Brinegar; (second row) Frank Williams and Leary Cashwell; (third row) Grant Daniel, Gaither Campbell, Aaron Bowles, J. K. Sheek, and R. O. Jenkins (teacher).

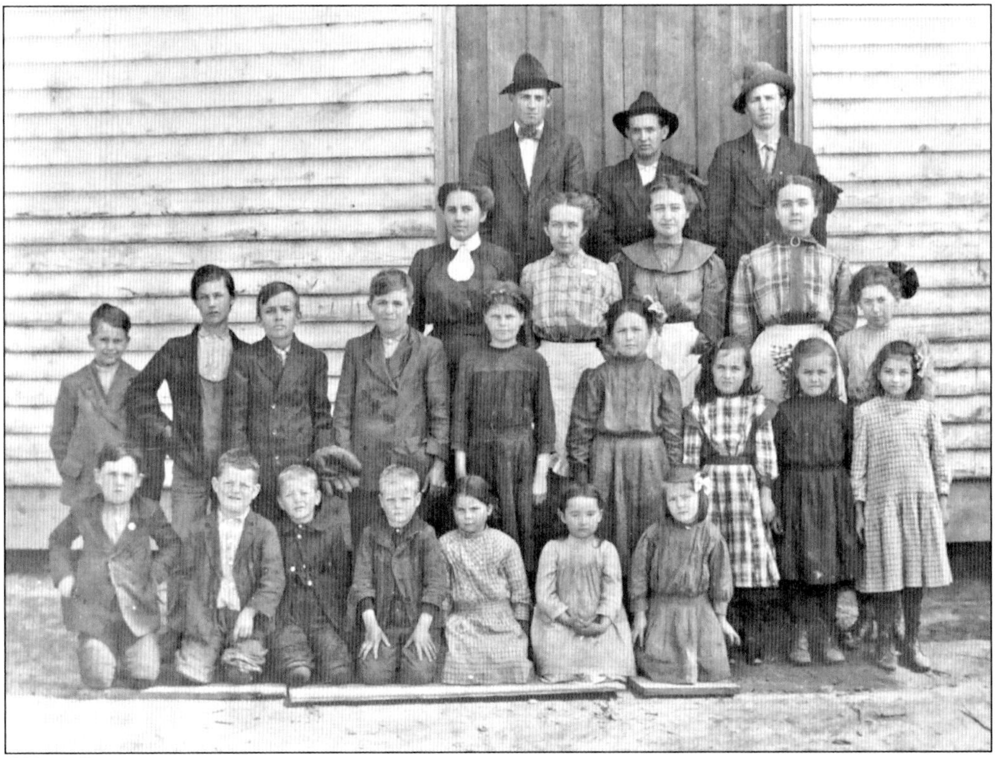

Center School, 1911. School members included, from left to right, (first row) Elmer Tutterow, Cleo Tutterow, Floyd Tutterow, Otis Tutterow, Delia Tutterow, Exia Clayton, and Grace Dwiggins; (second row) Roy Clayton, Rufus Dwiggins, Lonnie Dwiggins, Fred Walker, Nellie Tutterow, Annie Walker, Kitty Dwiggins, Mary Walker, and Mary Clayton; (third row) Mattie Eaton (teacher), Bessie Barneycastle, Minnie Walker, Lucy Dwiggins, and Rosie Clayton; (fourth row) Ben Tutterow, Holt Barneycastle, and Stokes Dwiggins.

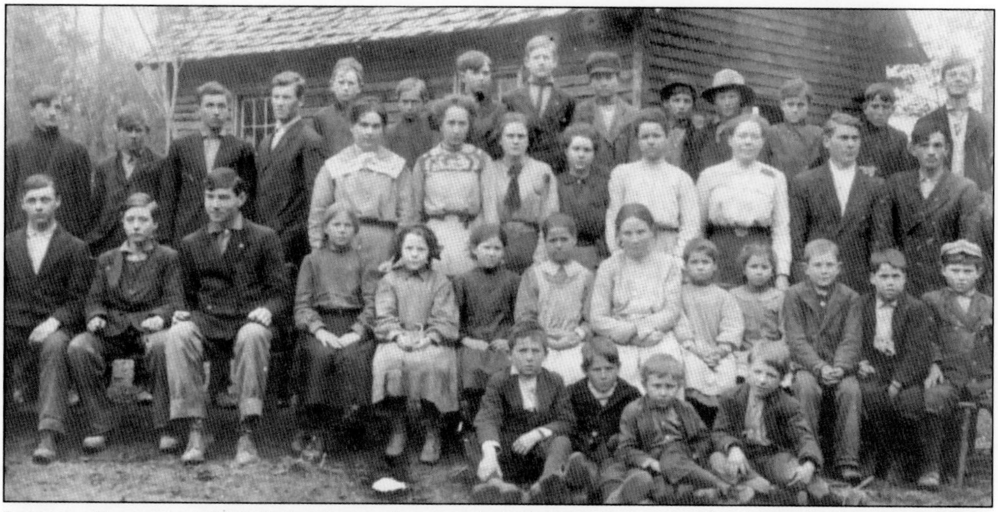

JERICHO SCHOOL, 1911. School members included, from left to right, (first row) "Mutt" Allen Grant, Charlie Bowles, Cling Green, and Oscar Keller; (second row) Frank Dwiggins, Gilbert Kurfees, Demas Foster, Edna Bowles, Edna Kurfees, Clayton Ijames, Flora Wilson, Etta Taylor, Amelia Wilson, Pearl Prather, Calvin Snider, William Wilson, and Burres Green; (third row) Gert Keller, Elva Click, Ollie Brown, Ila Snider, Ines Wilson, Susan Moore (teacher), William McSwain, John Smith, and Robert McSwain (partially visible); (fourth row) Albert Smith, Jim Bowles, Rike Wilson, Lee Bowles, Richard Emerson, Fletcher Click, Grady Ijames, Thurmond Bradford, Neal Smith, Oscar Prather, Marsh Bowles, Jim Wilson, Maxie Godby, and Clarence Grant.

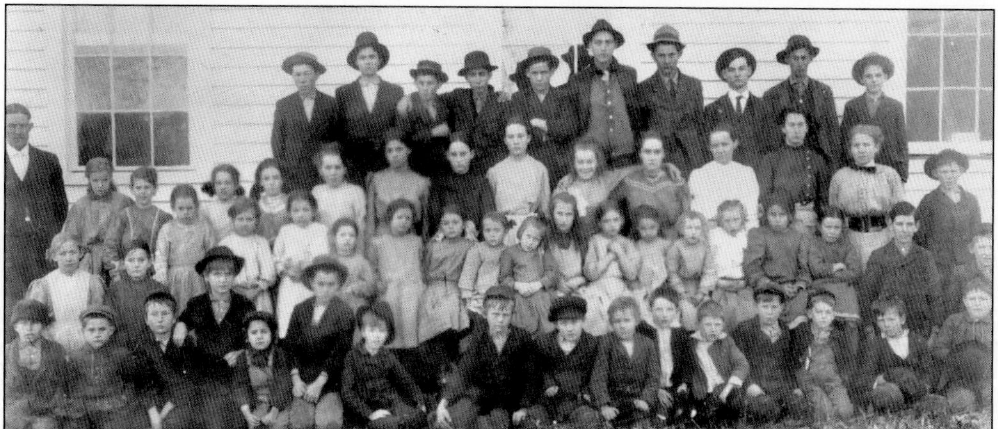

HOLMAN'S CROSSROADS, 1911. Members of Holman's School, located near the present intersection of Cana Road and U.S. 601 North, included, from left to right, (first row) Freddy McDaniel, Teeny Boger, Clyde Hutchens, Bob Baker, Halloway Boger, Earl Gaither, J. Hugh Gaither, Bud Allen, Dewitt Halton, Walter Allen, Walter Anderson, Clarence Anderson, Paul Allen, Rupert Boger, and Albert Boger; (second row) Mary Allen, Lacy Boger, Lillian Hutchens, Mable Hutchins, Tempie Boger, Minnie Boger, Selma Nichols, Bessie Cheshire, Isadora Halton, Juanita Halton, Ruth Baker, Polly Baker, ? McDaniel, ? McDaniel, Mattie Barneycastle, Lizzie Barneycastle, Will Booe, and Berry Neely; (third row) Charles Eaton (teacher), Effie Crater, Elma Booe, Minnie Cheshire, Viola Booe, Mae Neely, Ellen Gaither, Ella Nichols, Ivy Boger, Dotie Boger, Gertrude Gaither, Susie Hunter, Maggie Boger, Floyd Boger, Annie Halton, and Burley Boger; (fourth row) Bob Gaither, Mack Baker, Calvin Barneycastle, Charles Brown, Tom Allen, Lee Baker, John Boger, Grady Boger, Malcus Boger, and Tally Baker.

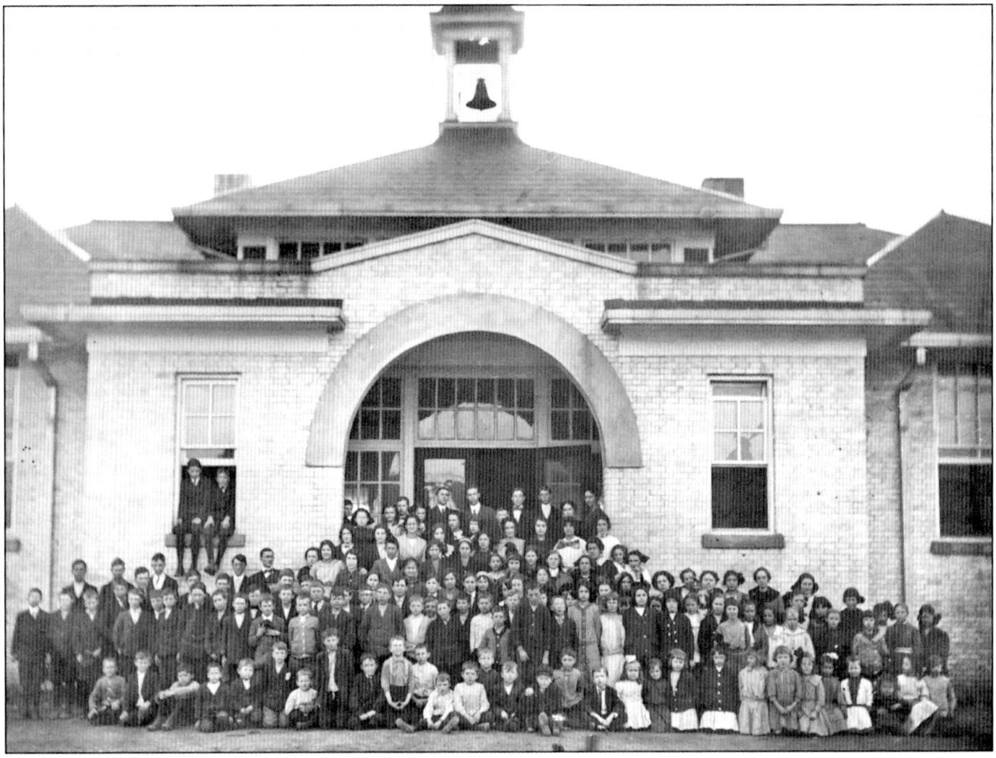

Mocksville Graded School, c. 1913. The school opened on Cherry Street in 1911 with an auditorium serving as the first indoor basketball court in the area. The ringing bells each day signaled the start of school, the recess hour, and the dinner hour. Principal E. C. Byerly led teachers Linda Clement, Sarah Gaither, Mary J. Heitman, Mattie Eaton, Rose Owens, and Margaret Bell.

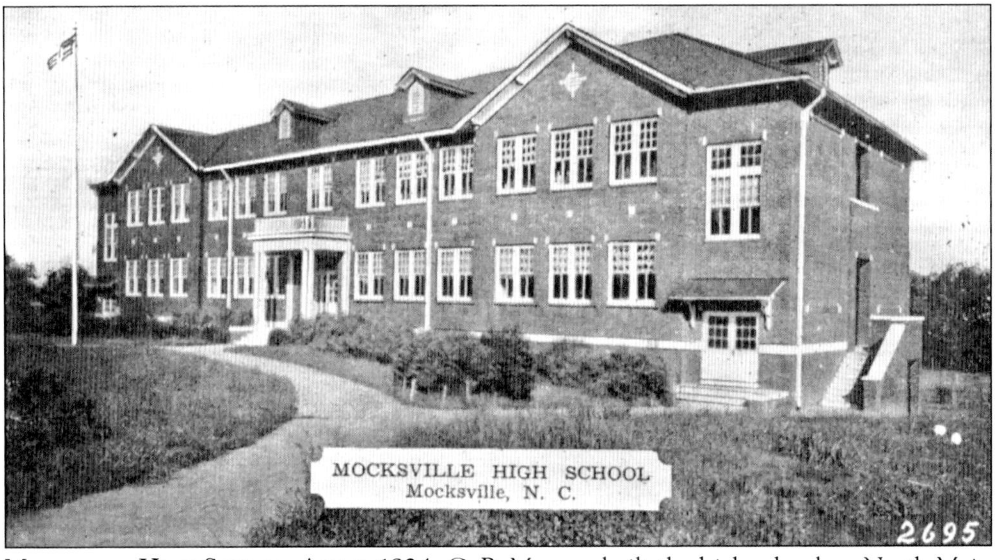

Mocksville High School, After 1924. C. B. Mooney built the high school on North Main Street for $70,000 in 1924. The two-story school contained many modern features: steam heat throughout the building, electrical lights, and a first-class water and sewer system. The Brock Center now stands on the site of the old school, which was demolished in 1972.

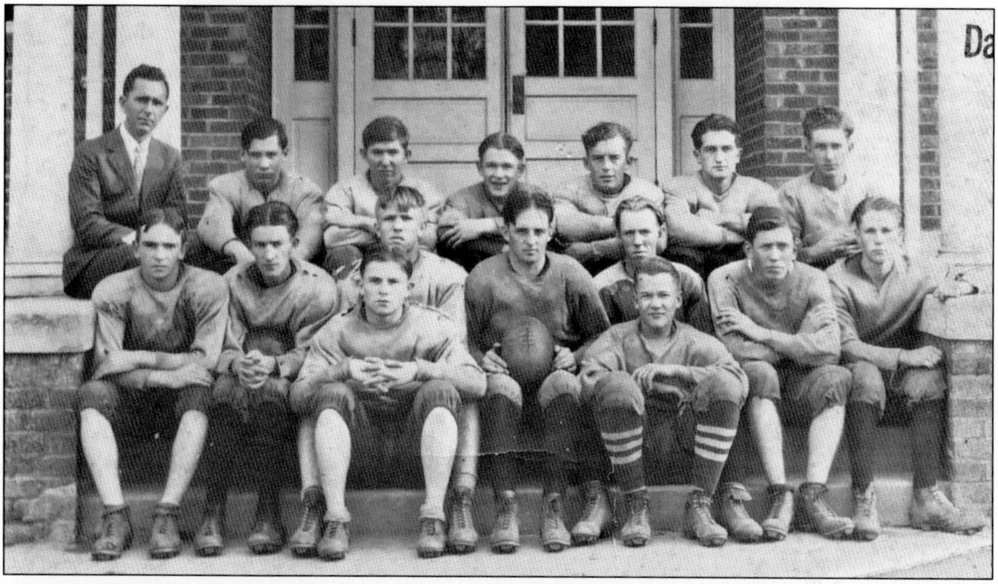

MOCKSVILLE HIGH SCHOOL FOOTBALL SQUAD, 1927. The coach and players sit on the steps of the high school.

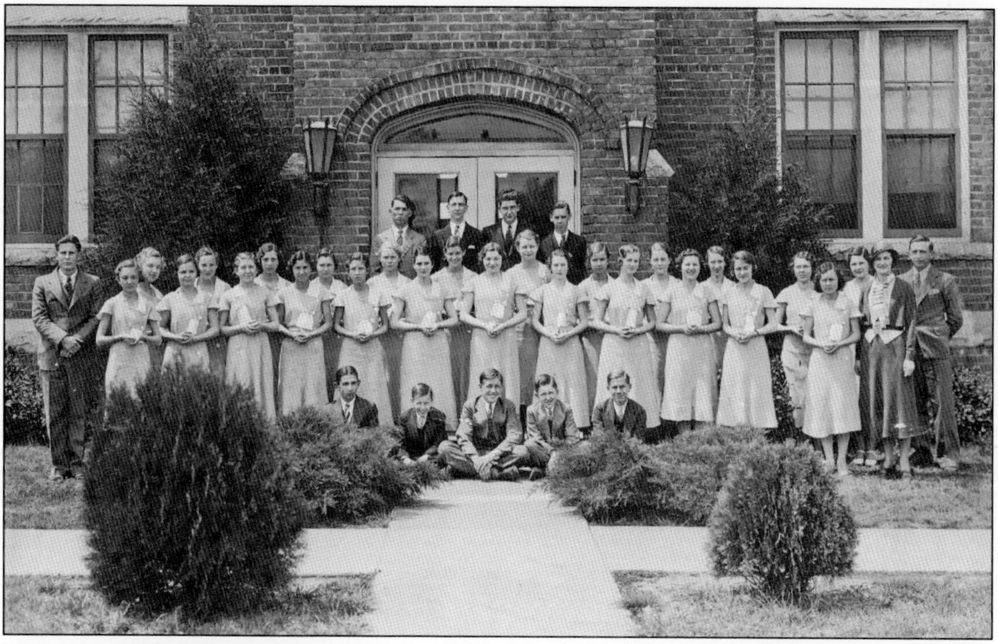

MOCKSVILLE HIGH SCHOOL GLEE CLUB, C. 1933. Members of the club posing at Catawba College in Salisbury include, from left to right, (first row) Lester Richie, James Thompson, Bill (Ralph) Mooney, James Wall, and Burton Killian; (second row) Everette Horn, Ruby Walker, Margaret Smith, Louise Frost, Louise Hendricks, Helen Ida Kirk, Ruth Hendricks, Helen Holthouser, Jane Crow, Pauline Campbell, Annie Ruth Call, Irene Horn, Aileen McClamrock, Annie Mae Benton (music teacher), and Johnny Smith; (third row) Mary Catherine Walker, Emily Rodwell, Francis Foster, Elma Hendricks, Helen Craven, Margaret Blackwood, Annie Mae Anderson, Helen Daniel, Dorothy Craven, Hayden Sanford, Rebecca Foster, and Elaine Call; (fourth row) Paul Eaton, Marshall Sanford, Ted Ward, and Bob Waters. (Courtesy of James Wall.)

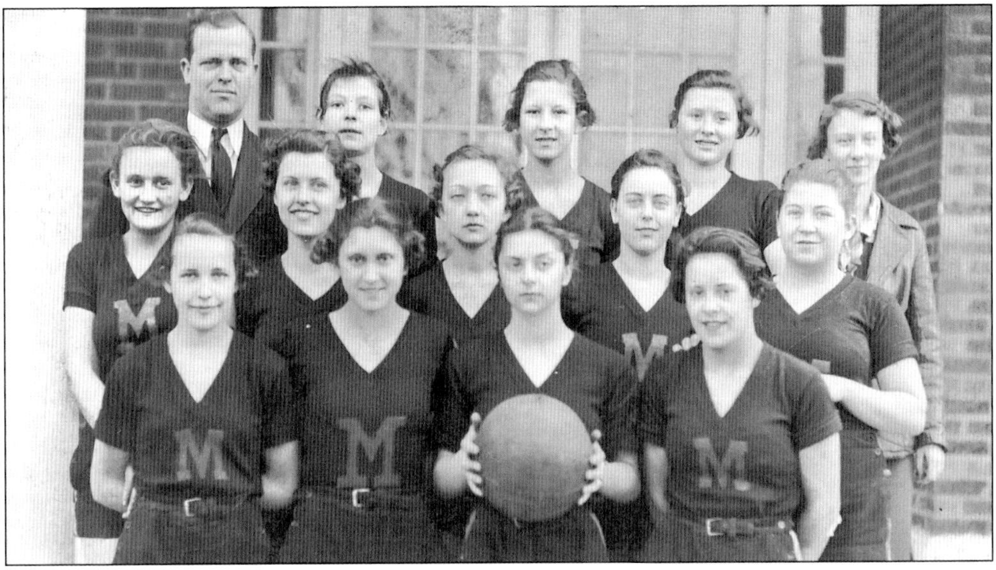

Mocksville High School Girls' Basketball Team, 1935. Team members included, from left to right, (first row) Martha Lee Craven, Louise Hendricks, Alice Carr Choate, and Margaret Craven; (second row) Eleanor Woodruff, Margaret Ward, Ruby Walker, Mary Waters, and Louise Frost; (third row) G. O. Boose (coach), Ozelle Miller, Helen Ida Kirk, Mildred Blackwood, and Hayden Sanford.

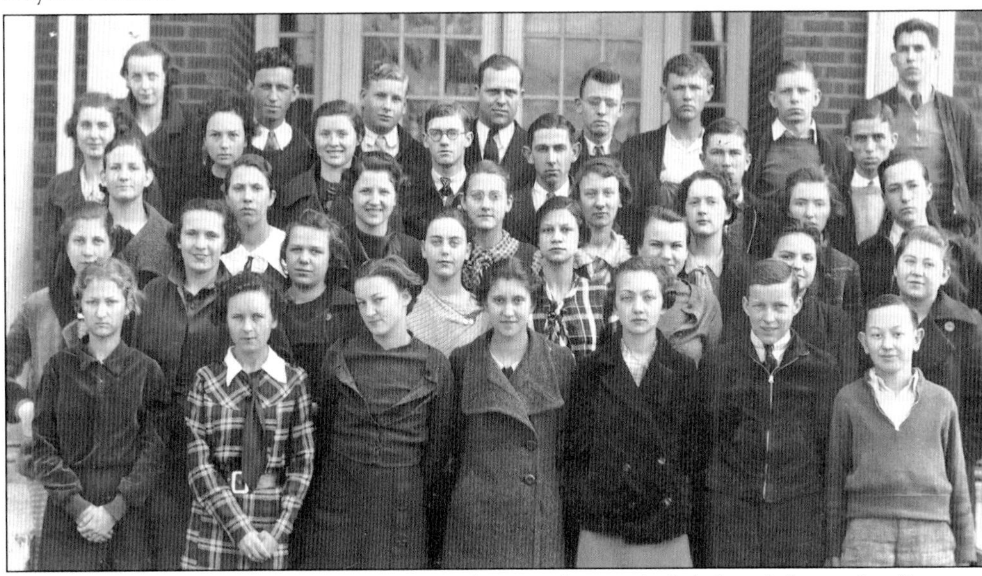

Mocksville High School Class of 1935. Class members included, from left to right, (first row) Mabel Wilson, Aileen McClamrock, Frances Allen, Louise Hendrix, Ruby Walker, Jim Thompson, and Bill Nail; (second row) Ruth Hethcox, Bertha Jones, Myra McAllister, Mary Waters, Sarah Grant, Evelyn Smith, Margaret Smith, and Louise Frost; (third row) Ruth Angell, Elizabeth Brewer, Annie Ruth Call, Irene Horn, Hayden Sanford, Gladys Cain, Helen Holman, and Joe Leagans; (fourth row) Katherine Anderson, Margaret Tutterow, Mildred Blackwood, Roy Walker, Lester Ritchie, Jim Wall, and Frank Hendricks; (fifth row) Earle Anderson, William Anderson, Duke Tutterow, G. O. Boose (teacher), Bill Eaton, Norman Leach, Sheek Miller, and Marshall Howard. (Courtesy of James Wall.)

Seven

PEOPLE

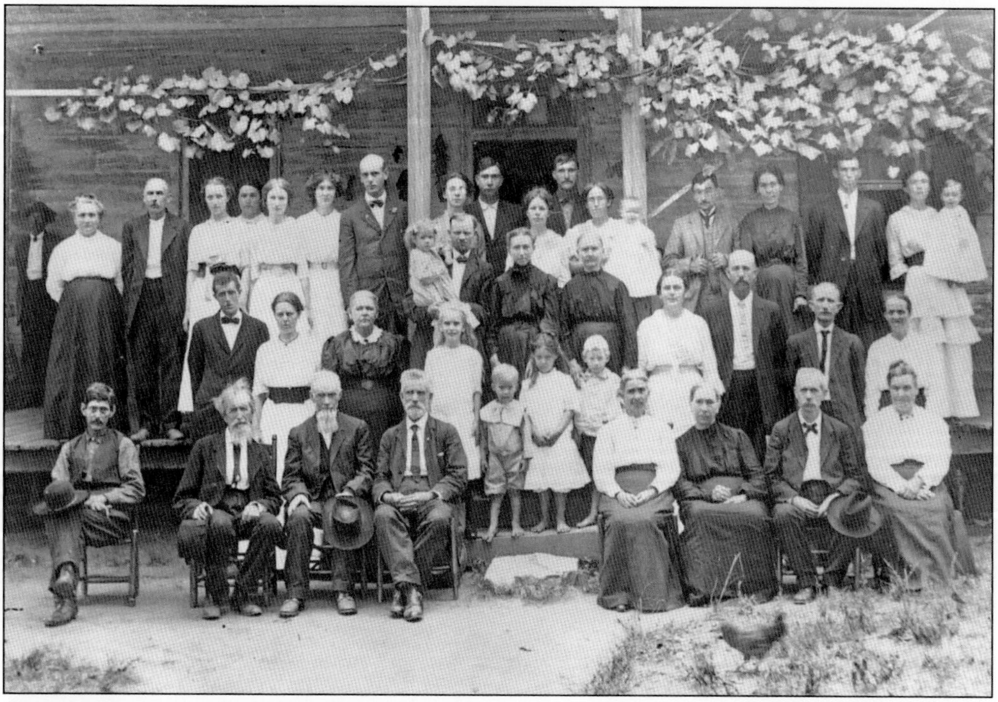

TURNER FAMILY. At the Turner Reunion in August 1914, the former Confederate soldier Pinkney Turner appears as the second man from the left on the first row. Turner wrote to his cousin James McGuire in June 1862, "I have had the flu very bad. They sent me to Richmond and I soon found that the doctor had nothing to give me more than turpentine." Less than a month before Gen. Robert E. Lee surrendered at the Appomattox Courthouse in April 1865, Turner wrote from near Petersburg, Virginia, to his sister, "I think the war may end in the course of a couple of months, and when I come, I want it to be at the right time. So that no one can point at me as a deserter or coward."

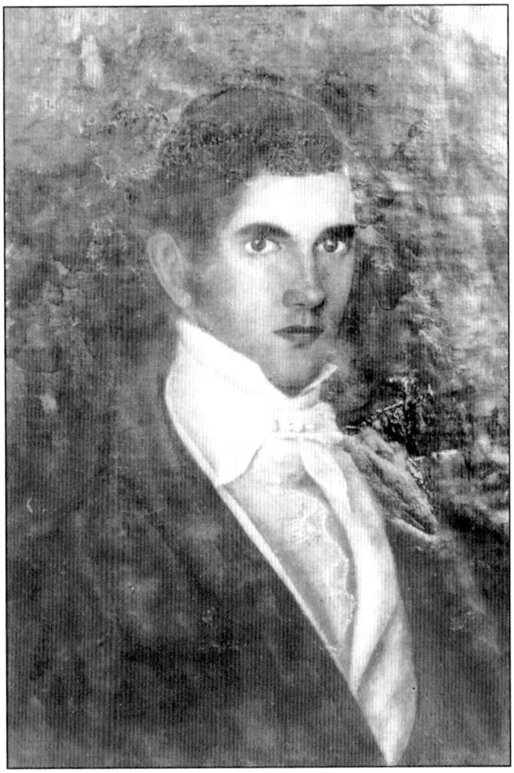

THOMAS MCNEELY (1796–1866). McNeely stands out as a prominent civic leader in early Mocksville. He served as postmaster from 1830 to 1847, magistrate of the first county court in 1837, and chairman of the town's first board of commissioners in 1839. McNeely laid out the original plat for downtown Mocksville, reserving space for the First Presbyterian Church, which he served as its first known clerk (1832–1849). The lots sold well enough at auction in 1837 to finance the building of the courthouse and jail. He built and owned a cotton factory operated by steam, an important advantage over water-operated mills in times of drought. Financial setbacks and the bankruptcy of the mill led to his relocation to Philadelphia in 1849. He later returned to Salisbury, North Carolina, where he died in 1866.

RICHMOND MUMFORD PEARSON (1805–1878). Pearson, born on June 28, 1805, at "Richmond Hill" near the town of Cooleemee, graduated from the University of North Carolina (1823), studied law under Leonard Henderson, received his law license (1826), and practiced in Salisbury. Highlights of his distinguished career include the North Carolina House of Commons (1829–1832), North Carolina Superior Court (1836–1849), North Carolina Supreme Court judge (1849), and chief justice (1858–1878). In addition, Pearson established a law school in Mocksville in about 1835, later moving it to Richmond Hill in Yadkin County when he inherited land there. Pearson taught at the law school until his sudden death in early 1878. In 1881, lawyers who had studied under Pearson erected a monument at his grave site in Raleigh inscribed, "His epitaph is written by his own hand in the North Carolina Reports."

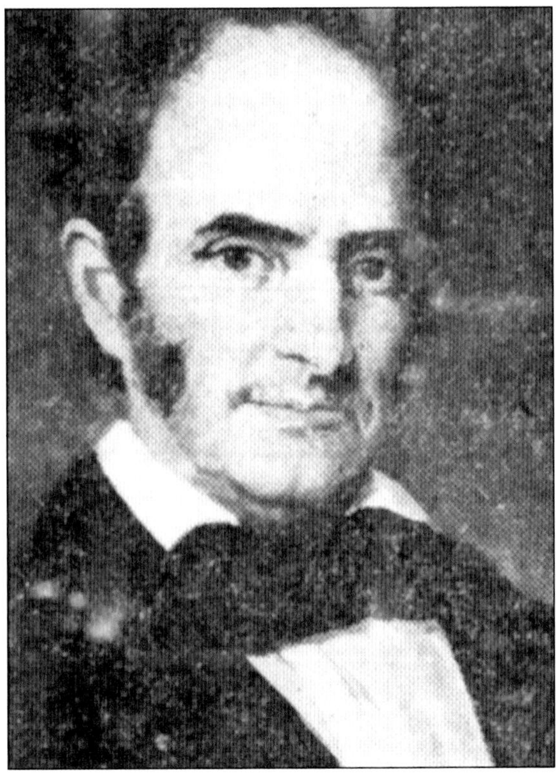

JESSE A. PEARSON (1776–1823). Pearson, who was born in Rowan County, served as a major general in the War of 1812, as a member in the House of Commons of the North Carolina General Assembly (1807–1808 and 1812–1815), and as a member in the North Carolina Senate (1816). The owner of Cooleemee Hill Plantation beginning in 1804, Pearson sold it to Peter Hairston of Stokes County in 1817. Later that year, he became involved in the Yadkin Navigation Company, attempting to make the Yadkin River navigable for freight and passenger boats with links all the way to Wilmington, North Carolina. Pearson also helped organize the Clinton Town Company in 1818, which mapped out a new town on 327 acres of land in "the Point" where the Yadkin and South Yadkin Rivers meet. Plans for the town floundered when the navigation project failed. Pearson also served as a manager of the Jockey Club of Salisbury. He died in 1823 from injuries sustained when he was thrown by his horse while returning from a funeral in Salisbury. He lies buried in the Pearson graveyard in southern Davie County.

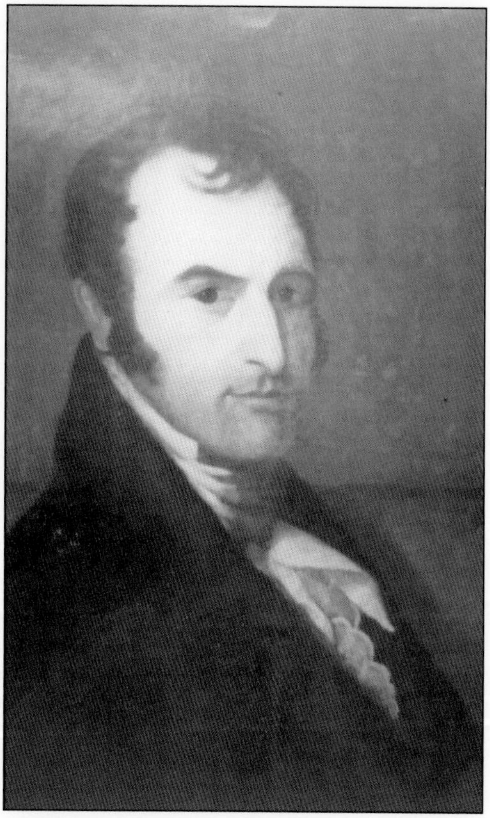

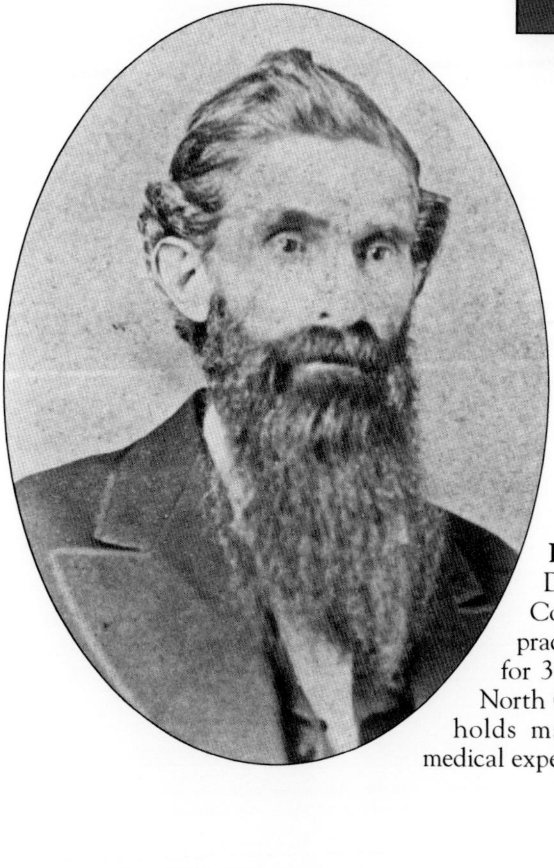

DR. WILLIAM REESE SHARPE (1820–1877). Dr. Sharpe graduated from Jefferson Medical College in Philadelphia, Pennsylvania, and practiced medicine in the Fulton community for 36 years (1840–1876). The University of North Carolina's Southern Historical Collection holds many of Dr. Sharpe's writings on his medical experiences.

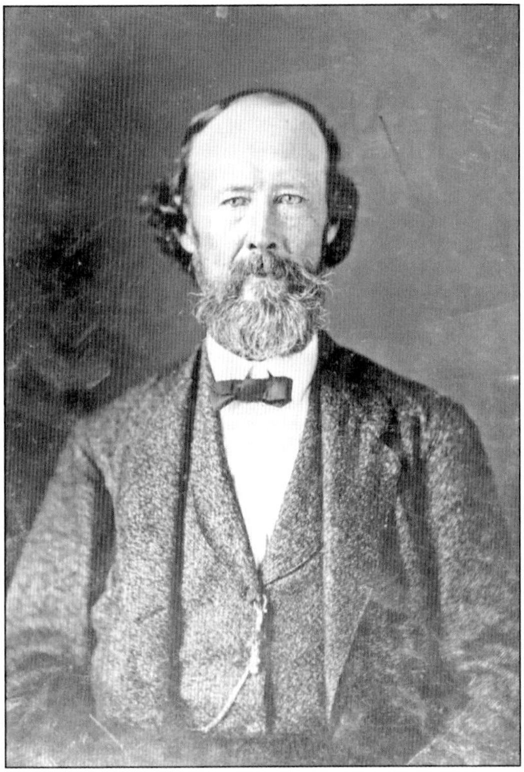

Dr. Leonard Hamilton Cash (1825–1905). Dr. Cash studied at Jefferson Medical College in Philadelphia, obtained his medical degree (1852), opened his first medical office in Clemmons, North Carolina, and later practiced at Smith Grove for 40 years. From his office on the west side of Salem Road, Dr. Cash made house calls to patients on his horse, Johnny Morgan.

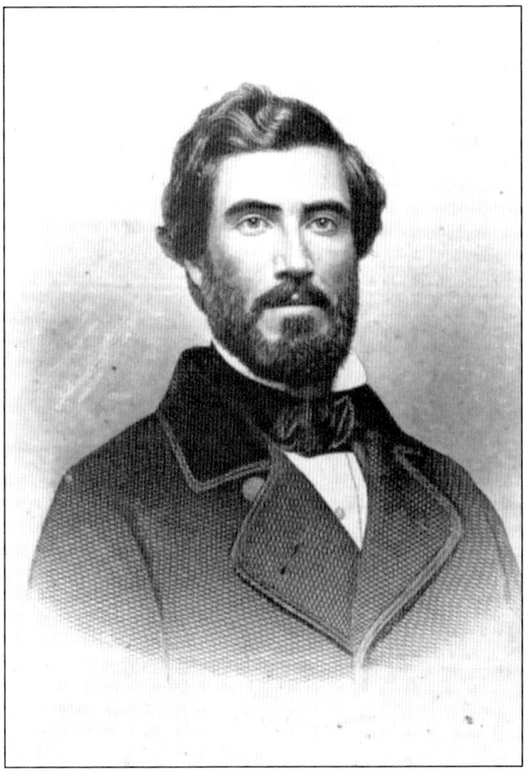

Hinton Rowan Helper (1829–1909). Helper, born on the Squire Boone home site in Davie County, received his education at the Mocksville Academy under Peter Stuart Ney. Helper authored a book, *The Impending Crisis of the South: How to Meet It*, which helped to inflame opposing sentiments leading up to the Civil War. Published in 1857, the book proposed abolishing slavery and influenced Lincoln's election to the presidency. Helper was vilified throughout the South. In 1861, Lincoln appointed Helper as consul to Buenos Aires. He later returned to the United States and, after brief stints as a lobbyist and envoy in Washington, spent the rest of his life promoting the idea of a Three Americas Railway linking North, Central, and South America. He became mentally unstable and committed suicide in March 1909. The National Park Service listed the Helper house on the National Register of Historic Places in 1973.

DR. JAMES MCGUIRE (1829–1909). Dr. McGuire received his degree in medicine from the University of New York (1857). He practiced medicine with Dr. James F. Martin until 1860 and then alone for a decade in Mocksville and County Line (1860–1870). After a brief period in Jersey County, Illinois (1870), McGuire returned to Mocksville to work with Dr. Dewitt C. Clement and then Dr. Marmaduke Kimbrough (1896–1900). Dr. McGuire held the office of county physician and county superintendent of health for more than 20 years, represented Davie County in the state House of Representatives for one session, and served as county treasurer for 16 years beginning in 1882.

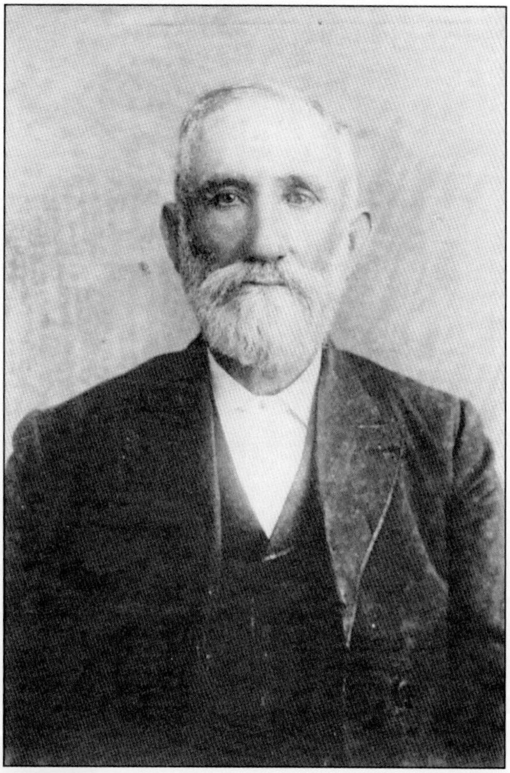

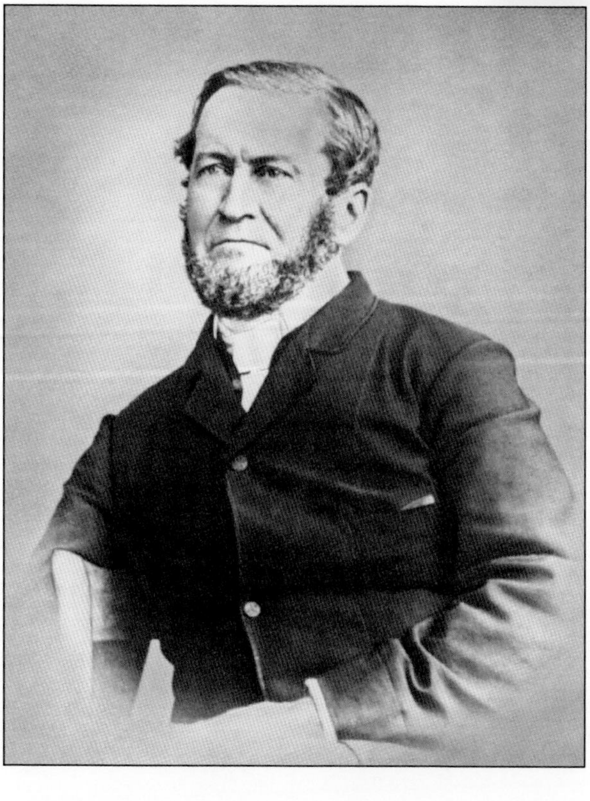

DR. JAMES WASHINGTON WISEMAN (1825–1899). Dr. Wiseman studied at the University of Pennsylvania Medical School in Philadelphia and practiced in the Farmington community. Affectionately known as Dr. Wash, he served one term in the North Carolina Senate (1885) and as the first master of the Masonic Lodge in Farmington.

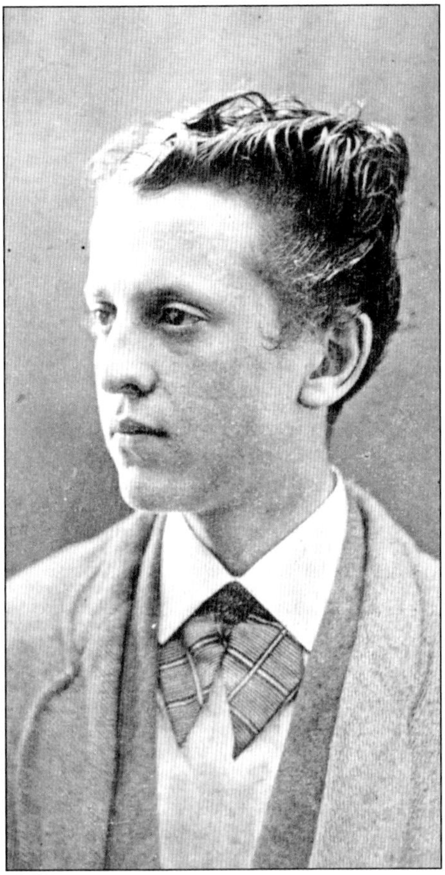

DR. ALFRED WILSON WISEMAN (1834–1907). Dr. Alfred Wiseman, the brother of Dr. James Washington Wiseman, studied at the University Medical Center in New York. While an assistant surgeon for the 7th North Carolina Infantry during the Civil War, Union soldiers captured Dr. Wiseman, who had stayed behind to care for the wounded, in Sharpsburg, Maryland, on September 19, 1862. After the war, Dr. Wiseman practiced medicine in the Jerusalem community of Davie County.

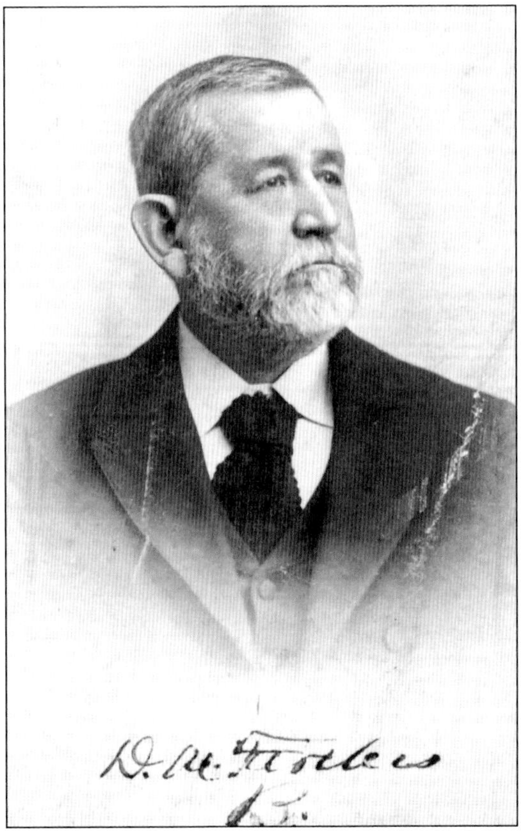

JUDGE DAVID MOFFATT FURCHES (1832–1908). Judge Furches, born on April 21, 1832, in Davie County, studied at the Richmond Hill Law School and began practicing law at age 26 in Mocksville. Furches served as a county solicitor, delegate to the Constitutional Convention in Raleigh after the Civil War (1865), and justice on the North Carolina Supreme Court (1894–1901), becoming chief justice in 1901.

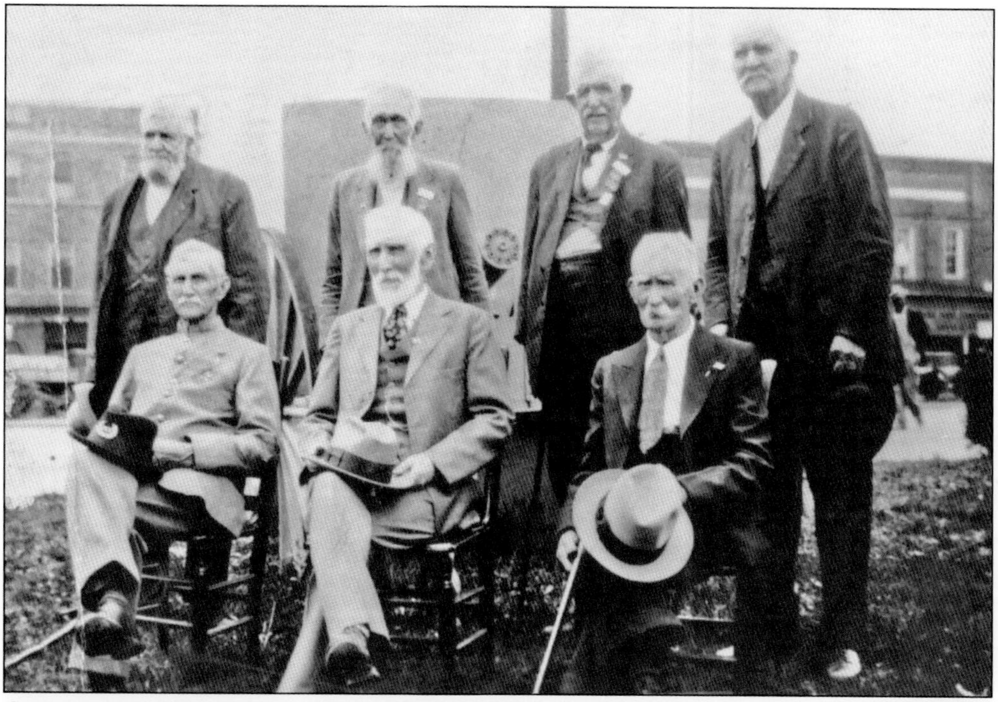

CONFEDERATE VETERANS OF DAVIE COUNTY. This photograph, taken after a reunion dinner given by the Davie County chapter of the United Daughters of the Confederacy at the March House in 1932, shows seven veterans: from left to right, (first row) Col. John D. Hodges, Jesse Lee Clement, and Simeon Goins; (second row) J. L. Glasscock, W. P. Ray, William Henderson Clement, and Leo A. Sheek.

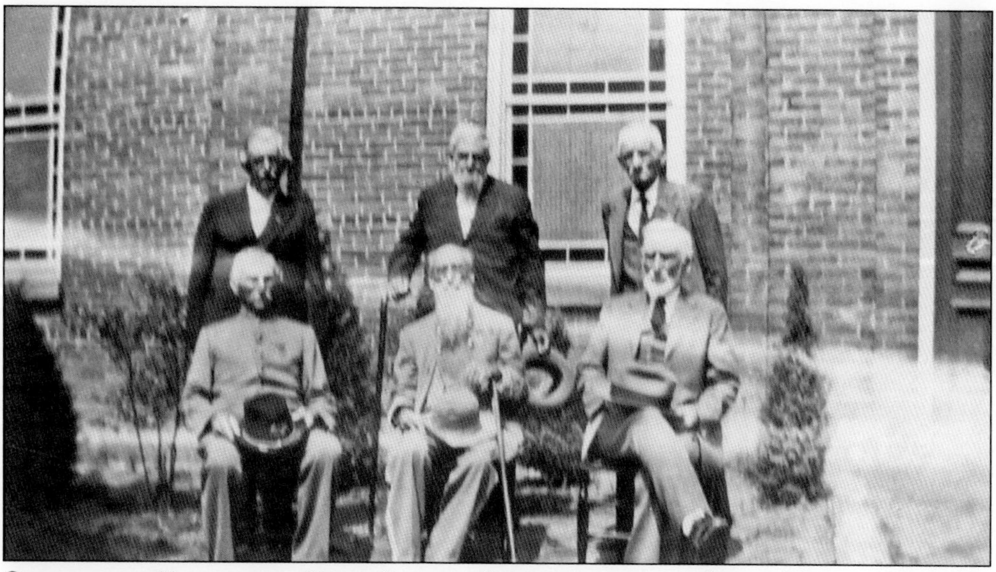

CONFEDERATE VETERANS OF DAVIE COUNTY. Six veterans pose in front of the First Methodist Church in Mocksville on North Carolina Confederate Memorial Day, May 10th. From left to right are (first row) Col. J. D. Hodges, Simeon Goins, and Jesse Lee Clement; (second row) W. P. Ray, J. L. Glasscock, and William Henderson Clement.

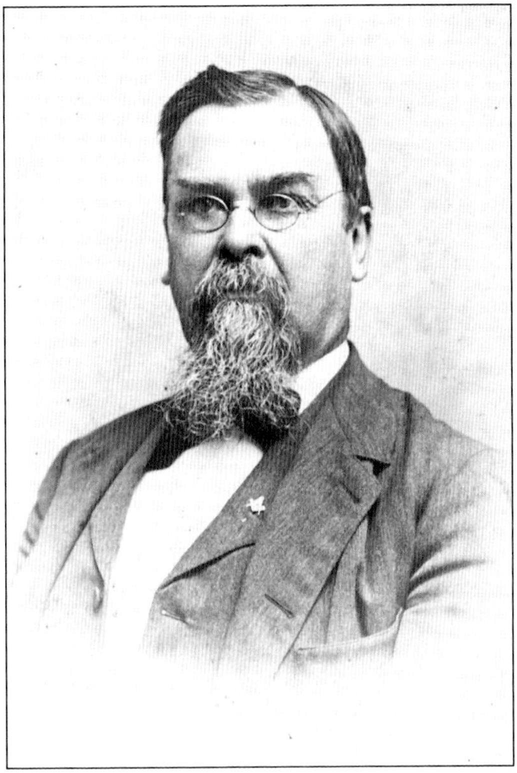

Dr. Marmaduke D. Kimbrough (1838–1910). Dr. Kimbrough served as a surgeon with the Forsyth County Militia during the Civil War (1862–1865). After the war, he practiced medicine in Smith Grove, chaired the Davie County Republican Executive Committee (1884–1896), and chaired the Congressional and Judicial District Committee (1882–1896).

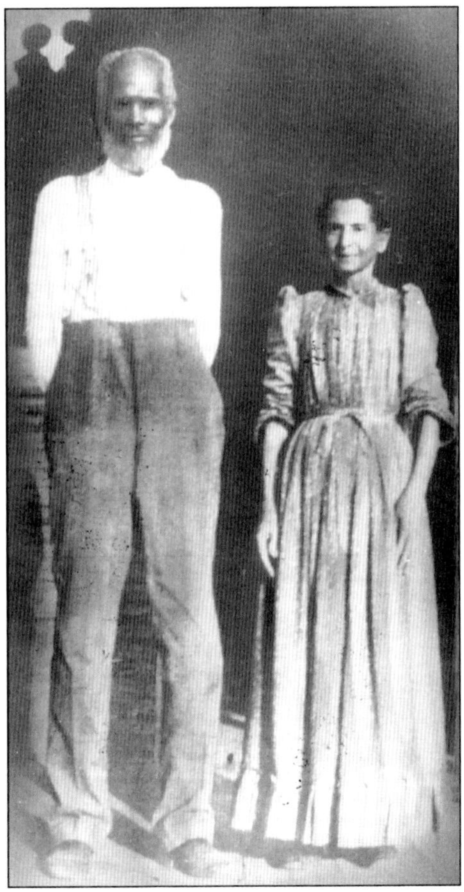

George Washington Clement (1836?–1910). The photograph shows Clement with his wife, Melinda Brown Clement. George, born into slavery about 1836, rose to become a successful farmer and landowner. In 1850, Davie County court records show that Elizabeth Clement inherited George, a boy of about 14, at the death of her father, Henry Clement Sr. In 1870, after the Civil War, George appears as a landowner in Davie County. He later moved to Rowan County near Livingstone College to enhance educational opportunities for his children. Two children, Fannie and Della, attended Livingstone College and became teachers. His son, George Addison, received his medical degree from Shaw University.

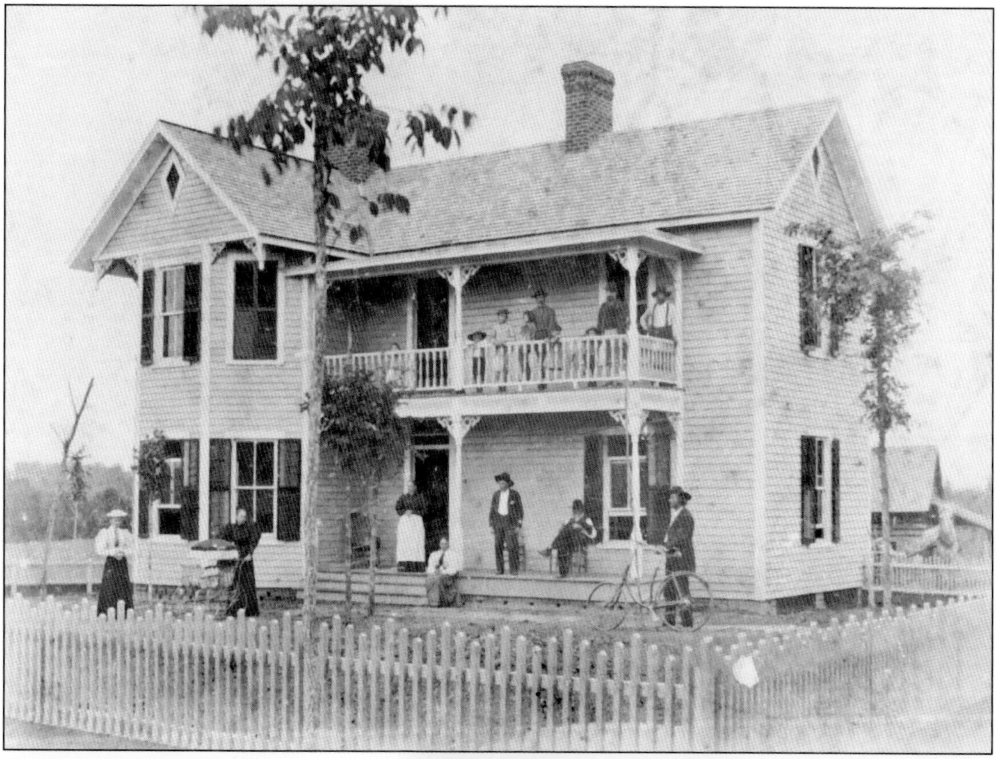

Home of Dr. Charles F. Anderson (1859–1903). Dr. Anderson, born in the Calahaln community, studied medicine under his uncle, Dr. John Anderson. After graduating from medical school, he lived and practiced in the Fork Church community until his death in 1903.

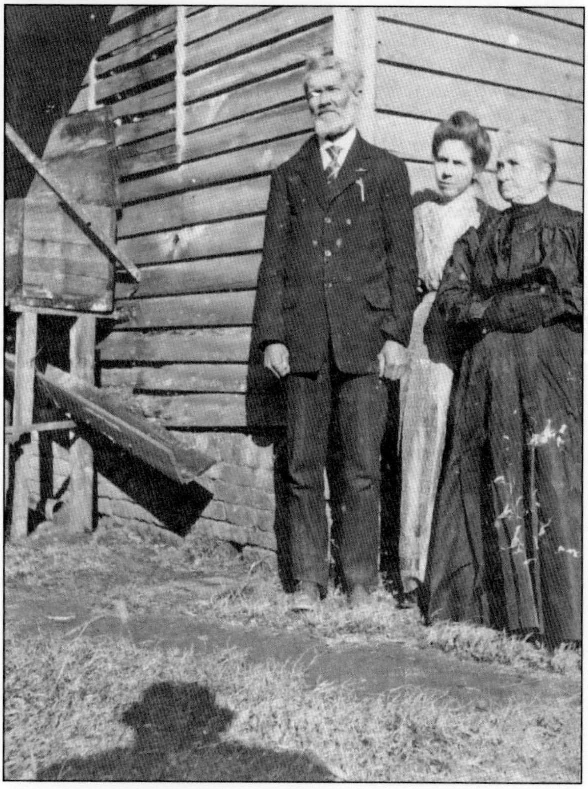

William C. P. Etchison (1846–1923). Shown here with his wife, Nancy, and daughter, Sallie, Mocksville's first police officer lit the kerosene lamps around the square at dusk. As police chief, Etchison supervised road projects. The *Davie Record* reported on July 27, 1910, "Chief Etchison has made some noted improvements around the old court house. In muddy weather one may now get by without using a boat and life preserver." The family's home on Salisbury Street burned about 1920. (Courtesy of Gwynn Meroney.)

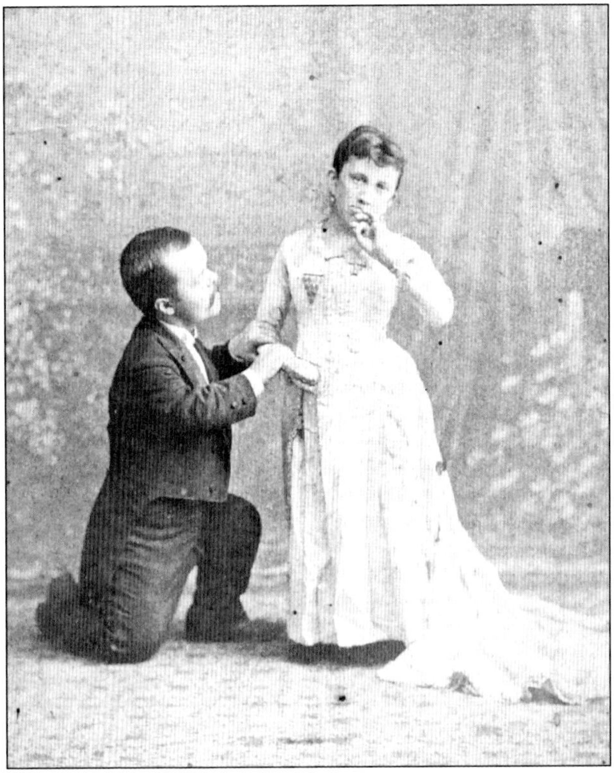

MAJ. JOHN MERTZ (1853–1938) AND MARIAH NAIL MERTZ (1852–1922). Mocksville native Mariah Elizabeth Nail only stood 36 inches tall and weighed 48 pounds. She traveled throughout the United States and Europe with the circus as one of the world's smallest women. She met her diminutive husband, Maj. John Mertz, "Major Mite," while touring. John Mertz, born in Austria in 1853, had joined the circus at age 21. The couple traveled with the Barnum Circus, Adam Forepaugh, and John Robinson shows. They retired from the circus in 1911 and lived in Salisbury until their deaths.

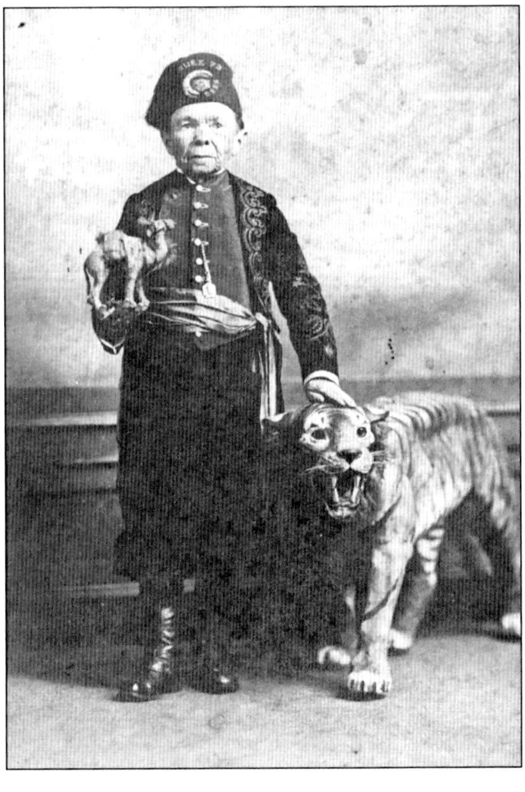

Henry Meroney (1869–1957). The 18-year-old Meroney joined Capt. Frank Brown in a federal project to make the Yadkin River navigable for steamboats in the 1880s. The men worked and lived on houseboats, bunking six to a boat. They drilled, blasted, and cleared rock and snags from the riverbed. After five seasons, Brown abandoned the project and returned home to Salisbury, ending the dream of steamboats on the Yadkin. Meroney went on to work at the Mocksville bus station for many years.

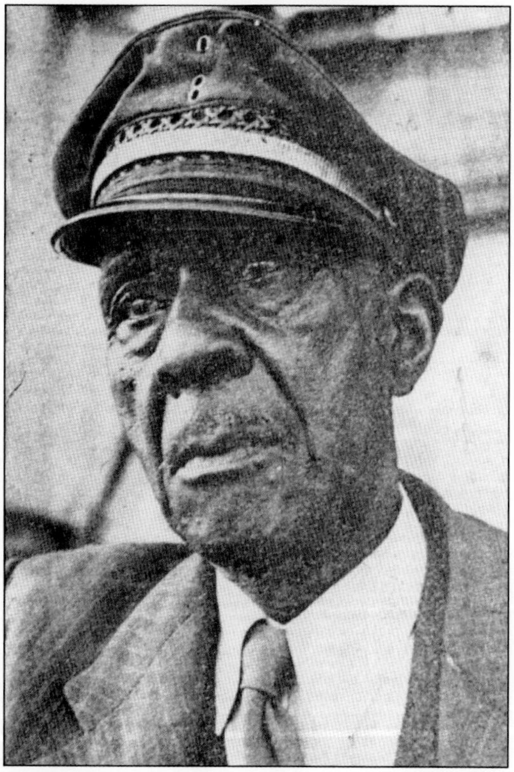

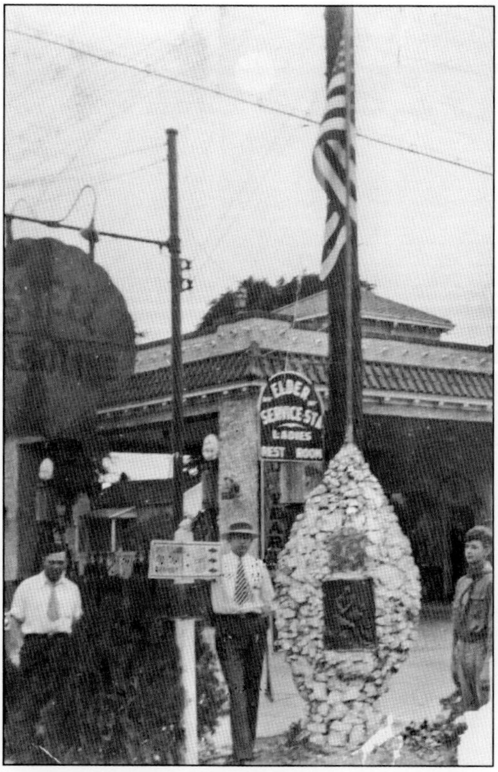

J. Hampton Rich (1874–1949). Rich, born on July 14, 1874, in the Cana community, founded the Boone Trail Highway and Memorial Association in 1913. To commemorate Daniel Boone, Rich erected arrowhead-shaped monuments of rocks and concrete typically containing a metal plaque depicting Boone sitting on a boulder looking westward. Each plaque contained a small amount of metal from 400 pounds of scrap salvaged from the USS *Maine*. Rich, dressed in a coonskin cap and carrying a long rifle, appeared throughout the country promoting the legend of Daniel Boone; he claimed to have placed over 350 memorial tablets.

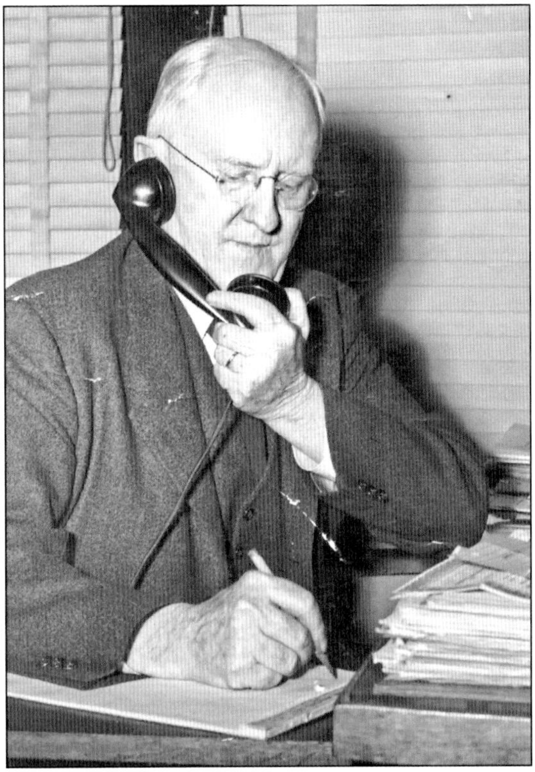

John Calvin Sanford (1886–1953). A Mocksville business and civic leader, Sanford received his education at the Fishburne Military Academy and Davidson College. He entered the family businesses and with his brother, Rufus B. Sanford, held management positions in Sanford Brothers, Inc.; C. C. Sanford and Sons; Rankin-Sanford Implement Company; the Sanford-Mando Company; and the Sanford Motor Company, as well as the Bank of Davie. Sanford served as a member of the Mocksville Town Board and an elder of the First Presbyterian Church.

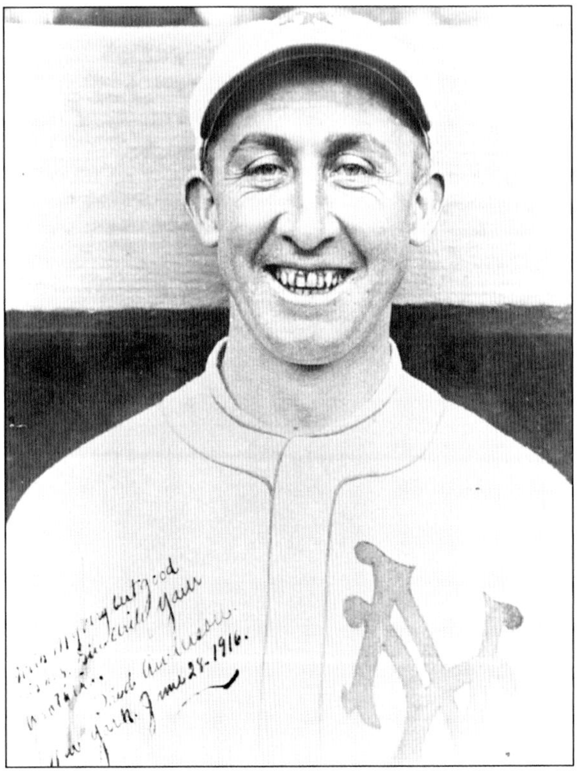

Dr. Fred Anderson (1886–1957). Anderson, son of Dr. John Anderson of Calahaln, never lost a college game as a baseball pitcher for Davidson College and the University of Maryland, graduating in 1909 in dentistry. The "star spitballist" played professionally with the Boston Red Sox (1909 and 1913), Federal (minor) League's Buffalo Buffeds (1914–1915), and the New York Giants (1916–1918). Anderson pitched in the 1917 World Series against the Chicago White Sox; the Sox won. After service in World War I as an army dentist, Anderson practiced dentistry in Winston-Salem. Anderson also coached baseball at North Carolina State University for at least one year. (Courtesy of Neil Anderson.)

GOAT MAN. Charles "Ches" McCartney wandered throughout the country in a wagon pulled by a team of nine goats for close to 40 years (1930–1968). The wagon, loaded with pots, pans, pails, and other items he found by the road, also contained his bed and a potbellied stove. Wearing goatskin clothes, drinking goat's milk, and rarely bathing, the Goat Man preached and told tall tales wherever he went. Muggs Smith recalls seeing the Goat Man in Mocksville during the 1950s. (Right, courtesy of the Davie County Public Library; below, courtesy of Charles "Muggs" Smith.)

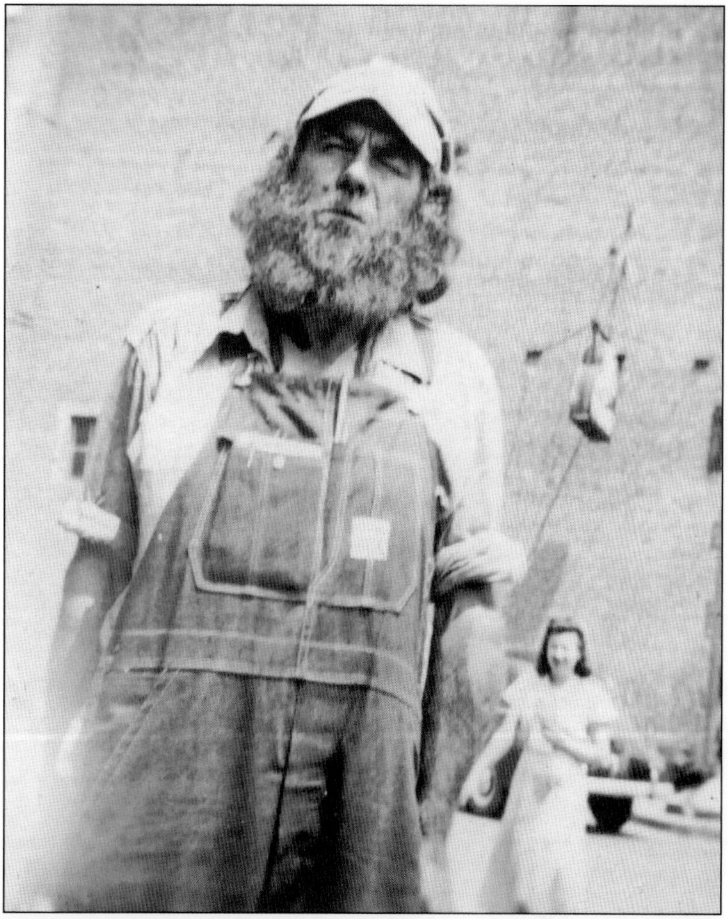

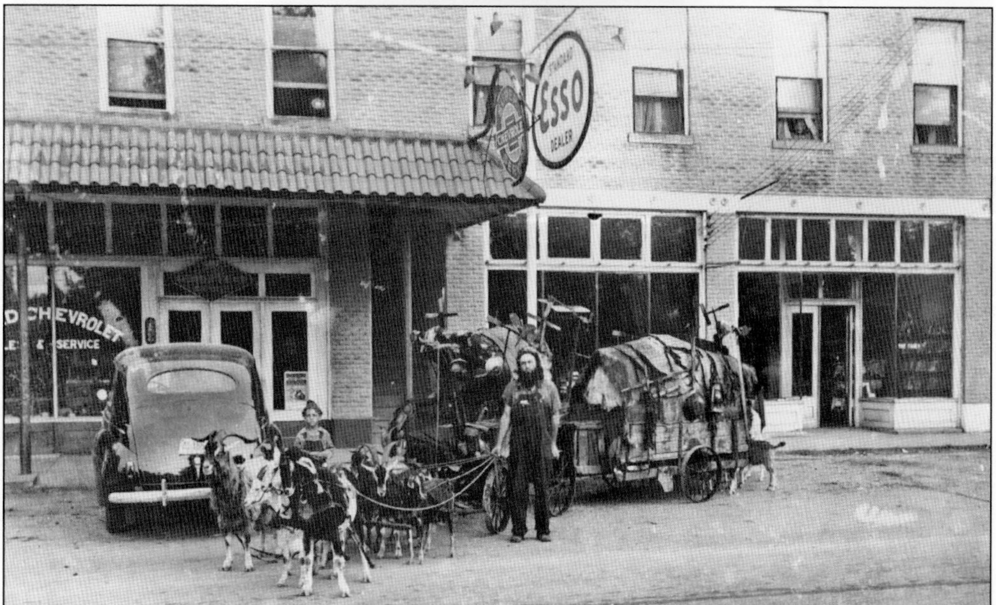

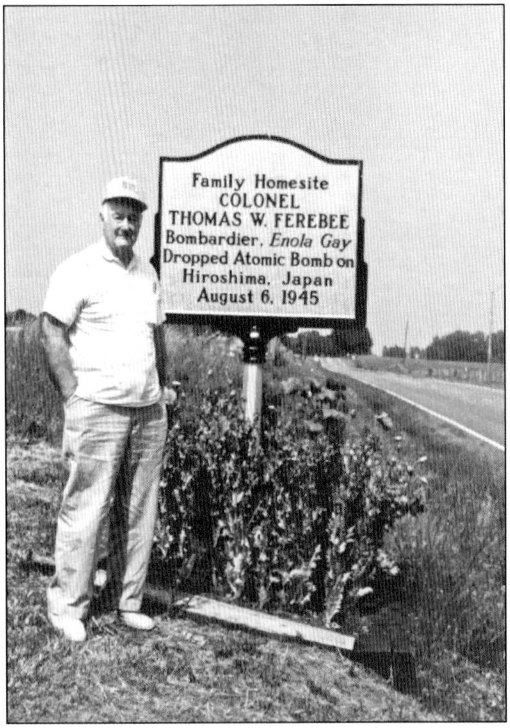

COL. THOMAS W. FEREBEE (1918–2000). On August 6, 1945, during World War II, Davie County native and *Enola Gay* bombardier Ferebee released the first atomic bomb over Hiroshima, Japan, contributing to the unconditional surrender by Japan eight days later. Ferebee stands beside the highway marker for the Ferebee family home place on U.S. 64 West, dedicated on Memorial Day 1991.

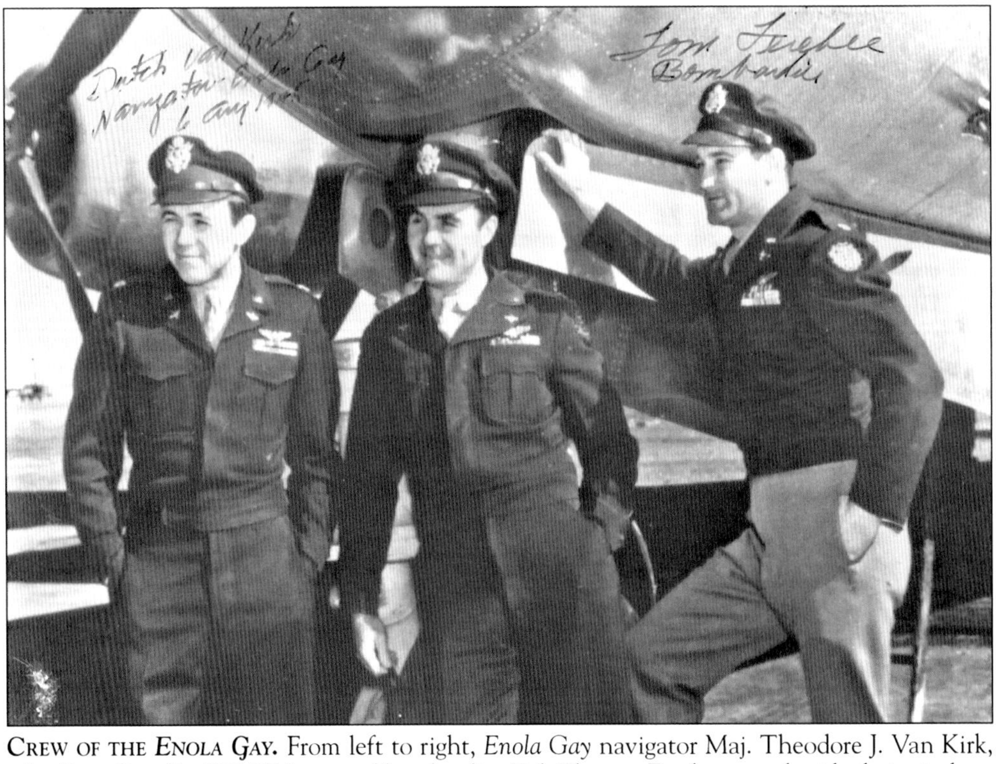

CREW OF THE *ENOLA GAY*. From left to right, *Enola Gay* navigator Maj. Theodore J. Van Kirk, pilot Brig. Gen. Paul W. Tibbets, and bombardier Col. Thomas Ferebee pose beside their airplane in late 1945. (Courtesy of William Ferebee.)

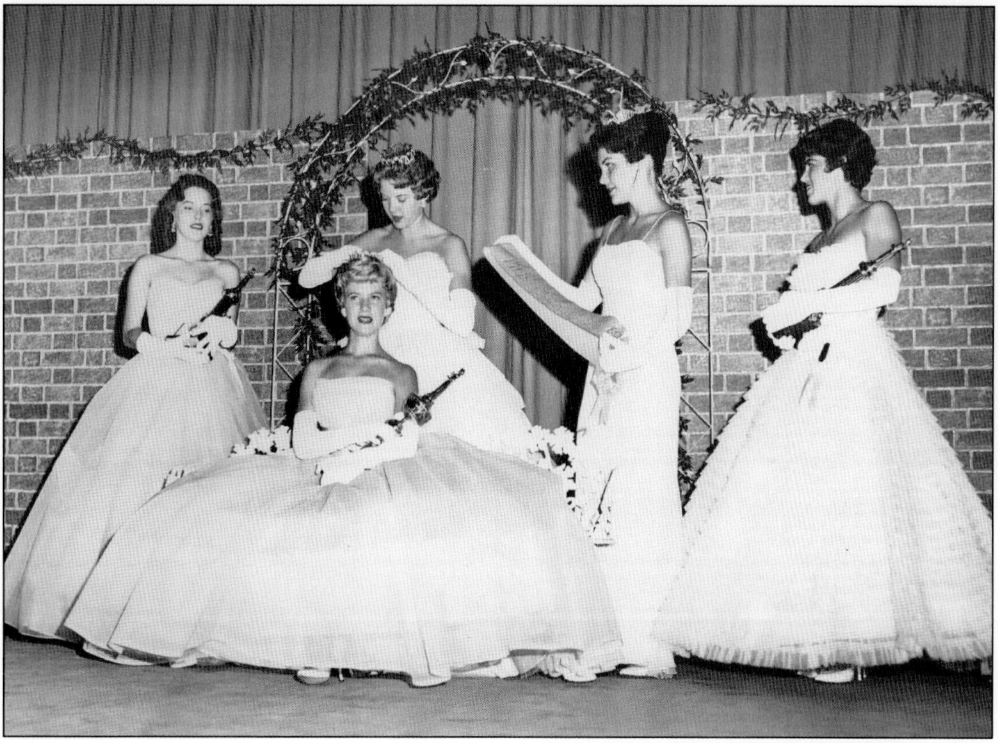

MISS MOCKSVILLE CORONATION, 1962. Beauty pageant contestants pose with the winner. From left to right are Sue Kimmer, second runner-up; Connie Wagner, Miss Mocksville 1962; Diana Groce, Miss Mocksville 1963; Susan Kay Woodall, Miss North Carolina 1962; and Brenda Zimmerman, first runner-up.

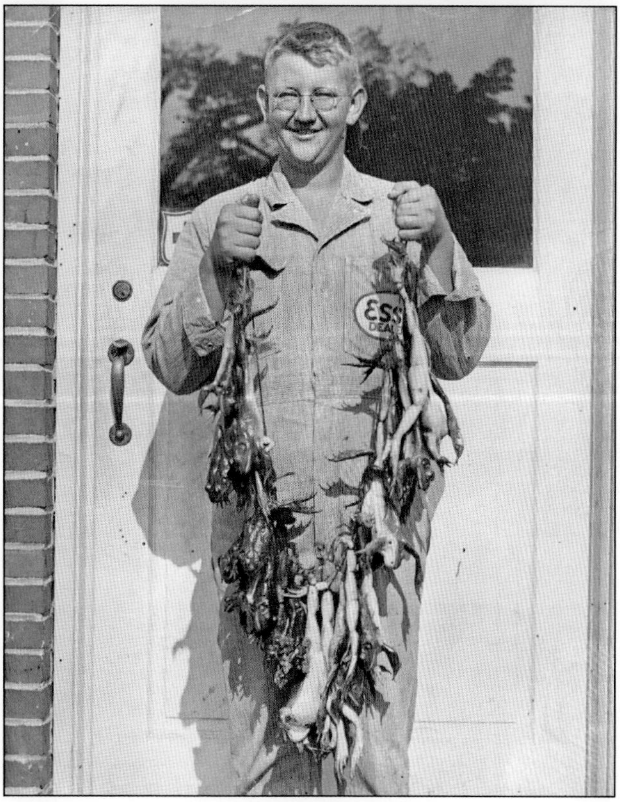

FROG LEGS FOR SUPPER! Jack Sanford poses after a successful frog gigging expedition.

Consistent with our mission to preserve history on a local level, this book was printed in South Carolina on American-made paper and manufactured entirely in the United States. Products carrying the accredited Forest Stewardship Council (FSC) label are printed on 100 percent FSC-certified paper.